(ISC)²®

SSCP® Systems Security Certified Practitioner

Official Practice Tests

Second Edition

T0188768

(ISC)²®
SSCP® Systems Security Certified Practitioner

Official Practice Tests

Second Edition

Mike Chapple

David Seidl

SYBEX®
A Wiley Brand

Acknowledgments

The authors would like to thank the many people who made this book possible. First, Ricky Chapple and Matthew Chapple provided crucial assistance in formatting and laying out the chapters for this book. Without their help, we would never have completed this project on schedule.

We also owe our thanks to a large supporting team from the publishing world. Jim Minatel at Wiley Publishing helped us extend the Sybex security certification franchise to include this new title and gain important support from the International Information Systems Security Consortium (ISC)². Carole Jelen, our agent, worked on a myriad of logistic details and handled the business side of the book with her usual grace and commitment to excellence. Ben Malisow, our technical editor, continues to provide wonderful input and suggestions that keep us on our toes and help us produce a high-quality final product. Lily Miller served as the project editor and managed the project smoothly.

About the Authors

Mike Chapple, Ph.D., Security+, CISSP, CISA, PenTest+, CySA+, is teaching professor of IT, analytics, and operations at the University of Notre Dame. He is also academic director of the university's master's program in business analytics.

Mike is a cybersecurity professional with more than 20 years of experience in the field. Prior to his current role, Mike served as the senior director for IT service delivery at Notre Dame, where he oversaw the university's cybersecurity program, cloud computing efforts, and other areas. Mike also previously served as chief information officer of Brand Institute and an information security researcher with the National Security Agency and the U.S. Air Force.

Mike is a frequent contributor to several magazines and websites and is the author or coauthor of more than 25 books including *CISSP Official (ISC)² Study Guide, CISSP Official (ISC)² Practice Tests, CompTIA CySA+ Study Guide*, and *CompTIA CySA+ Practice Tests*, all from Wiley, and *Cyberwarfare: Information Operations in a Connected World* from Jones and Bartlett.

Mike offers free study groups for the PenTest+, CySA+, Security+, CISSP, and SSCP certifications at his website, certmike.com.

David Seidl is the Vice President for Information Technology and CIO at Miami University of Ohio. During his more than 23 years in information technology, he has served in a variety of leadership, technical, and information security roles, including leading the University of Notre Dame's Campus Technology Services operations and infrastructure division as well as heading up Notre Dame's information security team as Notre Dame's director of information security.

He has written books on security certification and cyberwarfare, including co-authoring *CompTIA CySA+ Study Guide: Exam CS0-002, CompTIA CySA+ Practice Tests: Exam CS0-002*, and *CISSP Official (ISC)² Practice Tests* and *CompTIA Security+ Study Guide: Exam SY0-601* and *CompTIA Security+ Practice Tests: Exam SY0-601*, all from Wiley, and *Cyberwarfare: Information Operations in a Connected World* from Jones and Bartlett.

David holds a bachelor's degree in communication technology and a master's degree in information security from Eastern Michigan University, as well as CISSP, GPEN, GCIH, CySA+, and PenTest+ certifications.

About the Technical Editor

Ben Malisow is a consultant and writer with more than 25 years of experience in the fields of information, security, and information security. He teaches SSCP, CISSP, and CCSP preparation courses for (ISC)² and has written the *Official (ISC)² CCSP Study Guide* and the *Official (ISC)² Practice Tests* books, among other titles; his latest works include *CCSP Practice Tests* and *Exposed: How Revealing Your Data and Eliminating Privacy Increases Trust and Liberates Humanity*. He and his partner, Robin Cabe, host the weekly podcast "The Sensuous Sounds of INFOSEC," from his website, www.securityzed.com.

Contents

Contents

Introduction

(ISC)² SSCP Systems Security Certified Practitioner Official Practice Tests, 2nd Edition is a companion volume to the *SSCP (ISC)² Systems Security Certified Practitioner Official Study Guide, 3rd Edition.* If you're looking to test your knowledge before you take the SSCP exam, this book will help you by providing a combination of practice questions that cover the SSCP Common Body of Knowledge and easy-to-understand explanations of both right and wrong answers. This book as well as the 3rd edition of the *Study Guide* are updated according to the Exam Outline effective November 2021.

If you're just starting to prepare for the SSCP exam, we highly recommend that you use the *SSCP (ISC)² Certified Information Systems Security Professional Official Study Guide, 3rd Edition* to help you learn about each of the domains covered by the SSCP exam. Once you're ready to test your knowledge, use this book to help find places where you may need to study more, or to practice for the exam itself.

Since this is a companion to the SSCP Study Guide, this book is designed to be similar to taking the SSCP exam. It contains multipart scenarios as well as standard multiple-choice questions similar to those you may encounter in the certification exam itself. The book itself is broken up into 9 chapters: 7 domain-centric chapters covering each domain, and 2 chapters that contain full-length practice tests to simulate taking the exam itself.

SSCP Certification

The SSCP certification is offered by the International Information System Security Certification Consortium, or (ISC)², a global nonprofit. The mission of (ISC)² is to support and provide members and constituents with credentials, resources, and leadership to address cyber, information, software, and infrastructure security to deliver value to society. They achieve this mission by delivering the world's leading information security certification program. The SSCP is the entry-level credential in this series and is accompanied by several other (ISC)² programs:

- Certified Information Systems Security Professional (CISSP)
- Certified Authorization Professional (CAP)
- Certified Secure Software Lifecycle Professional (CSSLP)
- Certified Cyber Forensic Professional (CCFP)
- HealthCare Information Security Privacy Practitioner (HCISPP)
- Certified Cloud Security Professional (CCSP)

There are also three advanced CISSP certifications for those who wish to move on from the base credential to demonstrate advanced expertise in a domain of information security:

- Information Systems Security Architecture Professional (CISSP-ISSAP)
- Information Systems Security Engineering Professional (CISSP-ISSEP)
- Information Systems Security Management Professional (CISSP-ISSMP)

The SSCP certification covers seven domains of information security knowledge. These domains are meant to serve as the broad knowledge foundation required to succeed in the information security profession. They include:

- Access Controls
- Security Operations and Administration
- Risk Identification, Monitoring, and Analysis
- Incident Response and Recovery
- Cryptography
- Network and Communications Security
- Systems and Application Security

Complete details on the SSCP Common Body of Knowledge (CBK) are contained in the Candidate Information Bulletin (CIB). The CIB, which includes a full outline of exam topics, can be found on the ISC[2] website at www.isc2.org.

Taking the SSCP Exam

The SSCP exam is a 3-hour exam that consists of 125 questions covering the seven domains. Passing requires achieving a score of at least 700 out of 1,000 points. It's important to understand that this is a scaled score, meaning that not every question is worth the same number of points. Questions of differing difficulty may factor into your score more or less heavily. That said, as you work through these practice exams, you might want to use 70 percent as a yardstick to help you get a sense of whether you're ready to sit for the actual exam. When you're ready, you can schedule an exam via links provided on the (ISC)[2] website—tests are offered in locations throughout the world.

The questions on the SSCP exam are all multiple choice questions with four answer options. You will be asked to select the one correct answer for each question. Watch out for questions that ask you to exercise judgement—these are commonly used on (ISC)[2] exams. You might be asked to identify the "best" option or select the "least" expensive approach. These questions require that you use professional judgement to come to the correct answer.

Computer-Based Testing Environment

Almost all SSCP exams are now administered in a computer-based testing (CBT) format. You'll register for the exam through the Pearson Vue website and may take the exam in the language of your choice. It is offered in English, Japanese, and Brazilian Portuguese.

You'll take the exam in a computer-based testing center located near your home or office. The centers administer many different exams, so you may find yourself sitting in the same room as a student taking a school entrance examination and a healthcare professional earning a medical certification. If you'd like to become more familiar with the testing environment, the Pearson Vue website offers a virtual tour of a testing center: `https://home .pearsonvue.com/test-taker/Pearson-Professional-Center-Tour.aspx`.

When you sit down to take the exam, you'll be seated at a computer that has the exam software already loaded and running. It's a pretty straightforward interface that allows you to navigate through the exam. You can download a practice exam and tutorial from Pearson at: `http://www.vue.com/athena/athena.asp`.

Be aware that the testing software will not let you move back to questions that you previously saw. Each time a question is presented to you, you must provide your answer before moving on to the next question. Be sure to read each question carefully and thoroughly before advancing because you will not have any other opportunity to check your work.

Exam Retake Policy

If you don't pass the SSCP exam, you shouldn't panic. Many individuals don't reach the bar on their first attempt but gain valuable experience that helps them succeed the second time around. When you retake the exam, you'll have the benefit of familiarity with the CBT environment and SSCP exam format. You'll also have time to study up on the areas where you felt less confident.

After your first exam attempt, you must wait 30 days before retaking the computer-based exam. If you're not successful on that attempt, you must then wait 60 more days before your third attempt and 90 more days before any additional attempt. You may only attempt the SSCP exam four times within any 12-month period. For more information on the Retake Policy, see `https://www.isc2.org/Exams/After-Your-Exam`.

 (ISC)² exam policies are subject to change. Please be sure to check www. isc2.org for the current policies before you register and take the exam.

Work Experience Requirement

Candidates who wish to earn the SSCP credential must not only pass the exam but also demonstrate that they have at least one year of work experience in the information security field. Your work experience must cover activities in at least one of the seven domains of the SSCP program and must be paid employment.

You may be eligible to waive the work experience requirement based on your educational achievements. If you hold a bachelor's or master's degree in cybersecurity, you may be eligible for a degree waiver that covers one of those years. For more information see `https:// www.isc2.org/Certifications/SSCP/experience-requirements`.

If you haven't yet completed your work experience requirement, you may still attempt the SSCP exam. Individuals who pass the exam are designated Associates of (ISC)² and have two years to complete the work experience requirement.

Recertification Requirements

Once you've earned your SSCP credential, you'll need to maintain your certification by paying maintenance fees and participating in continuing professional education (CPE). As long as you maintain your certification in good standing, you will not need to retake the SSCP exam. Currently, the annual maintenance fees for the SSCP credential are $125 per year.

To maintain your SSCP certification, you must earn at least 60 CPE credits during each three-year renewal period. (ISC)² provides an online portal where members may submit CPE completion for review and approval. The portal also tracks annual maintenance fee payments and progress toward recertification.

Using This Book to Practice

This book is composed of 9 chapters. Each of the first seven chapters covers a domain, with a variety of questions that can help you test your knowledge of real-world, scenario, and best practices–based security knowledge. The final two chapters are complete practice exams that can serve as timed practice tests to help determine if you're ready for the SSCP exam.

We recommend taking the first practice exam to help identify where you may need to spend more study time, and then using the domain-specific chapters to test your domain knowledge where it is weak. Once you're ready, take the second practice exam to make sure you've covered all of the material and are ready to attempt the SSCP exam.

Using the Online Practice Tests

All of the questions in this book are also available in Sybex's online practice test tool. To get access to this online format, go to www.wiley.com/go/sybextestprep and start by registering your book. You'll receive a pin code and instructions on where to create an online test bank account. Once you have access, you can use the online version to create your own sets of practice tests from the book questions and practice in a timed and graded setting.

Do you need more? If you are not seeing passing grades on these practice tests, look for the all new *(ISC)² SSCP Systems Security Certified Practitioner Official Study Guide, Third Edition* by Michael S. Wills (ISBN: 978-1-119-85498-2). This book is an excellent resource to master any SSCP topics causing problems. This book maps every official exam objective to the corresponding chapter in the book to help track exam prep objective-by-objective, challenging review questions in each chapter to prepare for exam day, and online test prep materials with flashcards and additional practice tests.

Chapter

1

Security Operations and Administration (Domain 1)

THE SSCP EXAM TOPICS COVERED IN THIS CHAPTER INCLUDE:

✓ **Domain 1.0: Security Operations and Administration**

- **1.1 Comply with codes of ethics**
  - (ISC)² Code of Ethics
  - Organizational code of ethics
- **1.2 Understand security concepts**
  - Confidentiality
  - Integrity
  - Availability
  - Accountability
  - Privacy
  - Non-repudiation
  - Least privilege
  - Segregation of duties (SoD)
- **1.3 Identify and implement security controls**
  - Technical controls (e.g., session timeout, password aging)
  - Physical controls (e.g., mantraps, cameras, locks)
  - Administrative controls (e.g., security policies, standards, procedures, baselines)
  - Assessing compliance
  - Periodic audit and review
- **1.4 Document and maintain functional security controls**
  - Deterrent controls
  - Preventative controls

- Detective controls
- Corrective controls
- Compensating controls

■ **1.5 Participate in asset management lifecycle (hardware, software, and data)**

- Process, planning, design, and initiation
- Development/Acquisition
- Inventory and licensing
- Implementation/Assessment
- Operation/Maintenance
- Archiving and retention requirements
- Disposal and destruction

■ **1.6 Participate in change management lifecycle**

- Change management (e.g., roles, responsibilities, processes)
- Security impact analysis
- Configuration management (CM)

■ **1.7 Participate in implementing security awareness and training (e.g., social engineering/phishing)**

■ **1.8 Collaborate with physical security operations (e.g., data center assessment, badging)**

1. Maddox is conducting an information audit for his organization. Which one of the following elements that he discovered is least likely to be classified as PII when used in isolation?

    A. Street addresses

    B. Item codes

    C. Mobile phone numbers

    D. Social Security numbers

2. Carl recently assisted in the implementation of a new set of security controls designed to comply with legal requirements. He is concerned about the long-term maintenance of those controls. Which one of the following is a good way for Carl to ease his concerns?

    A. Firewall rules

    B. Policy documents

    C. Security standards

    D. Periodic audits

3. Darlene was recently offered a consulting opportunity as a side job. She is concerned that the opportunity might constitute a conflict of interest. Which one of the following sources is most likely to provide her with appropriate guidance?

    A. Organizational code of ethics

    B. (ISC)² code of ethics

    C. Organizational security policy

    D. (ISC)² security policy

4. Which one of the following is an administrative control that can protect the confidentiality of information?

    A. Encryption

    B. Nondisclosure agreement

    C. Firewall

    D. Fault tolerance

5. Chris is worried that the laptops that his organization has recently acquired were modified by a third party to include keyloggers before they were delivered. Where should he focus his efforts to prevent this?

    A. His supply chain

    B. His vendor contracts

    C. His post-purchase build process

    D. The original equipment manufacturer (OEM)

6. The (ISC)² code of ethics applies to all SSCP holders. Which of the following is not one of the four mandatory canons of the code?

    A. Protect society, the common good, the necessary public trust and confidence, and the infrastructure.

    B. Disclose breaches of privacy, trust, and ethics.

    C. Provide diligent and competent service to the principles.

    D. Advance and protect the profession.

7. Which one of the following control categories does not accurately describe a fence around a facility?

    A. Physical

    B. Detective

    C. Deterrent

    D. Preventive

8. Which one of the following actions might be taken as part of a business continuity plan?

    A. Restoring from backup tapes

    B. Implementing RAID

    C. Relocating to a cold site

    D. Restarting business operations

9. Which one of the following is an example of physical infrastructure hardening?

    A. Antivirus software

    B. Hardware-based network firewall

    C. Two-factor authentication

    D. Fire suppression system

10. Mary is helping a computer user who sees the following message appear on his computer screen. What type of attack has occurred?

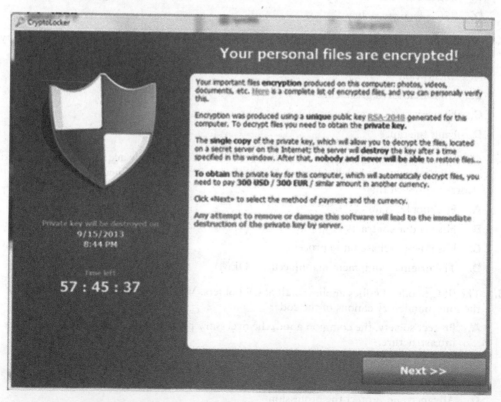

    A. Availability

    B. Confidentiality

    C. Disclosure

    D. Distributed

11. The Acme Widgets Company is putting new controls in place for its accounting department. Management is concerned that a rogue accountant may be able to create a new false vendor and then issue checks to that vendor as payment for services that were never rendered. What security control can best help prevent this situation?

    A. Mandatory vacation

    B. Separation of duties

    C. Defense in depth

    D. Job rotation

12. Beth is the security administrator for a public school district. She is implementing a new student information system and is testing the code to ensure that students are not able to alter their own grades. What principle of information security is Beth enforcing?

    A. Integrity

    B. Availability

    C. Confidentiality

    D. Denial

For questions 13–15, please refer to the following scenario.

Juniper Content is a web content development company with 40 employees located in two offices: one in New York and a smaller office in the San Francisco Bay Area. Each office has a local area network protected by a perimeter firewall. The local area network (LAN) contains modern switch equipment connected to both wired and wireless networks.

Each office has its own file server, and the information technology (IT) team runs software every hour to synchronize files between the two servers, distributing content between the offices. These servers are primarily used to store images and other files related to web content developed by the company. The team also uses a SaaS-based email and document collaboration solution for much of their work.

You are the newly appointed IT manager for Juniper Content, and you are working to augment existing security controls to improve the organization's security.

13. Users in the two offices would like to access each other's file servers over the Internet. What control would provide confidentiality for those communications?

    A. Digital signatures

    B. Virtual private network

    C. Virtual LAN

    D. Digital content management

14. You are also concerned about the availability of data stored on each office's server. You would like to add technology that would enable continued access to files located on the server even if a hard drive in a server fails. What integrity control allows you to add robustness without adding additional servers?

   A. Server clustering

   B. Load balancing

   C. RAID

   D. Scheduled backups

15. Finally, there are historical records stored on the server that are extremely important to the business and should never be modified. You would like to add an integrity control that allows you to verify on a periodic basis that the files were not modified. What control can you add?

   A. Hashing

   B. ACLs

   C. Read-only attributes

   D. Firewalls

16. An accounting employee at Doolittle Industries was recently arrested for participation in an embezzlement scheme. The employee transferred money to a personal account and then shifted funds around between other accounts every day to disguise the fraud for months. Which one of the following controls might have best allowed the earlier detection of this fraud?

   A. Separation of duties

   B. Least privilege

   C. Defense in depth

   D. Mandatory vacation

17. Yolanda is writing a document that will provide configuration information regarding the minimum level of security that every system in the organization must meet. What type of document is she preparing?

   A. Policy

   B. Baseline

   C. Guideline

   D. Procedure

18. Frank discovers a keylogger hidden on the laptop of his company's chief executive officer. What information security principle is the keylogger most likely designed to disrupt?

   A. Confidentiality

   B. Integrity

   C. Availability

   D. Denial

19. Susan is working with the management team in her company to classify data in an attempt to apply extra security controls that will limit the likelihood of a data breach. What principle of information security is Susan trying to enforce?

    A. Availability

    B. Denial

    C. Confidentiality

    D. Integrity

20. Gary is implementing a new website architecture that uses multiple small web servers behind a load balancer. What principle of information security is Gary seeking to enforce?

    A. Denial

    B. Confidentiality

    C. Integrity

    D. Availability

21. Which one of the following is not an example of a technical control?

    A. Session timeout

    B. Password aging

    C. Encryption

    D. Data classification

For questions 22–25, please refer to the following scenario.

Jasper Diamonds is a jewelry manufacturer that markets and sells custom jewelry through their website. Bethany is the manager of Jasper's software development organization, and she is working to bring the company into line with industry standard practices. She is developing a new change management process for the organization and wants to follow commonly accepted approaches.

22. Jasper would like to establish a governing body for the organization's change management efforts. What individual or group within an organization is typically responsible for reviewing the impact of proposed changes?

    A. Chief information officer

    B. Senior leadership team

    C. Change control board

    D. Software developer

23. During what phase of the change management process does the organization conduct peer review of the change for accuracy and completeness?

    A. Recording

    B. Analysis/Impact Assessment

    C. Approval

    D. Decision Making and Prioritization

24. Who should the organization appoint to manage the policies and procedures surrounding change management?

    A. Project manager

    B. Change manager

    C. System security officer

    D. Architect

25. Which one of the following elements is not a crucial component of a change request?

    A. Description of the change

    B. Implementation plan

    C. Backout plan

    D. Incident response plan

26. Ben is designing a messaging system for a bank and would like to include a feature that allows the recipient of a message to prove to a third party that the message did indeed come from the purported originator. What goal is Ben trying to achieve?

    A. Authentication

    B. Authorization

    C. Integrity

    D. Nonrepudiation

27. What principle of information security states that an organization should implement overlapping security controls whenever possible?

    A. Least privilege

    B. Separation of duties

    C. Defense in depth

    D. Security through obscurity

28. Which one of the following is not a goal of a formal change management program?

    A. Implement change in an orderly fashion.

    B. Test changes prior to implementation.

    C. Provide rollback plans for changes.

    D. Inform stakeholders of changes after they occur.

29. Ben is assessing the compliance of his organization with credit card security requirements. He finds payment card information stored in a database. Policy directs that he remove the information from the database, but he cannot do this for operational reasons. He obtained an exception to policy and is seeking an appropriate compensating control to mitigate the risk. What would be his best option?

    A. Purchasing insurance

    B. Encrypting the database contents

    C. Removing the data

    D. Objecting to the exception

30. You discover that a user on your network has been using the Wireshark tool, as shown here. Further investigation revealed that he was using it for illicit purposes. What pillar of information security has most likely been violated?

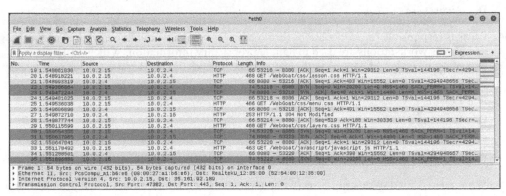

    A. Integrity

    B. Denial

    C. Availability

    D. Confidentiality

31. Which one of the following is the first step in developing an organization's vital records program?

    A. Identifying vital records

    B. Locating vital records

    C. Archiving vital records

    D. Preserving vital records

32. Which one of the following security programs is designed to provide employees with the knowledge they need to perform their specific work tasks?

    A. Awareness

    B. Training

    C. Education

    D. Indoctrination

33. Which one of the following security programs is designed to establish a minimum standard common denominator of security understanding?

    A. Training

    B. Education

    C. Indoctrination

    D. Awareness

34. Chris is responsible for workstations throughout his company and knows that some of the company's workstations are used to handle proprietary information. Which option best describes what should happen at the end of their lifecycle for workstations he is responsible for?

    A. Erasing

    B. Clearing

    C. Sanitization

    D. Destruction

35. What term is used to describe a set of common security configurations, often provided by a third party?

    A. Security policy

    B. Baseline

    C. DSS

    D. NIST SP 800-53

36. Which one of the following administrative processes assists organizations in assigning appropriate levels of security control to sensitive information?

    A. Information classification

    B. Remanence

    C. Transmitting data

    D. Clearing

37. Ben is following the National Institute of Standards and Technology (NIST) Special Publication 800-88 guidelines for sanitization and disposition as shown here. He is handling information that his organization classified as sensitive, which is a moderate security categorization in the NIST model. If the media is going to be sold as surplus, what process does Ben need to follow?

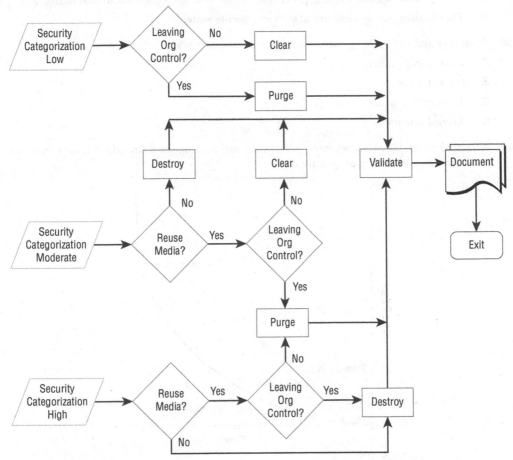

Source: NIST SP 800-88

A. Destroy, validate, document

B. Clear, purge, document

C. Purge, document, validate

D. Purge, validate, document

38. Ben has been tasked with identifying security controls for systems covered by his organization's information classification system. Why might Ben choose to use a security baseline?

    A. It applies in all circumstances, allowing consistent security controls.

    B. They are approved by industry standards bodies, preventing liability.

    C. They provide a good starting point that can be tailored to organizational needs.

    D. They ensure that systems are always in a secure state.

39. Retaining and maintaining information for as long as it is needed is known as what?

    A. Data storage policy

    B. Data storage

    C. Asset maintenance

    D. Record retention

40. Referring to the figure shown here, what is the earliest stage of a fire where it is possible to use detection technology to identify it?

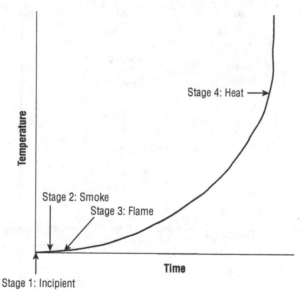

Image reprinted from *CISSP (ISC)² Certified Information Systems Security Professional Official Study Guide, 7th Edition* © John Wiley & Sons 2015, reprinted with permission.

    A. Incipient

    B. Smoke

    C. Flame

    D. Heat

41. What type of fire suppression system fills with water when the initial stages of a fire are detected and then requires a sprinkler head heat activation before dispensing water?

   A. Wet pipe

   B. Dry pipe

   C. Deluge

   D. Preaction

42. Ralph is designing a physical security infrastructure for a new computing facility that will remain largely unstaffed. He plans to implement motion detectors in the facility but would also like to include a secondary verification control for physical presence. Which one of the following would best meet his needs?

   A. CCTV

   B. IPS

   C. Turnstiles

   D. Faraday cages

43. Referring to the figure shown here, what is the name of the security control indicated by the arrow?

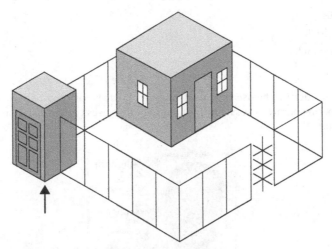

Image reprinted from *CISSP (ISC)² Certified Information Systems Security Professional Official Study Guide, 7th Edition* © John Wiley & Sons 2015, reprinted with permission.

   A. Mantrap

   B. Turnstile

   C. Intrusion prevention system

   D. Portal

44. Which one of the following does not describe a standard physical security requirement for wiring closets?

    A. Place only in areas monitored by security guards.

    B. Do not store flammable items in the closet.

    C. Use sensors on doors to log entries.

    D. Perform regular inspections of the closet.

45. Betty is concerned about the use of buffer overflow attacks against a custom application developed for use in her organization. What security control would provide the strongest defense against these attacks?

    A. Firewall

    B. Intrusion detection system

    C. Parameter checking

    D. Vulnerability scanning

46. Juan is retrofitting an existing door to his facility to include a lock with automation capabilities. Which one of the following types of lock is easiest to install as a retrofit to the existing door?

    A. Mantrap

    B. Electric lock

    C. Magnetic lock

    D. Turnstile

47. Rhonda is considering the use of new identification cards for physical access control in her organization. She comes across a military system that uses the card shown here. What type of card is this?

A. Smart card

B. Proximity card

C. Magnetic stripe card

D. Phase three card

48. Which one of the following facilities would have the highest level of physical security requirements?

A. Data center

B. Network closet

C. SCIF

D. Cubicle work areas

49. Glenda is investigating a potential privacy violation within her organization. The organization notified users that it was collecting data for product research that would last for six months and then disposed of the data at the end of that period. During the time that they had the data, they also used it to target a marketing campaign. Which principle of data privacy was most directly violated?

A. Data minimization

B. Accuracy

C. Storage limitations

D. Purpose limitations

50. What type of access control is composed of policies and procedures that support regulations, requirements, and the organization's own policies?

A. Corrective

B. Logical

C. Compensating

D. Administrative

51. Match each of the numbered security controls listed with exactly one of the lettered categories shown. Choose the category that best describes each control. You may use each control category once, more than once, or not at all.

Controls

1. Password

2. Account reviews

3. Badge readers

4. MFA

5. IDP

Categories

A. Administrative

B. Technical

C. Physical

52. Which of the following access control categories would not include a door lock?

A. Physical

B. Corrective

C. Preventative

D. Deterrent

For questions 53–54, please refer to the following scenario.

Gary was recently hired as the first chief information security officer (CISO) for a local government agency. The agency recently suffered a security breach and is attempting to build a new information security program. Gary would like to apply some best practices for security operations as he is designing this program.

53. As Gary decides what access permissions he should grant to each user, what principle should guide his decisions about default permissions?

A. Separation of duties

B. Least privilege

C. Aggregation

D. Separation of privileges

54. As Gary designs the program, he uses the matrix shown here. What principle of information security does this matrix most directly help enforce?

Roles/Tasks	Application Programmer	Security Administrator	Database Administrator	Database Server Administrator	Budget Analyst	Accounts Receivable	Accounts Payable	Deploy Patches	Verify Patches
Application Programmer		X	X	X					
Security Administrator	X		X	X	X	X	X	X	
Database Administrator	X	X		X					
Database Server Administrator	X	X	X						
Budget Analyst		X				X	X		
Accounts Receivable		X			X		X		
Accounts Payable		X			X	X			
Deploy Patches		X							X
Verify Patches								X	
Potential Areas of Conflict									

A. Segregation of duties

B. Aggregation

C. Two-person control

D. Defense in depth

55. Lydia is processing access control requests for her organization. She comes across a request where the user does have the required security clearance, but there is no business justification for the access. Lydia denies this request. What security principle is she following?

   A. Need to know

   B. Least privilege

   C. Separation of duties

   D. Two-person control

56. Helen is implementing a new security mechanism for granting employees administrative privileges in the accounting system. She designs the process so that both the employee's manager and the accounting manager must approve the request before the access is granted. What information security principle is Helen enforcing?

   A. Least privilege

   B. Two-person control

   C. Job rotation

   D. Separation of duties

57. Which of the following is not true about the (ISC)² code of ethics?

   A. Adherence to the code is a condition of certification.

   B. Failure to comply with the code may result in revocation of certification.

   C. The code applies to all members of the information security profession.

   D. Members who observe a breach of the code are required to report the possible violation.

58. Javier is verifying that only IT system administrators have the ability to log on to servers used for administrative purposes. What principle of information security is he enforcing?

   A. Need to know

   B. Least privilege

   C. Two-person control

   D. Transitive trust

59. Connor's company recently experienced a denial-of-service attack that Connor believes came from an inside source. If true, what type of event has the company experienced?

   A. Espionage

   B. Confidentiality breach

   C. Sabotage

   D. Integrity breach

60. Which one of the following is not a canon of the (ISC)² code of ethics?

   A. Protect society, the common good, necessary public trust and confidence, and the infrastructure.

   B. Promptly report security vulnerabilities to relevant authorities.

   C. Act honorably, honestly, justly, responsibly, and legally.

   D. Provide diligent and competent service to principals.

61. When designing an access control scheme, Hilda set up roles so that the same person does not have the ability to provision a new user account and assign superuser privileges to an account. What information security principle is Hilda following?

    A. Least privilege

    B. Separation of duties

    C. Job rotation

    D. Security through obscurity

62. Which one of the following tools helps system administrators by providing a standard, secure template of configuration settings for operating systems and applications?

    A. Security guidelines

    B. Security policy

    C. Baseline configuration

    D. Running configuration

63. Tracy is preparing to apply a patch to her organization's enterprise resource planning system. She is concerned that the patch may introduce flaws that did not exist in prior versions, so she plans to conduct a test that will compare previous responses to input with those produced by the newly patched application. What type of testing is Tracy planning?

    A. Unit testing

    B. Acceptance testing

    C. Regression testing

    D. Vulnerability testing

64. Which one of the following security practices suggests that an organization should deploy multiple, overlapping security controls to meet security objectives?

    A. Defense in depth

    B. Security through obscurity

    C. Least privilege

    D. Separation of duties

65. What technology asset management practice would an organization use to ensure that systems meet baseline security standards?

    A. Change management

    B. Patch management

    C. Configuration management

    D. Identity management

66. The large business that Jack works for has been using noncentralized logging for years. They have recently started to implement centralized logging, however, and as they reviewed logs, they discovered a breach that appeared to have involved a malicious insider. How can Jack best ensure accountability for actions taken on systems in his environment?

 A. Review the logs and require digital signatures for each log.

 B. Require authentication for all actions taken and capture logs centrally.

 C. Log the use of administrative credentials and encrypt log data in transit.

 D. Require authorization and capture logs centrally.

67. Veronica is responsible for her organization's asset management program. During what stage of the process would she select the controls that will be used to protect assets from theft?

 A. Implementation/assessment

 B. Operation/maintenance

 C. Inventory and licensing

 D. Process, planning, design, and initiation

68. Under what type of software license does the recipient of software have an unlimited right to copy, modify, distribute, or resell a software package?

 A. GNU Public License

 B. Freeware

 C. Open source

 D. Public domain

69. When an attacker called an organization's help desk and persuaded them to reset a password due to the help desk employee's trust and willingness to help, what type of attack succeeded?

 A. Trojan horse

 B. Social engineering

 C. Phishing

 D. Whaling

Chapter 2

Access Controls (Domain 2)

THE SSCP EXAM TOPICS COVERED IN THIS CHAPTER INCLUDE:

✓ **Domain 2.0: Access Controls**

- **2.1 Implement and maintain authentication methods**
    - Single/multi-factor authentication (MFA)
    - Single sign-on (SSO) (e.g., Active Directory Federation Services (ADFS), OpenID Connect)
    - Device authentication
    - Federated access (e.g., Open Authorization 2 (OAuth2), Security Assertion Markup Language (SAML))
- **2.2 Support internetwork trust architectures**
    - Trust relationships (e.g., 1-way, 2-way, transitive, zero)
    - Internet, intranet, and extranet
    - Third-party connections
- **2.3 Participate in the identity management lifecycle**
    - Authorization
    - Proofing
    - Provisioning/de-provisioning
    - Maintenance
    - Entitlement
    - Identity and access management (IAM) systems
- **2.4 Understand and apply access controls**
    - Mandatory
    - Discretionary
    - Role-based (e.g., attribute-, subject-, object-based)
    - Rule-based

1. Greg is the network administrator for a large stadium that hosts many events throughout the course of the year. They equip ushers with handheld scanners to verify tickets. Ushers turn over frequently and are often hired at the last minute. Scanners are handed out to ushers before each event, but different ushers may use different scanners. Scanners are secured in a locked safe when not in use. What network access control approach would be most effective for this scenario?

    A. Multifactor authentication

    B. Device authentication

    C. Password authentication

    D. No authentication

2. Norma is helping her organization create a specialized third-party network connection for a set of vendors needing to connect to Norma's organization's network to process invoices and upload inventory. This network should be segmented from the rest of the corporate network but have a much higher degree of access than the general public. What type of network is Norma building?

    A. Internet

    B. Intranet

    C. Outranet

    D. Extranet

3. Which one of the following is an example of a nondiscretionary access control system?

    A. File ACLs

    B. MAC

    C. DAC

    D. Visitor list

4. Wanda is configuring device-based authentication for systems on her network. Which one of the following approaches offers the strongest way to authenticate devices?

    A. IP address

    B. MAC address

    C. Digital certificate

    D. Password

5. Kaiden is creating an extranet for his organization and is concerned about unauthorized eavesdropping on network communications. Which one of the following technologies can he use to mitigate this risk?

    A. VPN

    B. Firewall

    C. Content filter

    D. Proxy server

6. When Ben lists the files on a Linux system, he sees the set of attributes shown here.

```
[demo@ip-10-0-0-254 ~]$ ls -l
total 8
-rw-r--r-- 1 demo demo 93 Apr 11 23:38 example.txt
-rw-rw-r-- 1 demo demo 15 Apr 11 23:37 index.html
[demo@ip-10-0-0-254 ~]$ []
```

The letters rwx indicate different levels of what?

A. Identification

B. Authorization

C. Authentication

D. Accountability

7. Which one of the following tools is most often used for identification purposes and is not suitable for use as an authenticator?

A. Password

B. Retinal scan

C. Username

D. Token

8. Gary is preparing to create an account for a new user and assign privileges to the HR database. What two elements of information must Gary verify before granting this access?

A. Credentials and need to know

B. Clearance and need to know

C. Password and clearance

D. Password and biometric scan

Ben's organization is adopting biometric authentication for its high-security building's access control system. Use the following chart to answer questions 9–11 about the organization's adoption of the technology.

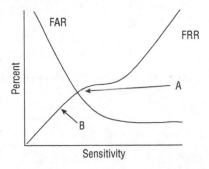

9. Ben's company is considering configuring its systems to work at the level shown by point A on the diagram. To what level is it setting the sensitivity?

    A. The FRR crossover

    B. The FAR point

    C. The CER

    D. The CFR

10. At point B, what problem is likely to occur?

    A. False acceptance will be very high.

    B. False rejection will be very high.

    C. False rejection will be very low.

    D. False acceptance will be very low.

11. What should Ben do if the FAR and FRR shown in this diagram does not provide an acceptable performance level for his organization's needs?

    A. Adjust the sensitivity of the biometric devices.

    B. Assess other biometric systems to compare them.

    C. Move the CER.

    D. Adjust the FRR settings in software.

12. When a subject claims an identity, what process is occurring?

    A. Login

    B. Identification

    C. Authorization

    D. Token presentation

13. Files, databases, computers, programs, processes, devices, and media are all examples of what?

    A. Subjects

    B. Objects

    C. File stores

    D. Users

14. MAC models use three types of environments. Which of the following is not a mandatory access control design?

    A. Hierarchical

    B. Bracketed

    C. Compartmentalized

    D. Hybrid

15. Ryan would like to implement an access control technology that is likely to both improve security and increase user satisfaction. Which one of the following technologies meets this requirement?

    A. Mandatory access controls

    B. Single sign-on

    C. Multifactor authentication

    D. Automated deprovisioning

16. The leadership at Susan's company has asked her to implement an access control system that can support rule declarations like "Only allow access to salespeople from managed devices on the wireless network between 8 a.m. and 6 p.m." What type of access control system would be Susan's best choice?

    A. ABAC

    B. Rule-based access control (RBAC)

    C. DAC

    D. MAC

17. What is the primary advantage of decentralized access control?

    A. It provides better redundancy.

    B. It provides control of access to people closer to the resources.

    C. It is less expensive.

    D. It provides more granular control of access.

18. Which of the following is best described as an access control model that focuses on subjects and identifies the objects that each subject can access?

    A. An access control list

    B. An implicit denial list

    C. A capability table

    D. A rights management matrix

19. Match each of the numbered authentication techniques with the appropriate lettered category. Each technique should be matched with exactly one category. Each category may be used once, more than once, or not at all.

Authentication technique	Category
1. Password	A. Something you have
2. ID card	B. Something you know
3. Retinal scan	C. Something you are
4. Smartphone token	
5. Fingerprint analysis	

20. Susan wants to integrate her website to allow users to use accounts from sites like Google. What technology should she adopt?

   A. Kerberos

   B. LDAP

   C. OpenID

   D. SESAME

21. Ben uses a software-based token that changes its code every minute. What type of token is he using?

   A. Asynchronous

   B. Smart card

   C. Synchronous

   D. Static

22. How does single sign-on increase security?

   A. It decreases the number of accounts required for a subject.

   B. It helps decrease the likelihood that users will write down their passwords.

   C. It provides logging for each system that it is connected to.

   D. It provides better encryption for authentication data.

23. Which of the following multifactor authentication technologies provides both low management overhead and flexibility?

   A. Biometrics

   B. Software tokens

   C. Synchronous hardware tokens

   D. Asynchronous hardware tokens

24. Tom is planning to terminate an employee this afternoon for fraud and expects that the meeting will be somewhat hostile. He is coordinating the meeting with human resources and wants to protect the company against damage. Which one of the following steps is most important to coordinate in time with the termination meeting?

   A. Informing other employees of the termination

   B. Retrieving the employee's photo ID

   C. Calculating the final paycheck

   D. Revoking electronic access rights

25. Jim wants to allow a partner organization's Active Directory forest (B) to access his domain forest's (A)'s resources but doesn't want to allow users in his domain to access B's resources. He also does not want the trust to flow upward through the domain tree as it is formed. What should he do?

    A. Set up a two-way transitive trust.

    B. Set up a one-way transitive trust.

    C. Set up a one-way nontransitive trust.

    D. Set up a two-way nontransitive trust.

26. The financial services company that Susan works for provides a web portal for its users. When users need to verify their identity, the company uses information from third-party sources to ask questions based on their past credit reports, such as "Which of the following streets did you live on in 2007?" What process is Susan's organization using?

    A. Identity proofing

    B. Password verification

    C. Authenticating with Type 2 authentication factor

    D. Out-of-band identity proofing

27. Lauren's team of system administrators each deal with hundreds of systems with varying levels of security requirements and find it difficult to handle the multitude of usernames and passwords they each have. What type of solution should she recommend to ensure that passwords are properly handled and that features such as logging and password rotation occur?

    A. A credential management system

    B. A strong password policy

    C. Separation of duties

    D. Single sign-on

28. What type of trust relationship extends beyond the two domains participating in the trust to one or more of their subdomains?

    A. Transitive trust

    B. Inheritable trust

    C. Nontransitive trust

    D. Noninheritable trust

29. Adam is accessing a standalone file server using a username and password provided to him by the server administrator. Which one of the following entities is guaranteed to have information necessary to complete the authorization process?

    A. Adam

    B. File server

    C. Server administrator

    D. Adam's supervisor

30. After 10 years working in her organization, Cassandra is moving into her fourth role, this time as a manager in the accounting department. What issue is likely to show up during an account review if her organization does not have strong account maintenance practices?

    A. An issue with least privilege

    B. Privilege creep

    C. Account creep

    D. Account termination

31. Adam recently configured permissions on an NTFS filesystem to describe the access that different users may have to a file by listing each user individually. What did Adam create?

    A. An access control list

    B. An access control entry

    C. Role-based access control

    D. Mandatory access control

32. Questions like "What is your pet's name?" are examples of what type of identity proofing?

    A. Knowledge-based authentication

    B. Dynamic knowledge-based authentication

    C. Out-of-band identity proofing

    D. A Type 3 authentication factor

33. What access management concept defines what rights or privileges a user has?

    A. Identification

    B. Accountability

    C. Authorization

    D. Authentication

34. Susan has been asked to recommend whether her organization should use a MAC scheme or a DAC scheme. If flexibility and scalability are important requirements for implementing access controls, which scheme should she recommend and why?

    A. MAC, because it provides greater scalability and flexibility because you can simply add more labels as needed

    B. DAC, because allowing individual administrators to make choices about the objects they control provides scalability and flexibility

    C. MAC, because compartmentalization is well suited to flexibility and adding compartments will allow it to scale well

    D. DAC, because a central decision process allows quick responses and will provide scalability by reducing the number of decisions required and flexibility by moving those decisions to a central authority

35. Which of the following tools is not typically used to verify that a provisioning process was followed in a way that ensures that the organization's security policy is being followed?

    A. Log review

    B. Manual review of permissions

    C. Signature-based detection

    D. Review the audit trail

36. Joe is the security administrator for an ERP system. He is preparing to create accounts for several new employees. What default access should he give to all of the new employees as he creates the accounts?

    A. Read only

    B. Editor

    C. Administrator

    D. No access

37. A new customer at a bank that uses fingerprint scanners to authenticate its users is surprised when he scans his fingerprint and is logged in to another customer's account. What type of biometric factor error occurred?

    A. A registration error

    B. A Type 1 error

    C. A Type 2 error

    D. A time-of-use, method-of-use error

38. Laura is in the process of logging into a system and she just entered her password. What term best describes this activity?

    A. Authentication

    B. Authorization

    C. Accounting

    D. Identification

39. Kelly is adjusting her organization's password requirements to make them consistent with best practice guidance from NIST. What should she choose as the most appropriate time period for password expiration?

    A. 30 days

    B. 90 days

    C. 180 days

    D. No expiration

40. Ben is working on integrating a federated identity management system and needs to exchange authentication and authorization information for browser-based single sign-on. What technology is his best option?

   A. HTML

   B. XACML

   C. SAML

   D. SPML

41. What access control scheme labels subjects and objects and allows subjects to access objects when the labels match?

   A. DAC

   B. MAC

   C. Rule-based access control (RBAC)

   D. Role-based access control (RBAC)

42. Mandatory access control is based on what type of model?

   A. Discretionary

   B. Group-based

   C. Lattice-based

   D. Rule-based

43. Ricky would like to access a remote file server through a VPN connection. He begins this process by connecting to the VPN and attempting to log in. Applying the subject/object model to this request, what is the subject of Ricky's login attempt?

   A. Ricky

   B. VPN

   C. Remote file server

   D. Files contained on the remote server

44. What type of access control is typically used by firewalls?

   A. Discretionary access controls

   B. Rule-based access controls

   C. Task-based access control

   D. Mandatory access controls

45. Gabe is concerned about the security of passwords used as a cornerstone of his organization's information security program. Which one of the following controls would provide the greatest improvement in Gabe's ability to authenticate users?

    A. More complex passwords

    B. User education against social engineering

    C. Multifactor authentication

    D. Addition of security questions based on personal knowledge

46. During a review of support incidents, Ben's organization discovered that password changes accounted for more than a quarter of its help desk's cases. Which of the following options would be most likely to decrease that number significantly?

    A. Two-factor authentication

    B. Biometric authentication

    C. Self-service password reset

    D. Passphrases

47. Jim wants to allow cloud-based applications to act on his behalf to access information from other sites. Which of the following tools can allow that?

    A. Kerberos

    B. OAuth

    C. OpenID

    D. LDAP

48. Which one of the following activities is an example of an authorization process?

    A. User providing a password

    B. User passing a facial recognition check

    C. System logging user activity

    D. System consulting an access control list

49. Raul is creating a trust relationship between his company and a vendor. He is implementing the system so that it will allow users from the vendor's organization to access his accounts payable system using the accounts created for them by the vendor. What type of authentication is Raul implementing?

    A. Federated authentication

    B. Transitive trust

    C. Multifactor authentication

    D. Single sign-on

50. In Luke's company, users change job positions on a regular basis. Luke would like the company's access control system to make it easy for administrators to adjust permissions when these changes occur. Which model of access control is best suited for Luke's needs?

    A. Mandatory access control

    B. Discretionary access control

    C. Rule-based access control

    D. Role-based access control

51. When you input a user ID and password, you are performing what important identity and access management activity?

    A. Authorization

    B. Validation

    C. Authentication

    D. Login

52. Which of the following is a ticket-based authentication protocol designed to provide secure communication?

    A. RADIUS

    B. OAuth

    C. SAML

    D. Kerberos

53. Which of the following authenticators is appropriate to use by itself rather than in combination with other biometric factors?

    A. Voice pattern recognition

    B. Hand geometry

    C. Palm scans

    D. Heart/pulse patterns

54. What type of token-based authentication system uses a challenge/response process in which the challenge must be entered on the token?

    A. Asynchronous

    B. Smart card

    C. Synchronous

    D. RFID

55. As part of hiring a new employee, Kathleen's identity management team creates a new user object and ensures that the user object is available in the directories and systems where it is needed. What is this process called?

A. Registration

B. Provisioning

C. Population

D. Authenticator loading

56. What access control system lets owners decide who has access to the objects they own?

A. Role-based access control

B. Task-based access control

C. Discretionary access control

D. Rule-based access control

57. When Alex sets the permissions shown in the following image as one of many users on a Linux server, what type of access control model is he leveraging?

```
$ chmod 731 alex.txt
$ ls -la
total 12
drwxr-xr-x 2 alex root 4096 Feb 27 19:26 .
drwxr-xr-x 3 root root 4096 Feb 27 19:25 ..
-rwx-wx--x 1 alex alex   15 Feb 27 19:26 alex.txt
$ ▮
```

A. Role-based access control

B. Rule-based access control

C. Mandatory access control (MAC)

D. Discretionary access control (DAC)

58. The U.S. government CAC is an example of what form of Type 2 authentication factor?

A. A token

B. A biometric identifier

C. A smart card

D. A PIV

59. Donna is conducting an ongoing review of her organization's identity and access management system and identifies a problem. She finds that when users change jobs, they never have the access rights associated with their old jobs removed. What term best describes this issue?

A. Rights management

B. Privilege creep

C. Two-person control

D. Least privilege

60. Which objects and subjects have a label in a MAC model?

    A. Objects and subjects that are classified as Confidential, Secret, or Top Secret have a label.

    B. All objects have a label, and all subjects have a compartment.

    C. All objects and subjects have a label.

    D. All subjects have a label and all objects have a compartment.

61. Jack's organization is a government agency that handles very sensitive information. They need to implement an access control system that allows administrators to set access rights but does not allow the delegation of those rights to other users. What is the best type of access control design for Jack's organization?

    A. Discretionary access control

    B. Mandatory access control

    C. Decentralized access control

    D. Rule-based access control

62. Kathleen works for a data center hosting facility that provides physical data center space for individuals and organizations. Until recently, each client was given a magnetic-strip-based keycard to access the section of the facility where their servers are located, and they were also given a key to access the cage or rack where their servers reside. In the past month, several servers have been stolen, but the logs for the pass cards show only valid IDs. What is Kathleen's best option to make sure that the users of the pass cards are who they are supposed to be?

    A. Add a reader that requires a PIN for passcard users.

    B. Add a camera system to the facility to observe who is accessing servers.

    C. Add a biometric factor.

    D. Replace the magnetic stripe keycards with smartcards.

63. What term is used to describe the default set of privileges assigned to a user when a new account is created?

    A. Aggregation

    B. Transitivity

    C. Baseline

    D. Entitlement

64. Kathleen is implementing an access control system for her organization and builds the following array:

    Reviewers: update files, delete files

    Submitters: upload files

    Editors: upload files, update files

    Archivists: delete files

What type of access control system has Kathleen implemented?

A. Role-based access control

B. Task-based access control

C. Rule-based access control

D. Discretionary access control

65. When a user attempts to log into their online account, Google sends a text message with a code to their cell phone. What type of verification is this?

A. Knowledge-based authentication

B. Dynamic knowledge-based authentication

C. Out-of-band identity proofing

D. Risk-based identity proofing

66. In a zero-trust network architecture, what criterion is used to make trust decisions?

A. Identity of a user or device

B. IP address

C. Network segment

D. VLAN membership

Chapter 3

Risk Identification, Monitoring, and Analysis (Domain 3)

THE SSCP EXAM TOPICS COVERED IN THIS CHAPTER INCLUDE:

✓ **Domain 3.0: Risk Identification, Monitoring, and Analysis**

- **3.1 Understand the risk management process**
  - Risk visibility and reporting (e.g., risk register, sharing threat intelligence/Indicators of Compromise (IOC), Common Vulnerability Scoring System (CVSS))
  - Risk management concepts (e.g., impact assessments, threat modeling)
  - Risk management frameworks (e.g., International Organization for Standardization (ISO), National Institute of Standards and Technology (NIST))
  - Risk tolerance (e.g., appetite)
  - Risk treatment (e.g., accept, transfer, mitigate, avoid, ignore)
- **3.2 Understand legal and regulatory concerns (e.g., jurisdiction, limitations, privacy)**
- **3.3 Participate in security assessment and vulnerability management activities**
  - Security testing
  - Risk review (e.g., internal, supplier, architecture)
  - Vulnerability management lifecycle
- **3.4 Operate and monitor security platforms (e.g., continuous monitoring)**
  - Source systems (e.g., applications, security appliances, network devices and hosts)

- ■ Events of interest (e.g., anomalies, intrusions, unauthorized changes, compliance monitoring)
- ■ Log management
- ■ Event aggregation and correlation
- ■ **3.5 Analyze monitoring results**
  - ■ Security baselines and anomalies
  - ■ Visualizations, metrics, and trends (e.g., notifications, dashboards, timelines)
  - ■ Event data analysis
  - ■ Document and communicate findings (e.g., escalation)

1. HAL Systems recently decided to stop offering public NTP services because of a fear that its NTP servers would be used in amplification DDoS attacks. What type of risk management strategy did HAL pursue with respect to its NTP services?

    A. Risk mitigation

    B. Risk acceptance

    C. Risk transference

    D. Risk avoidance

2. Tom is responding to a recent security incident and is seeking information on the approval process for a recent modification to a system's security settings. Where would he most likely find this information?

    A. Change log

    B. System log

    C. Security log

    D. Application log

3. Alex wants to use an automated tool to fill web application forms to test for format string vulnerabilities. What type of tool should he use?

    A. A black box

    B. A brute-force tool

    C. A fuzzer

    D. A static analysis tool

For questions 4–6, please refer to the following scenario.

Henry is the risk manager for Atwood Landing, a resort community in the midwestern United States. The resort's main data center is located in northern Indiana in an area that is prone to tornados. Henry recently undertook a replacement cost analysis and determined that rebuilding and reconfiguring the data center would cost $10 million.

Henry consulted with tornado experts, data center specialists, and structural engineers. Together, they determined that a typical tornado would cause approximately $5 million of damage to the facility. The meteorologists determined that Atwood's facility lies in an area where they are likely to experience a tornado once every 200 years.

4. Based upon the information in this scenario, what is the exposure factor for the effect of a tornado on Atwood Landing's data center?

    A. 10 percent

    B. 25 percent

    C. 50 percent

    D. 75 percent

5. Based upon the information in this scenario, what is the annualized rate of occurrence for a tornado at Atwood Landing's data center?

   A. 0.0025

   B. 0.005

   C. 0.01

   D. 0.015

6. Based upon the information in this scenario, what is the annualized loss expectancy for a tornado at Atwood Landing's data center?

   A. $25,000

   B. $50,000

   C. $250,000

   D. $500,000

7. Earlier this year, the information security team at Jim's employer identified a vulnerability in the web server that Jim is responsible for maintaining. He immediately applied the patch and is sure that it installed properly, but the vulnerability scanner has continued to incorrectly flag the system as vulnerable because of the version number it is finding even though Jim is sure the patch is installed. Which of the following options is Jim's best choice to deal with the issue?

   A. Uninstall and reinstall the patch.

   B. Ask the information security team to flag the system as patched and not vulnerable.

   C. Update the version information in the web server's configuration.

   D. Review the vulnerability report and use alternate remediation options.

8. Which NIST special publication covers the assessment of security and privacy controls?

   A. 800-12

   B. 800-53A

   C. 800-34

   D. 800-86

9. Selah's team is working to persuade their management that their network has extensive vulnerabilities that attackers could exploit. If she wants to conduct a realistic attack as part of a penetration test, what type of penetration test should she conduct?

   A. Full knowledge

   B. Partial knowledge

   C. Zero knowledge

   D. Specific knowledge

10. Tom enables an application firewall provided by his cloud infrastructure as a service provider that is designed to block many types of application attacks. When viewed from a risk management perspective, what metric is Tom attempting to lower?

    A. Impact

    B. RPO

    C. MTO

    D. Likelihood

11. Jim uses a tool that scans a system for available services and then connects to them to collect banner information to determine what version of the service is running. It then provides a report detailing what it gathers, basing results on service fingerprinting, banner information, and similar details it gathers combined with CVE information. What type of tool is Jim using?

    A. A port scanner

    B. A service validator

    C. A vulnerability scanner

    D. A patch management tool

12. What term describes software testing that is intended to uncover new bugs introduced by patches or configuration changes?

    A. Nonregression testing

    B. Evolution testing

    C. Smoke testing

    D. Regression testing

13. Mike recently implemented an intrusion prevention system designed to block common network attacks from affecting his organization. What type of risk management strategy is Mike pursuing?

    A. Risk acceptance

    B. Risk avoidance

    C. Risk mitigation

    D. Risk transference

14. During a port scan, Lauren found TCP port 443 open on a system. Which tool is best suited to scanning the service that is most likely running on that port?

    A. zzuf

    B. Nikto

    C. Metasploit

    D. sqlmap

15. When developing a business impact analysis, the team should first create a list of assets. What should happen next?

  A. Identify vulnerabilities in each asset.

  B. Determine the risks facing the asset.

  C. Develop a value for each asset.

  D. Identify threats facing each asset.

16. In this image, what issue may occur because of the log handling settings?

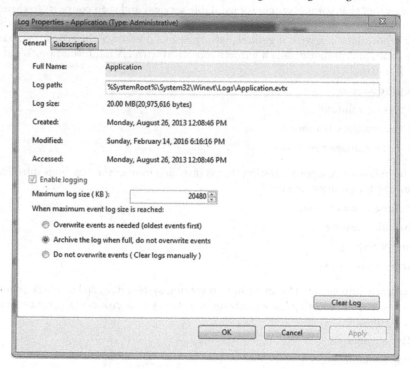

  A. Log data may be lost when the log is archived.

  B. Log data may be overwritten.

  C. Log data may not include needed information.

  D. Log data may fill the system disk.

17. What message logging standard is commonly used by network devices, Linux and Unix systems, and many other enterprise devices?

  A. Syslog

  B. Netlog

  C. Eventlog

  D. Remote Log Protocol (RLP)

18. Ryan is a security risk analyst for an insurance company. He is currently examining a scenario in which a malicious hacker might use a SQL injection attack to deface a web server because of a missing patch in the company's web application. In this scenario, what is the threat?

    A. Unpatched web application

    B. Web defacement

    C. Malicious hacker

    D. Operating system

19. Chris is responsible for his organization's security standards and has guided the selection and implementation of a security baseline for Windows PCs in his organization. How can Chris most effectively make sure that the workstations he is responsible for are being checked for compliance and that settings are being applied as necessary?

    A. Assign users to spot-check baseline compliance.

    B. Use Microsoft Group Policy.

    C. Create startup scripts to apply policy at system start.

    D. Periodically review the baselines with the data owner and system owners.

For questions 20–22, please refer to the following scenario.

The company that Jennifer works for has implemented a central logging infrastructure, as shown in the following image. Use this diagram and your knowledge of logging systems to answer the following questions.

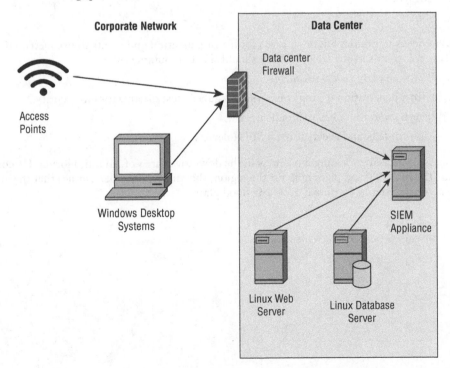

20. Jennifer needs to ensure that all Windows systems provide identical logging information to the SIEM. How can she best ensure that all Windows desktops have the same log settings?

    A. Perform periodic configuration audits.

    B. Use Group Policy.

    C. Use Local Policy.

    D. Deploy a Windows syslog client.

21. During normal operations, Jennifer's team uses the SIEM appliance to monitor for exceptions received via syslog. What system shown does not natively have support for syslog events?

    A. Enterprise wireless access points

    B. Windows desktop systems

    C. Linux web servers

    D. Enterprise firewall devices

22. What technology should an organization use for each of the devices shown in the diagram to ensure that logs can be time sequenced across the entire infrastructure?

    A. Syslog

    B. NTP

    C. Logsync

    D. SNAP

23. Susan needs to predict high-risk areas for her organization and wants to use metrics to assess risk trends as they occur. What should she do to handle this?

    A. Perform yearly risk assessments.

    B. Hire a penetration testing company to regularly test organizational security.

    C. Identify and track key risk indicators.

    D. Monitor logs and events using a SIEM device.

24. Tom is considering locating a business in the downtown area of Miami, Florida. He consults the FEMA flood plain map for the region, shown here, and determines that the area he is considering lies within a 100-year flood plain.

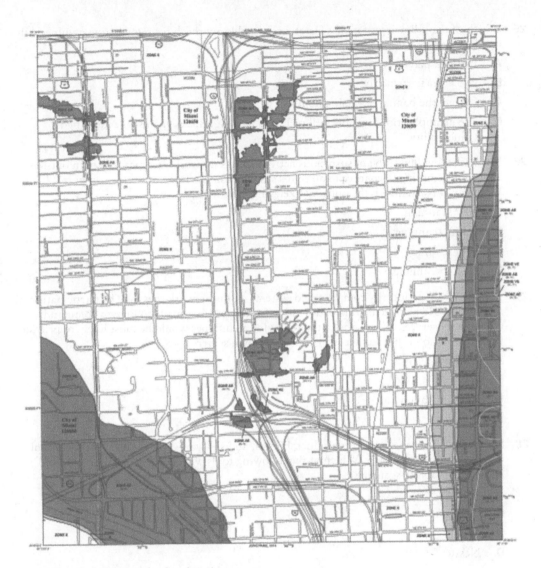

What is the ARO of a flood in this area?

A. 100

B. 1

C. 0.1

D. 0.01

25. Which of the following strategies is not a reasonable approach for remediating a vulnerability identified by a vulnerability scanner?

   A. Install a patch.

   B. Use a workaround fix.

   C. Update the banner or version number.

   D. Use an application layer firewall or IPS to prevent attacks against the identified vulnerability.

26. Bruce is seeing quite a bit of suspicious activity on his network. It appears that an outside entity is attempting to connect to all of his systems using a TCP connection on port 22. What type of scanning is the outsider likely engaging in?

   A. FTP scanning

   B. Telnet scanning

   C. SSH scanning

   D. HTTP scanning

27. Jim would like to identify compromised systems on his network that may be participating in a botnet. He plans to do this by watching for connections made to known command-and-control servers. Which one of the following techniques would be most likely to provide this information if Jim has access to a list of known servers?

   A. Netflow records

   B. IDS logs

   C. Authentication logs

   D. RFC logs

28. Susan needs to scan a system for vulnerabilities, and she wants to use an open source tool to test the system remotely. Which of the following tools will meet her requirements and allow vulnerability scanning?

   A. Nmap

   B. OpenVAS

   C. MBSA

   D. Nessus

29. Jim is designing his organization's log management systems and knows that he needs to carefully plan to handle the organization's log data. Which of the following is not a factor that Jim should be concerned with?

   A. The volume of log data

   B. A lack of sufficient log sources

   C. Data storage security requirements

   D. Network bandwidth

Kara used nmap to perform a scan of a system under her control and received the results shown here. Refer to these results to answer questions 30 and 31.

```
Starting Nmap 7.40 ( https://nmap.org ) at 2018-01-08 15:08 EST
Nmap scan report for myhost (192.168.107.9)
Host is up (0.033s latency).
Not shown: 997 filtered ports
PORT    STATE SERVICE
22/tcp  open  ssh
80/tcp  open  http
443/tcp open  https
```

30. If Kara's primary concern is preventing eavesdropping attacks, which port should she block?

   A. 22

   B. 80

   C. 443

   D. 1433

31. If Kara's primary concern is preventing administrative connections to the server, which port should she block?

   A. 22

   B. 80

   C. 443

   D. 1433

32. During a port scan, Susan discovers a system running services on TCP and UDP 137-139 and TCP 445, as well as TCP 1433. What type of system is she likely to find if she connects to the machine?

   A. A Linux email server

   B. A Windows SQL server

   C. A Linux file server

   D. A Windows workstation

33. After conducting a qualitative risk assessment of her organization, Sally recommends purchasing cybersecurity breach insurance. What type of risk response behavior is she recommending?

   A. Accept

   B. Transfer

   C. Reduce

   D. Reject

34. What is the best way to provide accountability for the use of identities?

   A. Logging

   B. Authorization

   C. Digital signatures

   D. Type 1 authentication

35. Robin recently conducted a vulnerability scan and found a critical vulnerability on a server that handles sensitive information. What should Robin do next?

   A. Patching

   B. Reporting

   C. Remediation

   D. Validation

36. Rolando is a risk manager with a large-scale enterprise. The firm recently evaluated the risk of California mudslides on its operations in the region and determined that the cost of responding outweighed the benefits of any controls it could implement. The company chose to take no action at this time. What risk management strategy did Rolando's organization pursue?

   A. Risk avoidance

   B. Risk mitigation

   C. Risk transference

   D. Risk acceptance

37. During a log review, Danielle discovers a series of logs that show login failures.

```
Jan 31 11:39:12 ip-10-0-0-2 sshd[29092]: Invalid user admin from remotehost passwd=aaaaaaaa
Jan 31 11:39:20 ip-10-0-0-2 sshd[29098]: Invalid user admin from remotehost passwd=aaaaaaab
Jan 31 11:39:23 ip-10-0-0-2 sshd[29100]: Invalid user admin from remotehost passwd=aaaaaaac
Jan 31 11:39:31 ip-10-0-0-2 sshd[29106]: Invalid user admin from remotehost passwd=aaaaaaad
Jan 31 20:40:53 ip-10-0-0-254 sshd[30520]: Invalid user admin from remotehost passwd=aaaaaaae
```

What type of attack has Danielle discovered?

   A. A pass-the-hash attack

   B. A brute-force attack

   C. A man-in-the-middle attack

   D. A dictionary attack

38. During a third-party audit, Jim's company receives a finding that states, "The administrator should review backup success and failure logs on a daily basis, and take action in a timely manner to resolve reported exceptions." What is the biggest issue that is likely to result if Jim's IT staff need to restore from a backup?

   A. They will not know if the backups succeeded or failed.

   B. The backups may not be properly logged.

   C. The backups may not be usable.

   D. The backup logs may not be properly reviewed.

For questions 39–41, please refer to the following scenario.

   Ben's organization has begun to use STRIDE to assess its software and has identified threat agents and the business impacts that these threats could have. Now they are working to identify appropriate controls for the issues they have identified.

39. Ben's development team needs to address an authorization issue, resulting in an elevation of privilege threat. Which of the following controls is most appropriate to this type of issue?

   A. Auditing and logging are enabled.

   B. Role-based access control is used for specific operations.

   C. Data type and format checks are enabled.

   D. User input is tested against a whitelist.

40. Ben's team is attempting to categorize a transaction identification issue that is caused by use of a symmetric key shared by multiple servers. What STRIDE category should this fall into?

   A. Information disclosure

   B. Denial of service

   C. Tampering

   D. Repudiation

41. Ben wants to prevent or detect tampering with data. Which of the following is not an appropriate solution?

   A. Hashes

   B. Digital signatures

   C. Filtering

   D. Authorization controls

42. During a port scan of his network, Alex finds that a number of hosts respond on TCP ports 80, 443, 515, and 9100 in offices throughout his organization. What type of devices is Alex likely discovering?

   A. Web servers

   B. File servers

   C. Wireless access points

   D. Printers

43. Alan is performing threat modeling and decides that it would be useful to decompose the system into the key elements shown here. What tool is he using?

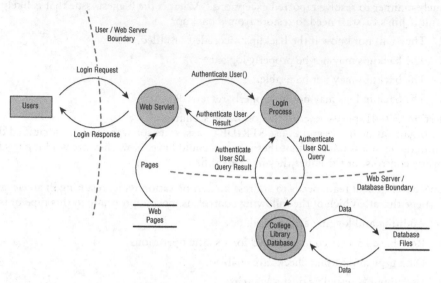

Image reprinted from *CISSP (ISC)² Certified Information Systems Security Professional Official Study Guide,* 7th Edition © John Wiley & Sons 2015, reprinted with permission.

    A. Vulnerability assessment

    B. Fuzzing

    C. Reduction analysis

    D. Data modeling

44. Which of the following is not a hazard associated with penetration testing?

    A. Application crashes

    B. Denial of service

    C. Exploitation of vulnerabilities

    D. Data corruption

45. Nmap is an example of what type of tool?

    A. Vulnerability scanner

    B. Web application fuzzer

    C. Network design and layout

    D. Port scanner

46. Which of the following is a method used to design new software tests and to ensure the quality of tests?

    A. Code auditing

    B. Static code analysis

    C. Regression testing

    D. Mutation testing

47. When a Windows system is rebooted, what type of log is generated?

    A. Error

    B. Warning

    C. Information

    D. Failure audit

48. What is the first step that should occur before a penetration test is performed?

    A. Data gathering

    B. Port scanning

    C. Getting permission

    D. Planning

49. Bobbi is investigating a security incident and discovers that an attacker began with a normal user account but managed to exploit a system vulnerability to provide that account with administrative rights. What type of attack took place under the STRIDE threat model?

    A. Spoofing

    B. Repudiation

    C. Tampering

    D. Elevation of privilege

For questions 50–53, please refer to the following scenario.

Ann is a security professional for a midsize business and typically handles log analysis and security monitoring tasks for her organization. One of her roles is to monitor alerts originating from the organization's intrusion detection system. The system typically generates several dozen alerts each day, and many of those alerts turn out to be false alarms after her investigation.

This morning, the intrusion detection system alerted because the network began to receive an unusually high volume of inbound traffic. Ann received this alert and began looking into the origin of the traffic.

50. At this point in the incident response process, what term best describes what has occurred in Ann's organization?

    A. Security occurrence

    B. Security incident

    C. Security event

    D. Security intrusion

51. Ann continues her investigation and realizes that the traffic generating the alert is abnormally high volumes of inbound UDP traffic on port 53. What service typically uses this port?

   A. DNS

   B. SSH/SCP

   C. SSL/TLS

   D. HTTP

52. As Ann analyzes the traffic further, she realizes that the traffic is coming from many different sources and has overwhelmed the network, preventing legitimate uses. The inbound packets are responses to queries that she does not see in outbound traffic. The responses are abnormally large for their type. What type of attack should Ann suspect?

   A. Reconnaissance

   B. Malicious code

   C. System penetration

   D. Denial of service

53. Now that Ann understands that an attack has taken place that violates her organization's security policy, what term best describes what has occurred in Ann's organization?

   A. Security occurrence

   B. Security incident

   C. Security event

   D. Security intrusion

54. During a log review, Saria discovers a series of logs that show login failures, as shown here:

```
Jan 31 11:39:12 ip-10-0-0-2 sshd[29092]: Invalid user admin from remotehost passwd=orange
Jan 31 11:39:20 ip-10-0-0-2 sshd[29098]: Invalid user admin from remotehost passwd=Orang3
Jan 31 11:39:23 ip-10-0-0-2 sshd[29100]: Invalid user admin from remotehost passwd=Orange93
Jan 31 11:39:31 ip-10-0-0-2 sshd[29106]: Invalid user admin from remotehost passwd=Orangutan1
Jan 31 20:40:53 ip-10-0-0-254 sshd[30520]: Invalid user admin from remotehost passwd=Orangemonkey
```

   What type of attack has Saria discovered?

   A. A brute-force attack

   B. A man-in-the-middle attack

   C. A dictionary attack

   D. A rainbow table attack

55. Ben is seeking a control objective framework that is widely accepted around the world and focuses specifically on information security controls. Which one of the following frameworks would best meet his needs?

    A. ITIL

    B. ISO 27002

    C. CMM

    D. PMBOK Guide

56. Alex is using nmap to perform port scanning of a system, and he receives three different port status messages in the results. Match each of the numbered status messages with the appropriate lettered description. You should use each item exactly once.

    Status message

    1. Open
    2. Closed
    3. Filtered

    Description

    A. The port is accessible on the remote system, but no application is accepting connections on that port.

    B. The port is not accessible on the remote system.

    C. The port is accessible on the remote system, and an application is accepting connections on that port.

57. Tony is developing a business continuity plan and is having difficulty prioritizing resources because of the difficulty of combining information about tangible and intangible assets. What would be the most effective risk assessment approach for him to use?

    A. Quantitative risk assessment

    B. Qualitative risk assessment

    C. Neither quantitative nor qualitative risk assessment

    D. Combination of quantitative and qualitative risk assessment

58. Angela wants to test a web browser's handling of unexpected data using an automated tool. What tool should she choose?

    A. Nmap

    B. zzuf

    C. Nessus

    D. Nikto

59. Saria wants to log and review traffic information between parts of her network. What type of network logging should she enable on her routers to allow her to perform this analysis?

    A. Audit logging

    B. Flow logging

    C. Trace logging

    D. Route logging

60. Jim is working with a penetration testing contractor who proposes using Metasploit as part of her penetration testing effort. What should Jim expect to occur when Metasploit is used?

   A. Systems will be scanned for vulnerabilities.

   B. Systems will have known vulnerabilities exploited.

   C. Services will be probed for buffer overflow and other unknown flaws.

   D. Systems will be tested for zero-day exploits.

61. You are completing your business continuity planning effort and have decided that you wish to accept one of the risks. What should you do next?

   A. Implement new security controls to reduce the risk level.

   B. Design a disaster recovery plan.

   C. Repeat the business impact assessment.

   D. Document your decision-making process.

For questions 62–64, please refer to the following scenario. During a port scan, Ben uses nmap's default settings and sees the following results.

```
Nmap scan report for 192.168.184.130
Host is up (1.0s latency).
Not shown: 977 closed ports
PORT      STATE SERVICE
21/tcp    open  ftp
22/tcp    open  ssh
23/tcp    open  telnet
25/tcp    open  smtp
53/tcp    open  domain
80/tcp    open  http
111/tcp   open  rpcbind
139/tcp   open  netbios-ssn
445/tcp   open  microsoft-ds
512/tcp   open  exec
513/tcp   open  login
514/tcp   open  shell
1099/tcp  open  rmiregistry
1524/tcp  open  ingreslock
2049/tcp  open  nfs
2121/tcp  open  ccproxy-ftp
3306/tcp  open  mysql
5432/tcp  open  postgresql
5900/tcp  open  vnc
6000/tcp  open  X11
6667/tcp  open  irc
8009/tcp  open  ajp13
8180/tcp  open  unknown

Nmap done: 1 IP address (1 host up) scanned in 54.69 seconds
```

62. If Ben is conducting a penetration test, what should his next step be after receiving these results?

   A. Connect to the web server using a web browser.

   B. Connect via Telnet to test for vulnerable accounts.

   C. Identify interesting ports for further scanning.

   D. Use sqlmap against the open databases.

63. Based on the scan results, what operating system (OS) was the system that was scanned most likely running?

    A. Windows Desktop

    B. Linux

    C. Network device

    D. Windows Server

64. Ben's manager expresses concern about the coverage of his scan. Why might his manager have this concern?

    A. Ben did not test UDP services.

    B. Ben did not discover ports outside the "well-known ports."

    C. Ben did not perform OS fingerprinting.

    D. Ben tested only a limited number of ports.

65. What is the formula used to determine risk?

    A. Risk = Threat * Vulnerability

    B. Risk = Threat / Vulnerability

    C. Risk = Asset * Threat

    D. Risk = Asset / Threat

66. A zero-day vulnerability is announced for the popular Apache web server in the middle of a workday. In Jacob's role as an information security analyst, he needs to quickly scan his network to determine what servers are vulnerable to the issue. What is Jacob's best route to quickly identify vulnerable systems?

    A. Immediately run Nessus against all of the servers to identify which systems are vulnerable.

    B. Review the CVE database to find the vulnerability information and patch information.

    C. Create a custom IDS or IPS signature.

    D. Identify affected versions and check systems for that version number using an automated scanner.

67. During a review of access logs, Alex notices that Danielle logged into her workstation in New York at 8 a.m. daily but that she was recorded as logging into her department's main web application shortly after 3 a.m. daily. What common logging issue has Alex likely encountered?

    A. Inconsistent log formatting

    B. Modified logs

    C. Inconsistent timestamps

    D. Multiple log sources

68. What is the final step of a quantitative risk analysis?

    A. Determine asset value.

    B. Assess the annualized rate of occurrence.

    C. Derive the annualized loss expectancy.

    D. Conduct a cost/benefit analysis.

69. Carrie is analyzing the application logs for her web-based application and comes across the following string:

    `../../../../../../../../../etc/passwd`

    What type of attack was likely attempted against Carrie's application?

    A. Command injection

    B. Session hijacking

    C. Directory traversal

    D. Brute force

70. Allie is responsible for reviewing authentication logs on her organization's network. She does not have the time to review all logs, so she decides to choose only records where there have been four or more invalid authentication attempts. What technique is Allie using to reduce the size of the pool?

    A. Sampling

    B. Random selection

    C. Clipping

    D. Statistical analysis

71. Isaac wants to be able to describe the severity of a vulnerability to his team. What standard could he use to easily describe vulnerabilities using a numerical score?

    A. CVSS

    B. ATT&CK

    C. MITRE

    D. SAML

72. Which type of business impact assessment tool is most appropriate when attempting to evaluate the impact of a failure on customer confidence?

    A. Quantitative

    B. Qualitative

    C. Annualized loss expectancy

    D. Reduction

73. What type of vulnerabilities will not be found by a vulnerability scanner?

   A. Local vulnerabilities

   B. Service vulnerabilities

   C. Zero-day vulnerabilities

   D. Vulnerabilities that require authentication

74. Which of the following vulnerabilities is unlikely to be found by a web vulnerability scanner?

   A. Path disclosure

   B. Local file inclusion

   C. Race condition

   D. Buffer overflow

75. Jim has been contracted to conduct a gray box penetration test, and his clients have provided him with the following information about their networks so that he can scan them:

   Data center: 10.10.10.0/24

   Sales: 10.10.11.0/24

   Billing: 10.10.12.0/24

   Wireless: 192.168.0.0/16

   What problem will Jim encounter if he is contracted to conduct a scan from offsite?

   A. The IP ranges are too large to scan efficiently.

   B. The IP addresses provided cannot be scanned.

   C. The IP ranges overlap and will cause scanning issues.

   D. The IP addresses provided are RFC 1918 addresses.

76. Naomi wants to put a system in place that will allow her team to aggregate and correlate event information from a variety of systems and devices in her organization. She then wants to automate the investigation process using workflows with the correlated data. What type of system should she put in place?

   A. A NAS

   B. An IPS

   C. A SOAR

   D. An MDR

77. Murali wants to determine if SQL injection attacks are being attempted against his web application. Which of the following potential source systems will not be useful when identifying SQL injection?

   A. Application logs

   B. WAF logs

   C. Network switch logs

   D. Database logs

78. Li has completed the discovery of assets across her organization's network. What is the most likely next step in her vulnerability management lifecycle?

A. Prioritizing the assets

B. Applying patches to any vulnerable systems

C. Testing the vulnerabilities using proof-of-concept exploits

D. Identifying all vulnerabilities that have not been patched since the last scan

79. Diego's organization has applied controls to all risks that it has prioritized. It would not be cost effective to remediate or prevent the remaining risks, and he needs to determine what to do with them. What risk response option is most appropriate to this scenario?

A. Transferring the risks

B. Ignoring the risks

C. Reviewing for possible new mitigations

D. Accepting the risks

80. Kathleen's organization has a mature risk assessment process with strong sponsorship from leadership, but also has very low tolerance for risk. Which of the following is most likely to be true about their process for handling risks?

A. They are likely to accept many risks.

B. They are likely to spend resources to mitigate as many risks as possible.

C. They are likely to ignore as many risks as possible.

D. They are likely to spend as few resources as possible to mitigate risks.

81. Megan is reviewing her organization's risks and identifies a single point of failure due to the fiber-optic cable connection to a local fiber ring that her organization built and maintains. What type of risk does this describe?

A. An intrinsic risk

B. An architecture risk

C. A supplier risk

D. A contractual risk

82. Unusual outbound network traffic, irregularities in geographic or time-based login information, privileged users account activity changes, and unexpected traffic on nonstandard ports are all common examples of what?

A. Vulnerability scanning artifacts

B. SQL injection log entries

C. Indicators of Compromise

D. Key performance indicators

83. Susan wants to use her SIEM to deliver notifications when events occur. Which of the following should she ensure is set to prevent responders from ignoring the notifications?

    A. An automated daily email with dashboard information

    B. A required login when notifications are sent

    C. Automated timeline creation for incident data

    D. Appropriate thresholds for notification

Chapter 4

Incident Response and Recovery (Domain 4)

THE SSCP EXAM TOPICS COVERED IN THIS CHAPTER INCLUDE:

✓ **Domain 4.0 Incident Response and Recovery**

- **4.1 Support incident lifecycle (e.g., National Institute of Standards and Technology (NIST), International Organization for Standardization (ISO))**

  - Preparation

  - Detection, analysis, and escalation

  - Containment

  - Eradication

  - Recovery

  - Lessons learned/implementation of new countermeasure

- **4.2 Understand and support forensic investigations**

  - Legal (e.g., civil, criminal, administrative) and ethical principles

  - Evidence handling (e.g., first responder, triage, chain of custody, preservation of scene)

  - Reporting of analysis

- **4.3 Understand and support Business Continuity Plan (BCP) and Disaster Recovery Plan (DRP) activities**

  - Emergency response plans and procedures (e.g., information system contingency plan, natural disaster, crisis management)

  - Interim or alternate processing strategies

  - Restoration planning

  - Backup and redundancy implementation

  - Testing and drills

1. Tara recently detected a security incident in progress on her network. What action should be her highest priority at this point?

   A. Eradication

   B. Recovery

   C. Containment

   D. Detection

2. Alan is responding to a security incident and receives a hard drive image from a cooperating organization that contains evidence. What additional information should he request to verify the integrity of the evidence?

   A. Private key

   B. Public key

   C. Hash

   D. Drive capacity

3. Jeff discovers a series of JPEG photos on a drive that he is analyzing for evidentiary purposes. He uses exiftool to collect metadata from those files. Which information is *not* likely to be included in that metadata?

   A. GPS location

   B. Camera type

   C. Number of copies made

   D. Timestamp

4. Chris would like to use John the Ripper to test the security of passwords on a compromised Linux system. What files does he need to conduct this analysis?

   A. /etc/shadow and /etc/user

   B. /etc/passwd and /etc/user

   C. /etc/user and /etc/account

   D. /etc/passwd and /etc/shadow

5. Alex's organization uses the NIST incident classification scheme. Alex discovers that a laptop belonging to a senior executive had keylogging software installed on it. How should Alex classify this occurrence?

   A. Event

   B. Adverse event

   C. Incident

   D. Policy violation

6. When working to restore systems to their original configuration after a long-term APT compromise, Charles has three options:

    Option 1: He can restore from a backup and then update patches on the system.

    Option 2: He can rebuild and patch the system using the original installation media and application software and his organization's build documentation.

    Option 3: He can remove the compromised accounts and rootkit tools and then fix the issues that allowed the attackers to access the systems.

    Which option should Charles choose in this scenario?

    A. Option 1

    B. Option 2

    C. Option 3

    D. None of the above. Charles should hire a third party to assess the systems before proceeding.

7. If Danielle wants to purge a drive, which of the following options will accomplish her goal?

    A. Cryptographic erase

    B. Reformat

    C. Overwrite

    D. Partition

8. Cynthia is building a series of scripts to detect malware beaconing behavior on her network. Which of the following is *not* a typical means of identifying malware beaconing?

    A. Persistence of the beaconing

    B. Beacon protocol

    C. Beaconing interval

    D. Removal of known traffic

9. While performing post-rebuild validation efforts, Scott scans a server from a remote network and sees no vulnerabilities. Joanna, the administrator of the machine, runs a scan and discovered two critical vulnerabilities and five moderate issues. What is most likely causing the difference in their reports?

    A. Different patch levels during the scans

    B. Scanning through a load balancer

    C. Firewall between the remote network and the server

    D. Running the scan with different settings

10. Mika wants to analyze the contents of a drive without causing any changes to the drive. What method is best suited to ensuring this?

    A. Set the read-only jumper on the drive.

    B. Use a write blocker.

    C. Use a read blocker.

    D. Use a forensic software package.

11. What type of forensic investigation-related form is shown here?

Case Number: _____ Item Number: _____
Evidence Description: _____
_____
_____
Collection method: _____
_____
Evidence storage method: _____
How is evidence secured? _____
Collected by: (Name/ID#) _____
Signature of collector: _____

Copy History		
Date	**Copied method**	**Disposition of original and all copies**

Item #	Date/Time	Released by (Signature & ID#)	Received by (Signature & ID#)	Comments/Location

    A. Chain of custody

    B. Report of examination

    C. Forensic discovery log

    D. Policy custody release

12. Eric has access to a full suite of network monitoring tools and wants to use appropriate tools to monitor network bandwidth consumption. Which of the following is *not* a common method of monitoring network bandwidth usage?

    A. SNMP

    B. Portmon

    C. Packet sniffing

    D. Netflow

13. After completing an incident response process and providing a final report to management, what step should Casey use to identify improvement to her incident response plan?

    A. Update system documentation.

    B. Conduct a lessons-learned session.

    C. Review patching status and vulnerability scans.

    D. Engage third-party consultants.

14. The senior management of Kathleen's company is concerned about rogue devices on the network. If Kathleen wants to identify rogue devices on her wired network, which of the following solutions will quickly provide the most accurate information?

    A. Discovery scan with a port scanner

    B. Router and switch-based MAC address reporting

    C. Physical survey

    D. Reviewing a central administration tool, such as SCCM

15. During a forensic investigation, Charles discovers that he needs to capture a virtual machine that is part of the critical operations of his company's website. If he cannot suspend or shut down the machine for business reasons, what imaging process should he follow?

    A. Perform a snapshot of the system, boot it, suspend the copied version, and copy the directory it resides in.

    B. Copy the virtual disk files and then use a memory capture tool.

    C. Escalate to management to get permission to suspend the system to allow a true forensic copy.

    D. Use a tool like the Volatility Framework to capture the live machine completely.

16. Lauren is the IT manager for a small company and occasionally serves as the organization's information security officer. Which of the following roles should she include as the leader of her organization's CSIRT?

    A. Her lead IT support staff technician

    B. Her organization's legal counsel

    C. A third-party IR team lead

    D. She should select herself.

17. Because of external factors, Eric has only a limited time period to collect an image from a workstation. If he collects only specific files of interest, what type of acquisition has he performed?

    A. Logical

    B. Bit-by-bit

    C. Sparse

    D. None of the above

18. NIST defines five major types of threat information types in NIST SP 800-150 the "Guide to Cyber Threat Information Sharing." They are:

1. Indicators, which are technical artifacts or observables that suggest an attack is imminent, currently underway, or compromise may have already occurred

2. Tactics, techniques, and procedures that describe the behavior of an actor

3. Security alerts like advisories and bulletins

4. Threat intelligence reports that describe actors, systems, and information being targeted and the methods being used

5. Tool configurations that support collection, exchange, analysis, and use of threat information

Which one of the following groups would be least likely to included in an organization's cybersecurity incident communications plans?

A. Law enforcement

B. Security vendors

C. Utilities

D. Media

19. Which of the following is not an important part of the incident response communication process?

A. Limiting communication to trusted parties

B. Disclosure based on public feedback

C. Using a secure method of communication

D. Preventing accidental release of incident related information

20. As the CISO of her organization, Jennifer is working on an incident classification scheme and wants to base her design on NIST's definitions. Which of the following options should she use to best describe a user accessing a file that they are not authorized to view?

A. An incident

B. An event

C. An adverse event

D. A security incident

21. In his role as a forensic examiner, Lucas has been asked to produce forensic evidence related to a civil case. What is this process called?

A. Criminal forensics

B. eDiscovery

C. Cyber production

D. Civil tort

22. Darcy is designing a fault-tolerant system and wants to implement RAID level 5 for her system. What is the minimum number of physical hard disks she can use to build this system?

   A. One

   B. Two

   C. Three

   D. Five

23. What important function do senior managers normally fill on a business continuity planning team?

   A. Arbitrating disputes about criticality

   B. Evaluating the legal environment

   C. Training staff

   D. Designing failure controls

24. Which one of the following is not normally included in business continuity plan documentation?

   A. Statement of accounts

   B. Statement of importance

   C. Statement of priorities

   D. Statement of organizational responsibility

25. Which one of the following is not normally considered a business continuity task?

   A. Business impact assessment

   B. Emergency response guidelines

   C. Electronic vaulting

   D. Vital records program

26. Who should receive initial business continuity plan training in an organization?

   A. Senior executives

   B. Those with specific business continuity roles

   C. Everyone in the organization

   D. First responders

27. Which one of the following components should be included in an organization's emergency response guidelines?

   A. List of individuals who should be notified of an emergency incident

   B. Long-term business continuity protocols

   C. Activation procedures for the organization's cold sites

   D. Contact information for ordering equipment

For questions 28–30, please refer to the following scenario.

Alejandro is an incident response analyst for a large corporation. He is on the midnight shift when an intrusion detection system alerts him to a potential brute-force password attack against one of the company's critical information systems. He performs an initial triage of the event before taking any additional action.

28. What stage of the incident response process is Alejandro currently conducting?
    A. Detection
    B. Response
    C. Recovery
    D. Mitigation

29. If Alejandro's initial investigation determines that a security incident is likely taking place, what should be his next step?
    A. Investigate the root cause.
    B. File a written report.
    C. Activate the incident response team.
    D. Attempt to restore the system to normal operations.

30. As the incident response progresses, during which stage should the team conduct a root-cause analysis?
    A. Response
    B. Reporting
    C. Remediation
    D. Lessons learned

31. The Domer Industries risk assessment team recently conducted a qualitative risk assessment and developed a matrix similar to the one shown here. Which quadrant contains the risks that require the most immediate attention?

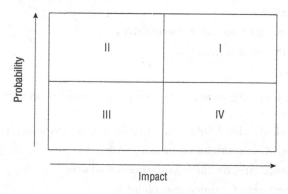

    A. I

    B. II

    C. III

    D. IV

32. Which one of the following stakeholders is not typically included on a business continuity planning team?

    A. Core business function leaders

    B. Information technology staff

    C. CEO

    D. Support departments

33. Craig is selecting the site for a new data center and must choose a location somewhere within the United States. He obtained the earthquake risk map shown here from the United States Geological Survey. Which of the following would be the safest location to build his facility if he were primarily concerned with earthquake risk?

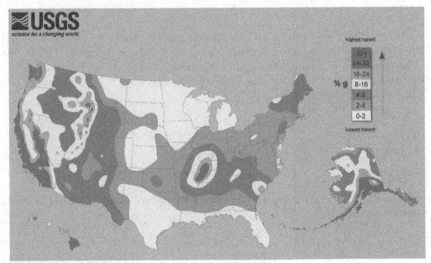

(Source: US Geological Survey)

Image reprinted from *CISSP (ISC)² Certified Information Systems Security Professional Official Study Guide*, 7th Edition © John Wiley & Sons 2015, reprinted with permission.

    A. New York

    B. North Carolina

    C. Indiana

    D. Florida

34. As part of his incident response process, Charles securely wipes the drive of a compromised machine and reinstalls the operating system (OS) from original media. Once he is done, he patches the machine fully and applies his organization's security templates before reconnecting the system to the network. Almost immediately after the system is returned to service, he discovers that it has reconnected to the same botnet it was part of before. Where should Charles look for the malware that is causing this behavior?

A. The operating system partition

B. The system BIOS or firmware

C. The system memory

D. The installation media

35. As part of his team's forensic investigation process, Matt signs drives and other evidence out of storage before working with them. What type of documentation is he creating?

A. Criminal

B. Chain of custody

C. Civil

D. CYA

36. Karen's organization has been performing system backups for years but has not used the backups frequently. During a recent system outage, when administrators tried to restore from backups, they found that the backups had errors and could not be restored. Which of the following options should Karen avoid when selecting ways to ensure that her organization's backups will work next time?

A. Log review

B. MTD verification

C. Hashing

D. Periodic testing

37. Referring to the following figure, what technology is shown that provides fault tolerance for the database servers?

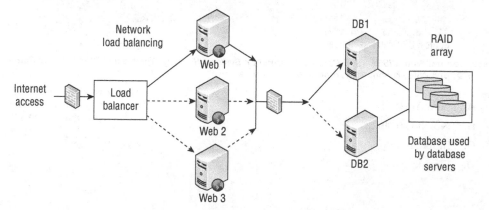

    A. Failover cluster

    B. UPS

    C. Tape backup

    D. Cold site

38. Which of the following is not a common ethical standard for computer forensics professionals?

    A. Maintaining objectivity

    B. Testimony must favor the client

    C. Avoiding conflict of interest

    D. Not concealing any findings

39. Glenda would like to conduct a disaster recovery test and is seeking a test that will allow a review of the plan with no disruption to normal information system activities and as minimal a commitment of time as possible. What type of test should she choose?

    A. Tabletop exercise

    B. Parallel test

    C. Full interruption test

    D. Checklist review

40. Which one of the following is not an example of a backup tape rotation scheme?

    A. Grandfather/Father/Son

    B. Meet-in-the-middle

    C. Tower of Hanoi

    D. Six Cartridge Weekly

41. Which one of the following is not a requirement for evidence to be admissible in court?

    A. The evidence must be relevant.

    B. The evidence must be material.

    C. The evidence must be tangible.

    D. The evidence must be competent.

42. Sam is responsible for backing up his company's primary file server. He configured a backup schedule that performs full backups every Monday evening at 9 p.m. and differential backups on other days of the week at that same time. Files change according to the information shown in the following figure. How many files will be copied in Wednesday's backup?

<u>File Modifications</u>
Monday 8 a.m. - File 1 created
Monday 10 a.m. - File 2 created
Monday 11 a.m. - File 3 created
Monday 4 p.m. - File 1 modified
Monday 5 p.m. - File 4 created
Tuesday 8 a.m. - File 1 modified
Tuesday 9 a.m. - File 2 modified
Tuesday 10 a.m. - File 5 created
Wednesday 8 a.m. - File 3 modified
Wednesday 9 a.m. - File 6 created

   A. 2

   B. 3

   C. 5

   D. 6

43. Tim is a forensic analyst who is attempting to retrieve information from a hard drive. It appears that the user attempted to erase the data, and Tim is trying to reconstruct it. What type of forensic analysis is Tim performing?

   A. Software analysis

   B. Media analysis

   C. Embedded device analysis

   D. Network analysis

44. Which one of the following is an example of a computer security incident?

   A. Completion of a backup schedule

   B. System access recorded in a log

   C. Unauthorized vulnerability scan of a file server

   D. Update of antivirus signatures

45. Florian is building a disaster recovery plan for his organization and would like to determine the amount of time that a particular IT service may be down without causing serious damage to business operations. What variable is Florian calculating?

   A. RTO

   B. MTD

   C. RPO

   D. SLA

46. During an incident investigation, investigators meet with a system administrator who may have information about the incident but is not a suspect. What type of conversation is taking place during this meeting?

   A. Interview

   B. Interrogation

   C. Both an interview and an interrogation

   D. Neither an interview nor an interrogation

47. Match each of the numbered types of recovery capabilities to their correct lettered definition:

Terms

   1. Hot site

   2. Cold site

   3. Warm site

   4. Service bureau

Definitions

   A. An organization that can provide on-site or off-site IT services in the event of a disaster

   B. A site with dedicated storage and real-time data replication, often with shared equipment that allows restoration of service in a very short time

   C. A site that relies on shared storage and backups for recovery

   D. A rented space with power, cooling, and connectivity that can accept equipment as part of a recovery effort

48. Veronica is considering the implementation of a database recovery mechanism recommended by a consultant. In the recommended approach, an automated process will move database backups from the primary facility to an off-site location each night. What type of database recovery technique is the consultant describing?

   A. Remote journaling

   B. Remote mirroring

   C. Electronic vaulting

   D. Transaction logging

49. Which one of the following events marks the completion of a disaster recovery process?

   A. Securing property and life safety

   B. Restoring operations in an alternate facility

   C. Restoring operations in the primary facility

   D. Standing down first responders

50. During what phase of the incident response process do administrators take action to limit the effect or scope of an incident?

    A. Detection

    B. Response

    C. Mitigation

    D. Recovery

51. Greg is redesigning his organization's incident response process, seeking to improve its efficiency and effectiveness. Which one of the following actions is not likely to improve his incident response plan?

    A. Create a mentoring program for technical staff

    B. Provide team members with opportunities to work on other tasks

    C. Keep all members of the team on permanent assignment to the team

    D. Conduct training exercises for the team

52. Gordon suspects that a hacker has penetrated a system belonging to his company. The system does not contain any regulated information, and Gordon wants to conduct an investigation on behalf of his company. He has permission from his supervisor to conduct the investigation. Which of the following statements is true?

    A. Gordon is legally required to contact law enforcement before beginning the investigation.

    B. Gordon may not conduct his own investigation.

    C. Gordon's investigation may include examining the contents of hard disks, network traffic, and any other systems or information belonging to the company.

    D. Gordon may ethically perform "hack back" activities after identifying the perpetrator.

53. You are performing an investigation into a potential bot infection on your network and want to perform a forensic analysis of the information that passed between different systems on your network and those on the Internet. You believe that the information was likely encrypted. You are beginning your investigation after the activity concluded. What would be the best and easiest way to obtain the source of this information?

    A. Packet captures

    B. Netflow data

    C. Intrusion detection system logs

    D. Centralized authentication records

54. What type of disaster recovery test activates the alternate processing facility and uses it to conduct transactions but leaves the primary site up and running?

    A. Full interruption test

    B. Parallel test

    C. Checklist review

    D. Tabletop exercise

55. During which phase of the incident response process would an analyst receive an intrusion detection system alert and verify its accuracy?

A. Response

B. Mitigation

C. Detection

D. Reporting

56. In what virtualization model do full guest operating systems run on top of a virtualization platform?

A. Virtual machines

B. Software-defined networking

C. Virtual SAN

D. Application virtualization

57. During what phase of the incident response process would security professionals analyze the process itself to determine whether any improvements are warranted?

A. Lessons learned

B. Remediation

C. Recovery

D. Reporting

58. Which one of the following information sources is most likely to detect a security incident involving unauthorized modification of information by an employee?

A. Intrusion detection system

B. Antivirus software

C. File integrity monitoring system

D. Firewall logs

59. During what phase of incident response is the primary goal to limit the damage caused by an incident?

A. Detection

B. Containment

C. Eradication

D. Recovery

60. Darcy is a computer security specialist who is assisting with the prosecution of a hacker. The prosecutor requests that Darcy give testimony in court about whether, in her opinion, the logs and other records in a case are indicative of a hacking attempt. What type of evidence is Darcy being asked to provide?

    A. Expert opinion

    B. Direct evidence

    C. Real evidence

    D. Documentary evidence

61. Jerome is conducting a forensic investigation and is reviewing database server logs to investigate query contents for evidence of SQL injection attacks. What type of analysis is he performing?

    A. Hardware analysis

    B. Software analysis

    C. Network analysis

    D. Media analysis

62. What documentation is typically prepared after a postmortem review of an incident has been completed?

    A. A lessons learned document

    B. A risk assessment

    C. A remediation list

    D. A mitigation checklist

63. Ed has been tasked with identifying a service that will provide a low-latency, high-performance, and high-availability way to host content for his employer. What type of solution should he seek out to ensure that his employer's customers around the world can access their content quickly, easily, and reliably?

    A. A hot site

    B. A CDN

    C. Redundant servers

    D. A P2P CDN

64. Who is the ideal person to approve an organization's business continuity plan?

    A. Chief information officer

    B. Chief executive officer

    C. Chief information security officer

    D. Chief operating officer

65. Which one of the following actions is not normally part of the project scope and planning phase of business continuity planning?

   A. Structured analysis of the organization

   B. Review of the legal and regulatory landscape

   C. Creation of a BCP team

   D. Documentation of the plan

66. Henry's company is being sued for breach of contract. What type of law will cover this?

   A. Civil law

   B. Administrative law

   C. Criminal law

   D. Ethical standards

67. The forensic investigation that Joanna has conducted is complete, and the report has been provided to organizational leadership in preparation for a human resources action. What should Joanna do once the report has been provided?

   A. Delete all files and notes about the forensic case.

   B. Notify the subject of the forensic investigation that it is complete.

   C. Notify law enforcement that the forensic investigation is complete.

   D. Preserve the forensic materials and notes in case they are needed.

68. Which of the following is not an event that is typically prepared for in an emergency response plan?

   A. A supply chain disruption

   B. A pandemic

   C. A natural disaster

   D. A man-made disaster

69. Miguel is preparing a crisis management process for his organization. What step will typically come after "Respond" in the following cycle?

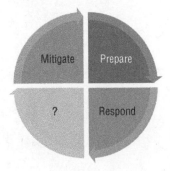

    A.   Analyze

    B.   Recover

    C.   Evaluate

    D.   Identify

70. Emma's organization is planning for natural disasters and wants to have a backup site available to move operations to. What important factor in backup site selection will help Emma avoid a single disaster disrupting operations for her organization?

    A.   Network bandwidth

    B.   Availability of backup power

    C.   Geographic location

    D.   Risk of natural disasters for the locations

Chapter 5

Cryptography (Domain 5)

THE SSCP EXAM TOPICS COVERED IN THIS CHAPTER INCLUDE:

✓ **Domain 5.0: Cryptography**

- **5.1 Understand reasons and requirements for cryptography**

  - Confidentiality

  - Integrity and authenticity

  - Data sensitivity (e.g., personally identifiable information (PII), intellectual property (IP), protected health information (PHI))

  - Regulatory and industry best practice (e.g., Payment Card Industry Data Security Standard (PCI DSS), International Organization for Standardization (ISO))

- **5.2 Apply cryptography concepts**

  - Hashing

  - Salting

  - Symmetric/asymmetric encryption/Elliptic Curve Cryptography (ECC)

  - Non-repudiation (e.g., digital signatures/certificates, Hash-based Message Authentication Code (HMAC), audit trails)

  - Strength of encryption algorithms and keys (e.g., Advanced Encryption Standard (AES), Rivest-Shamir-Adleman (RSA), 256-, 512-, 1024-, 2048-bit keys)

  - Cryptographic attacks, cryptanalysis, and countermeasures (e.g., quantum computing)

- **5.3 Understand and implement secure protocols**

  - Services and protocols (e.g., Internet Protocol Security (IPsec), Transport Layer Security (TLS), Secure/Multipurpose Internet Mail Extensions (S/MIME), DomainKeys Identified Mail (DKIM))

- Common use cases
- Limitations and vulnerabilities
- **5.4 Understand and support public key infrastructure (PKI) systems**
  - Fundamental key management concepts (e.g., storage, rotation, composition, generation, destruction, exchange, revocation, escrow)
  - Web of Trust (WoT) (e.g., Pretty Good Privacy (PGP), GNU Privacy Guard (GPG), blockchain)

1. Carla's organization recently suffered a data breach when an employee misplaced a laptop containing sensitive customer information. Which one of the following controls would be *least* likely to prevent this type of breach from reoccurring in the future?

   A. Full disk encryption

   B. File encryption

   C. File integrity monitoring

   D. Data minimization

2. Margot is considering the use of a self-signed certificate to reduce the costs associated with maintaining a public-facing web server. What is the primary risk associated with the use of self-signed certificates?

   A. Self-signed certificates use weak encryption.

   B. Self-signed certificates are not trusted by default.

   C. Self-signed certificates have short expiration periods.

   D. Self-signed certificates cannot be used with most browsers.

3. Which one of the following cryptographic systems is most closely associated with the Web of Trust?

   A. RC4

   B. SHA

   C. AES

   D. PGP

4. Kevin is an internal auditor at a major retailer and would like to ensure that the information contained in audit logs is not changed after it is created. Which one of the following controls would best meet his goal?

   A. Cryptographic hashing

   B. Data loss prevention

   C. File encryption

   D. Certificate management

5. Greg is designing a defense-in-depth approach to securing his organization's information and would like to select cryptographic tools that are appropriate for different use cases and provide strong encryption. Which one of the following pairings is the best use of encryption tools?

   A. SSL for data in motion and AES for data at rest

   B. VPN for data in motion and SSL for data at rest

   C. TLS for data in motion and AES for data at rest

   D. SSL for data in motion and TLS for data at rest

6. Max is the security administrator for an organization that uses a remote access VPN. The VPN depends upon RADIUS authentication, and Max would like to assess the security of that service. Which one of the following hash functions is the strongest cryptographic hash protocol supported by RADIUS?

    A. MD5

    B. SHA 2

    C. SHA-512

    D. HMAC

7. Angela is an information security architect at a bank and has been assigned to ensure that transactions are secure as they traverse the network. She recommends that all transactions use TLS. What threat is she most likely attempting to stop, and what method is she using to protect against it?

    A. Man-in-the-middle, VPN

    B. Packet injection, encryption

    C. Sniffing, encryption

    D. Sniffing, TEMPEST

For questions 8–10, please refer to the following scenario.

Your organization regularly handles three types of data: information that it shares with customers, information that it uses internally to conduct business, and trade secret information that offers the organization significant competitive advantages. Information shared with customers is used and stored on web servers, while both the internal business data and the trade secret information are stored on internal file servers and employee workstations.

8. What civilian data classifications best fit this data?

    A. Unclassified, confidential, top secret

    B. Public, sensitive, private

    C. Public, sensitive, proprietary

    D. Public, confidential, private

9. What technique could you use to mark your trade secret information in case it was released or stolen and you need to identify it?

    A. Classification

    B. Symmetric encryption

    C. Watermarks

    D. Metadata

10. What type of encryption should you use on the file servers for the proprietary data, and how might you secure the data when it is in motion?

   A. TLS at rest and AES in motion

   B. AES at rest and TLS in motion

   C. VPN at rest and TLS in motion

   D. DES at rest and AES in motion

The following diagram shows a typical workstation and server and their connections to each other and the Internet. For questions 11–13, please refer to this diagram.

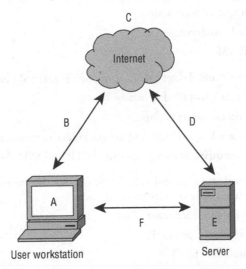

11. Which letters on this diagram are locations where you might find data at rest?

   A. A, B, and C

   B. C and E

   C. A and E

   D. B, D, and F

12. What would be the best way to secure data at points B, D, and F?

   A. AES-256

   B. SSL

   C. TLS

   D. 3DES

13. What is the best way to secure files that are sent from workstation A via the Internet service (C) to remote server E?

   A. Use AES at rest at point A, and use TLS in transit via B and D.

   B. Encrypt the data files and send them.

   C. Use 3DES and TLS to provide double security.

   D. Use full disk encryption at A and E, and use SSL at B and D.

14. What scenario describes data at rest?

   A. Data in an IPSec tunnel

   B. Data in an e-commerce transaction

   C. Data stored on a hard drive

   D. Data stored in RAM

15. What problem with FTP and Telnet makes using SFTP and SSH better alternatives?

   A. FTP and Telnet aren't installed on many systems.

   B. FTP and Telnet do not encrypt data.

   C. FTP and Telnet have known bugs and are no longer maintained.

   D. FTP and Telnet are difficult to use, making SFTP and SSH the preferred solution.

16. Information maintained about an individual that can be used to distinguish or trace their identity is known as what type of information?

   A. Personally identifiable information (PII)

   B. Personal health information (PHI)

   C. Social Security number (SSN)

   D. Secure identity information (SII)

17. Match each of the numbered data elements shown here with one of the lettered categories. You may use the categories once, more than once, or not at all. If a data element matches more than one category, choose the one that is most specific.

Data elements

   1. Medical records

   2. Credit card numbers

   3. Social Security numbers

   4. Driver's license numbers

Categories

   A. PCI DSS

   B. PHI

   C. PII

For question 18, please refer to the following scenario.

The healthcare company that Lauren works for handles HIPAA data as well as internal business data, protected health information, and day-to-day business communications. Its internal policy uses the following requirements for securing HIPAA data at rest and in transit.

Classification	Handling Requirements
Confidential (HIPAA)	Encrypt at rest and in transit.
	Full disk encryption is required for all workstations.
	Files can only be sent in encrypted form, and passwords must be transferred under separate cover.
	Printed documents must be labeled with "HIPAA handling required."
Private (PHI)	Encrypt at rest and in transit.
	PHI must be stored on secure servers, and copies should not be kept on local workstations.
	Printed documents must be labeled with "Private."
Sensitive (business confidential)	Encryption is recommended but not required.
Public	Information can be sent unencrypted.

18. What encryption technology would be appropriate for HIPAA documents in transit?
   A. BitLocker
   B. DES
   C. TLS
   D. SSL

19. Which one of the following ISO standards includes best-practice standards for developing an information security program?
   A. ISO 9000
   B. ISO 22301
   C. ISO 27001
   D. ISO 27701

20. Maria's organization is building a property records system that will rely upon a distributed immutable ledger to preserve transaction records. What technology is best suited to assist with this implementation?

    A. PKI

    B. Blockchain

    C. Digital signatures

    D. Digital certificates

21. What security measure can provide an additional security control in the event that backup tapes are stolen or lost?

    A. Keep multiple copies of the tapes.

    B. Replace tape media with hard drives.

    C. Use appropriate security labels.

    D. Use AES-256 encryption.

22. Joe works at a major pharmaceutical research and development company and has been tasked with writing his organization's data retention policy. As part of its legal requirements, the organization must comply with the U.S. Food and Drug Administration's Code of Federal Regulations Title 21. To do so, it is required to retain records with electronic signatures. Why would a signature be part of a retention requirement?

    A. It ensures that someone has reviewed the data.

    B. It provides confidentiality.

    C. It ensures that the data has not been changed.

    D. It validates who approved the data.

23. What protocol is preferred over Telnet for remote server administration via the command line?

    A. SCP

    B. SFTP

    C. WDS

    D. SSH

24. What methods are often used to protect data in transit?

    A. Telnet, ISDN, UDP

    B. BitLocker, FileVault

    C. AES, Serpent, IDEA

    D. TLS, VPN, IPSec

25. Linux systems that use bcrypt are using a tool based on what DES alternative encryption scheme?

    A. 3DES

    B. AES

    C. Diffie–Hellman

    D. Blowfish

26. Which one of the following is not considered PII under U.S. federal government regulations?

    A. Name

    B. Social Security number

    C. Student ID number

    D. ZIP code

27. What encryption algorithm would provide strong protection for data stored on a USB thumb drive?

    A. TLS

    B. SHA1

    C. AES

    D. DES

28. What type of encryption is typically used for data at rest?

    A. Asymmetric encryption

    B. Symmetric encryption

    C. DES

    D. OTP

29. Fred is preparing to send backup tapes off-site to a secure third-party storage facility. What steps should Fred take before sending the tapes to that facility?

    A. Ensure that the tapes are handled the same way the original media would be handled based on their classification.

    B. Increase the classification level of the tapes because they are leaving the possession of the company.

    C. Purge the tapes to ensure that classified data is not lost.

    D. Decrypt the tapes in case they are lost in transit.

30. Ed has been asked to send data that his organization classifies as confidential and proprietary via email. What encryption technology would be appropriate to ensure that the contents of the files attached to the email remain confidential as they traverse the Internet?

    A. SSL

    B. TLS

    C. PGP

    D. VPN

31. Chris wants to verify that a software package that he downloaded matches the original version. What hashing tool should he use if he believes that technically sophisticated attackers may have replaced the software package with a version containing a backdoor?

    A. MD5

    B. 3DES

    C. SHA1

    D. SHA 256

32. What name is given to the random value added to a password in an attempt to defeat rainbow table attacks?

    A. Hash

    B. Salt

    C. Extender

    D. Rebar

33. Which one of the following is not an attribute of a hashing algorithm?

    A. They require a cryptographic key.

    B. They are irreversible.

    C. It is very difficult to find two messages with the same hash value.

    D. They take variable-length input.

34. Susan would like to configure IPsec in a manner that provides confidentiality for the content of packets. What component of IPsec provides this capability?

    A. AH

    B. ESP

    C. IKE

    D. ISAKMP

For questions 35–38, please refer to the following scenario.

Alice and Bob would like to use an asymmetric cryptosystem to communicate with each other. They are located in different parts of the country but have exchanged encryption keys by using digital certificates signed by a mutually trusted certificate authority.

35. If Alice wants to send Bob an encrypted message, what key does she use to encrypt the message?

    A. Alice's public key

    B. Alice's private key

    C. Bob's public key

    D. Bob's private key

36. When Bob receives the encrypted message from Alice, what key does he use to decrypt the message?

    A. Alice's public key

    B. Alice's private key

    C. Bob's public key

    D. Bob's private key

37. Which one of the following keys would Bob not possess in this scenario?
    A. Alice's public key
    B. Alice's private key
    C. Bob's public key
    D. Bob's private key

38. Alice would also like to digitally sign the message that she sends to Bob. What key should she use to create the digital signature?
    A. Alice's public key
    B. Alice's private key
    C. Bob's public key
    D. Bob's private key

39. Which one of the following cryptographic goals protects against the risks posed when a device is lost or stolen?
    A. Nonrepudiation
    B. Authentication
    C. Integrity
    D. Confidentiality

40. Ethan is responsible for securing a credit card processing environment. He would like to apply encryption technology that meets all relevant standards. What set of requirements is most directly applicable to his work?
    A. GLBA
    B. HIPAA
    C. PCI DSS
    D. FERPA

41. Florian and Tobias would like to begin communicating using a symmetric cryptosystem, but they have no prearranged secret and are not able to meet in person to exchange keys. What algorithm can they use to securely exchange the secret key?
    A. IDEA
    B. Diffie-Hellman
    C. RSA
    D. MD5

42. Which one of the following is not one of the basic requirements for a cryptographic hash function?
    A. The function must work on fixed-length input.
    B. The function must be relatively easy to compute for any input.
    C. The function must be one way.
    D. The function must be collision free.

43. How many possible keys exist for a cipher that uses a key containing 5 bits?
    A. 10
    B. 16
    C. 32
    D. 64

44. What cryptographic principle stands behind the idea that cryptographic algorithms should be open to public inspection?
    A. Security through obscurity
    B. Kerckhoff's principle
    C. Defense in depth
    D. Heisenburg principle

45. Alice sent a message to Bob. Bob would like to demonstrate to Charlie that the message he received definitely came from Alice. What goal of cryptography is Bob attempting to achieve?
    A. Authentication
    B. Confidentiality
    C. Nonrepudiation
    D. Integrity

46. Sherry conducted an inventory of the cryptographic technologies in use within her organization and found the following algorithms and protocols in use. Which one of these technologies should she replace because it is no longer considered secure?
    A. MD5
    B. 3DES
    C. PGP
    D. WPA2

47. Tom is a cryptanalyst and is working on breaking a cryptographic algorithm's secret key. He has a copy of an intercepted message that is encrypted, and he also has a copy of the decrypted version of that message. He wants to use both the encrypted message and its decrypted plaintext to retrieve the secret key for use in decrypting other messages. What type of attack is Tom engaging in?
    A. Chosen ciphertext
    B. Chosen plaintext
    C. Known plaintext
    D. Brute force

48. What standard governs the creation and validation of digital certificates for use in a public key infrastructure?

- **A.** X.509
- **B.** TLS
- **C.** SSL
- **D.** 802.1x

49. Alan intercepts an encrypted message and wants to determine what type of algorithm was used to create the message. He first performs a frequency analysis and notes that the frequency of letters in the message closely matches the distribution of letters in the English language. What type of cipher was most likely used to create this message?

- **A.** Substitution cipher
- **B.** AES
- **C.** Transposition cipher
- **D.** 3DES

50. Brent is selecting an encryption algorithm that will protect data that has long-lasting sensitivity. He would like to select an algorithm that is most resistant to quantum computing attacks. Which algorithm would best meet his needs?

- **A.** AES
- **B.** RSA
- **C.** DES
- **D.** ECC

51. Raj is selecting an encryption algorithm for use in his organization and would like to be able to vary the strength of the encryption with the sensitivity of the information. Which one of the following algorithms allows the use of different key strengths?

- **A.** Blowfish
- **B.** DES
- **C.** Skipjack
- **D.** IDEA

52. Howard is choosing a cryptographic algorithm for his organization, and he would like to choose an algorithm that supports the creation of digital signatures. Which one of the following algorithms would meet his requirement?

- **A.** RSA
- **B.** DES
- **C.** AES
- **D.** Blowfish

53. In Transport Layer Security, what type of key is used to encrypt the actual content of communications between a web server and a client?

  A. Ephemeral session key

  B. Client's public key

  C. Server's public key

  D. Server's private key

54. Chris is designing a cryptographic system for use within his company. The company has 1,000 employees, and they plan to use an asymmetric encryption system. How many total keys will they need?

  A. 500

  B. 1,000

  C. 2,000

  D. 4,950

55. Todd wants to add a certificate to a certificate revocation list. What element of the certificate goes on the list?

  A. Serial number

  B. Public key

  C. Digital signature

  D. Private key

56. Alison is examining a digital certificate presented to her by her bank's website. Which one of the following requirements is not necessary for her to trust the digital certificate?

  A. She knows that the server belongs to the bank.

  B. She trusts the certificate authority.

  C. She verifies that the certificate is not listed on a CRL.

  D. She verifies the digital signature on the certificate.

57. Which one of the following would be a reasonable application for the use of self-signed digital certificates?

  A. E-commerce website

  B. Banking application

  C. Internal scheduling application

  D. Customer portal

58. Atwood Computing regularly ships tapes of backup data across the country to a secondary facility. These tapes contain confidential information. What is the most important security control that Atwood can use to protect these tapes?

  A. Locked shipping containers

  B. Private couriers

  C. Data encryption

  D. Media rotation

59. Alice is designing a cryptosystem for use by six users and would like to use a symmetric encryption algorithm. She wants any two users to be able to communicate with each other without worrying about eavesdropping by a third user. How many symmetric encryption keys will she need to generate?

   A. 6

   B. 12

   C. 15

   D. 30

60. Sally is using IPsec's ESP component in transport mode. What important information should she be aware of about transport mode?

   A. Transport mode provides full encryption of the entire IP packet.

   B. Transport mode adds a new, unencrypted header to ensure that packets reach their destination.

   C. Transport mode does not encrypt the header of the packet.

   D. Transport mode provides no encryption; only tunnel mode provides encryption.

61. Which one of the following cryptographic algorithms supports the goal of nonrepudiation?

   A. Blowfish

   B. DES

   C. AES

   D. RSA

62. Andrew believes that a digital certificate belonging to his organization was compromised and would like to add it to a Certificate Revocation List. Who must add the certificate to the CRL?

   A. Andrew

   B. The root authority for the top-level domain

   C. The CA that issued the certificate

   D. The revocation authority for the top-level domain

63. Attackers who compromise websites often acquire databases of hashed passwords. What technique can best protect these passwords against automated password cracking attacks that use precomputed values?

   A. Using the MD5 hashing algorithm

   B. Using the SHA-1 hashing algorithm

   C. Salting

   D. Double-hashing

64. Barry recently received a message from Melody that Melody encrypted using symmetric cryptography. What key should Barry use to decrypt the message?

A. Barry's public key

B. Barry's private key

C. Melody's public key

D. Shared secret key

65. Skip needs to transfer files from his PC to a remote server. What protocol should he use instead of FTP?

A. SCP

B. SSH

C. HTTP

D. Telnet

Chapter
6

Network and Communications Security (Domain 6)

THE SSCP EXAM TOPICS COVERED IN THIS CHAPTER INCLUDE:

✓ **Domain 6.0: Network and Communications Security**

- **6.1 Understand and apply fundamental concepts of networking**

- **6.2 Understand network attacks (e.g., distributed denial of service (DDoS), man-in-the-middle (MITM), Domain Name System (DNS) poisoning) and countermeasures (e.g., content delivery networks (CDN))**

- **6.3 Manage network access controls**

  - Network access controls, standards and protocols (e.g., Institute of Electrical and Electronics Engineers (IEEE) 802.1X, Remote Authentication Dial-In User Service (RADIUS), Terminal Access Controller Access-Control System Plus (TACACS+))

  - Remote access operation and configuration (e.g., thin client, virtual private network (VPN))

- **6.4 Manage network security**

  - Logical and physical placement of network devices (e.g., inline, passive, virtual)

  - Segmentation (e.g., physical/logical, data/control plane, virtual local area network (VLAN), access control list (ACL), firewall zones, micro-segmentation)

  - Secure device management

- **6.5 Operate and configure network-based security devices**

  - Firewalls and proxies (e.g., filtering methods, web application firewall (WAF))

  - Intrusion detection systems (IDS) and intrusion prevention systems (IPS)

- Routers and switches
- Traffic-shaping devices (e.g., wide area network (WAN) optimization, load balancing)
- **6.6 Secure wireless communications**
- Technologies (e.g., cellular network, Wi-Fi, Bluetooth, Near-Field Communication (NFC))
- Authentication and encryption protocols (e.g., Wired Equivalent Privacy (WEP), Wi-Fi Protected Access (WPA), Extensible Authentication Protocol (EAP))
- Internet of Things (IoT)

1. Which information security goal is impacted when an organization experiences a DoS or DDoS attack?

    A. Confidentiality

    B. Integrity

    C. Availability

    D. Denial

2. Chris is building an Ethernet network and knows that he needs to span a distance of more than 150 meters with his 1000BaseT network. What network technology should he use to help with this?

    A. Install a repeater or a concentrator before 100 meters.

    B. Use Category 7 cable, which has better shielding for higher speeds.

    C. Install a gateway to handle the distance.

    D. Use STP cable to handle the longer distance at high speeds.

3. What topology correctly describes Ethernet?

    A. A ring

    B. A star

    C. A mesh

    D. A bus

4. During a wireless network penetration test, Susan runs aircrack-ng against the network using a password file. What might cause her to fail in her password-cracking efforts?

    A. Use of WPA2 encryption

    B. Running WPA2 in Enterprise mode

    C. Use of WEP encryption

    D. Running WPA2 in PSK mode

5. What network topology is shown here?

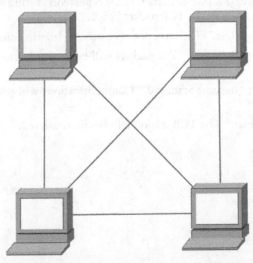

    A. A ring

    B. A bus

    C. A star

    D. A mesh

6. During a review of her organization's network, Angela discovered that it was suffering from broadcast storms and that contractors, guests, and organizational administrative staff were on the same network segment. What design change should Angela recommend?

    A. Require encryption for all users.

    B. Install a firewall at the network border.

    C. Enable spanning tree loop detection.

    D. Segment the network based on functional requirements.

7. In her role as an information security professional, Susan has been asked to identify areas where her organization's wireless network may be accessible even though it isn't intended to be. What should Susan do to determine where her organization's wireless network is accessible?

    A. A site survey

    B. Warwalking

    C. Wardriving

    D. A design map

8. Which OSI layer includes electrical specifications, protocols, and interface standards?

    A. The Transport layer

    B. The Device layer

    C. The Physical layer

    D. The Data Link layer

9. Sarah is manually reviewing a packet capture of TCP traffic and finds that a system is setting the RST flag in the TCP packets it sends repeatedly during a short period of time. What does this flag mean in the TCP packet header?

    A. RST flags mean "Rest." The server needs traffic to briefly pause.

    B. RST flags mean "Relay-set." The packets will be forwarded to the address set in the packet.

    C. RST flags mean "Resume Standard." Communications will resume in their normal format.

    D. RST means "Reset." The TCP session will be disconnected.

10. Place the layers of the OSI model shown here in the appropriate order, from layer 1 to layer 7.

    A. Application

    B. Data Link

    C. Network

    D. Physical

    E. Presentation

    F. Session

    G. Transport

11. Sue's organization recently failed a security assessment because their network was a single flat broadcast domain, and sniffing traffic was possible between different functional groups. What solution should she recommend to help prevent the issues that were identified?

    A. Use VLANs.

    B. Change the subnet mask for all systems.

    C. Deploy gateways.

    D. Turn on port security.

12. Lauren wants to provide port-based authentication on her network to ensure that clients must authenticate before using the network. What technology is an appropriate solution for this requirement?

    A. 802.11a

    B. 802.3

    C. 802.15.1

    D. 802.1x

13. Michelle knows that WEP is no longer used in modern wireless networks, but she needs to explain the problem with WEP to a customer who has an older wireless network still in production that must be upgraded to be secure. What issue should she explain to the customer?

    A. WEP does not provide encryption and instead uses hashing for security.

    B. WEP uses DES encryption and is not secure because DES is easily crackable.

    C. WEP provides data encryption for only part of the traffic sent to clients.

    D. WEP uses an initialization vector that is too small and does not change.

Chris is designing layered network security for his organization. Using the following diagram, answer questions 14 through 16.

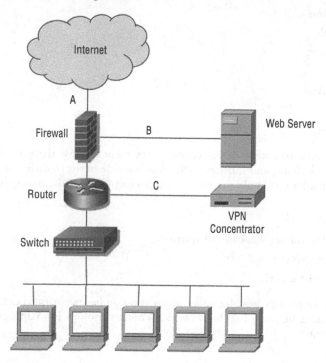

14. What type of firewall design is shown in the diagram?

   A.   A single-tier firewall

   B.   A two-tier firewall

   C.   A three-tier firewall

   D.   A four-tier firewall

15. If the VPN grants remote users the same access to network and system resources as local workstations have, what security issue should Chris raise?

   A.   VPN users will not be able to access the web server.

   B.   There is no additional security issue; the VPN concentrator's logical network location matches the logical network location of the workstations.

   C.   Web server traffic is not subjected to stateful inspection.

   D.   VPN users should only connect from managed PCs.

16. If Chris wants to stop cross-site scripting attacks against the web server, what is the best device for this purpose, and where should he put it?

   A.   A firewall, location A

   B.   An IDS, location A

   C.   An IPS, location B

   D.   A WAF, location C

17. What network topology is shown in the following image?

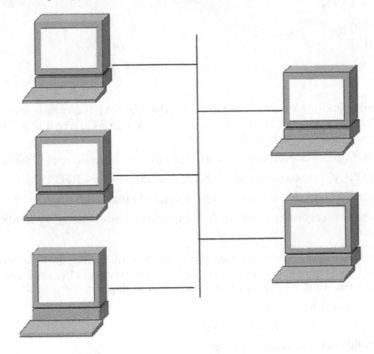

   A. A ring

   B. A star

   C. A bus

   D. A mesh

18. A remote access tool that copies what is displayed on a desktop PC to a remote computer is an example of what type of technology?

   A. Remote node operation

   B. Screen scraping

   C. Remote control

   D. RDP

19. Ben is designing a Wi-Fi network and has been asked to choose the most secure option for the network. Which wireless security standard should he choose?

   A. WPA2

   B. WPA

   C. WEP

   D. AES

20. Which one of the following protocols is commonly used to provide backend authentication services for a VPN?

    A. HTTPS

    B. RADIUS

    C. ESP

    D. AH

21. Ben is troubleshooting a network and discovers that the NAT router he is connected to has the 192.168.x.x subnet as its internal network and that its external IP is 192.168.1.40. What problem is he encountering?

    A. 192.168.x.x is a nonroutable network and will not be carried to the Internet.

    B. 192.168.1.40 is not a valid address because it is reserved by RFC 1918.

    C. Double NATing is not possible using the same IP range.

    D. The upstream system is unable to de-encapsulate his packets, and he needs to use PAT instead.

22. Susan sets up a firewall that keeps track of the status of the communication between two systems and allows a remote system to respond to a local system after the local system starts communication. What type of firewall is Susan using?

    A. A static packet filtering firewall

    B. An application-level gateway firewall

    C. A stateful packet inspection firewall

    D. A circuit-level gateway firewall

23. What type of networking device is most commonly used to assign endpoint systems to VLANs?

    A. Firewall

    B. Router

    C. Switch

    D. Hub

24. Chris needs to design a firewall architecture that can support a DMZ, a database, and a private internal network in a secure manner that separates each function. What type of design should he use, and how many firewalls does he need?

    A. A four-tier firewall design with two firewalls

    B. A two-tier firewall design with three firewalls

    C. A three-tier firewall design with at least one firewall

    D. A single-tier firewall design with three firewalls

25. Which of the following is not a potential problem with active wireless scanning?

    A. Accidently scanning apparent rogue devices that actually belong to guests

    B. Causing alarms on the organization's wireless IPS

    C. Scanning devices that belong to nearby organizations

    D. Misidentifying rogue devices

26. The Address Resolution Protocol (ARP) and the Reverse Address Resolution Protocol (RARP) operate at what layer of the OSI model?

    A. Layer 1

    B. Layer 2

    C. Layer 3

    D. Layer 4

27. John's network begins to experience symptoms of slowness. Upon investigation, he realizes that the network is being bombarded with TCP SYN packets and believes that his organization is the victim of a denial-of-service attack. What principle of information security is being violated?

    A. Availability

    B. Integrity

    C. Confidentiality

    D. Denial

28. What speed is Category 3 UTP cable rated for?

    A. 5 Mbps

    B. 10 Mbps

    C. 100 Mbps

    D. 1000 Mbps

Lauren's organization has used a popular messaging service for a number of years. Recently, concerns have been raised about the use of messaging. Using the following diagram, answer questions 29–31 about messaging.

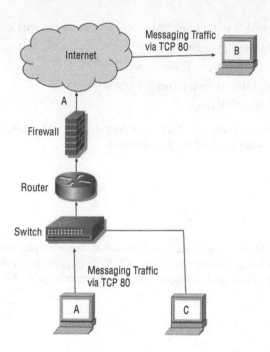

29. What protocol is the messaging traffic most likely to use based on the diagram?

    A. SLACK

    B. HTTP

    C. SMTP

    D. HTTPS

30. What security concern does sending internal communications from A to B raise?

    A. The firewall does not protect system B.

    B. System C can see the broadcast traffic from system A to B.

    C. It is traveling via an unencrypted protocol.

    D. Messaging does not provide nonrepudiation.

31. How could Lauren's company best address a desire for secure messaging for users of internal systems A and C?

    A. Use a third-party messaging service.

    B. Implement and use a locally hosted service.

    C. Use HTTPS.

    D. Discontinue use of messaging and instead use email, which is more secure.

32. Chris is configuring an IDS to monitor for unencrypted FTP traffic. What ports should Chris use in his configuration?

   A. TCP 20 and 21

   B. TCP 21 only

   C. UDP port 69

   D. TCP port 21 and UDP port 21

33. During a penetration test, Lauren is asked to test the organization's Bluetooth security. Which of the following is not a concern she should explain to her employers?

   A. Bluetooth scanning can be time-consuming.

   B. Many devices that may be scanned are likely to be personal devices.

   C. Bluetooth passive scans may require multiple visits at different times to identify all targets.

   D. Bluetooth active scans can't evaluate the security mode of Bluetooth devices.

34. What network tool can be used to protect the identity of clients while providing Internet access by accepting client requests, altering the source addresses of the requests, mapping requests to clients, and sending the modified requests out to their destination?

   A. A gateway

   B. A proxy

   C. A router

   D. A firewall

35. In the OSI model, when a packet changes from a datastream to a segment or a datagram, what layer has it traversed?

   A. The Transport layer

   B. The Application layer

   C. The Data Link layer

   D. The Physical layer

36. The Windows ipconfig command displays the following information:

   BC-5F-F4-7B-4B-7D

   What term describes this, and what information can usually be gathered from it?

   A. The IP address, the network location of the system

   B. The MAC address, the network interface card's manufacturer

   C. The MAC address, the media type in use

   D. The IPv6 client ID, the network interface card's manufacturer

37. Why should passive scanning be conducted in addition to implementing wireless security technologies like wireless intrusion detection systems?

   A. It can help identify rogue devices.

   B. It can test the security of the wireless network via scripted attacks.

   C. Their short dwell time on each wireless channel can allow them to capture more packets.

   D. They can help test wireless IDS or IPS systems.

38. What network topology is shown in the following image?

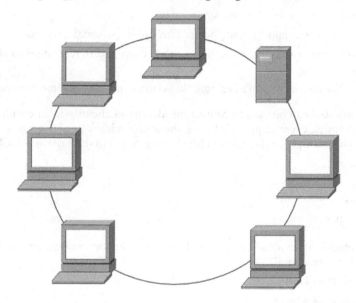

   A. A ring

   B. A bus

   C. A star

   D. A mesh

39. Chris is setting up a hotel network and needs to ensure that systems in each room or suite can connect to each other, but systems in other suites or rooms cannot. At the same time, he needs to ensure that all systems in the hotel can reach the Internet. What solution should he recommend as the most effective business solution?

   A. Per-room VPNs

   B. VLANs

   C. Port security

   D. Firewalls

40. Match each of the numbered TCP ports listed with the associated lettered protocol provided:

TCP ports	Protocols
1. 23	**A.** SMTP
2. 25	**B.** LPD
3. 143	**C.** IMAP
4. 515	**D.** Telnet

41. John deploys his website to multiple regions using load balancers around the world through his cloud infrastructure as a service provider. What availability concept is he using?

   A. Multiple processing sites

   B. Warm sites

   C. Cold sites

   D. A honeynet

42. There are four common VPN protocols. Which group listed contains all of the common VPN protocols?

   A. PPTP, LTP, L2TP, IPsec

   B. PPP, L2TP, IPsec, VNC

   C. PPTP, L2F, L2TP, IPsec

   D. PPTP, L2TP, IPsec, SPAP

43. Lauren's organization has deployed VoIP phones on the same switches that the desktop PCs are on. What security issue could this create, and what solution would help?

   A. VLAN hopping; use physically separate switches.

   B. VLAN hopping; use encryption.

   C. Caller ID spoofing; MAC filtering

   D. Denial-of-service attacks; use a firewall between networks.

44. Staff from Susan's company often travel internationally. Susan believes that they may be targeted for corporate espionage activities because of the technologies that her company is developing. What practice should Susan recommend that they adopt for connecting to networks while they travel?

   A. Only connect to public Wi-Fi.

   B. Use a VPN for all connections.

   C. Only use websites that support TLS.

   D. Do not connect to networks while traveling.

45. One of Susan's attacks during a penetration test involves inserting false ARP data into a system's ARP cache. When the system attempts to send traffic to the address it believes belongs to a legitimate system, it will instead send that traffic to a system she controls. What is this attack called?

    A. RARP flooding

    B. ARP cache poisoning

    C. A denial-of-ARP attack

    D. ARP buffer blasting

46. Which one of the following traffic types should not be blocked by an organization's egress filtering policy?

    A. Traffic destined to a private IP address

    B. Traffic with a broadcast destination

    C. Traffic with a source address from an external network

    D. Traffic with a destination address on an external network

47. A denial-of-service (DoS) attack that sends fragmented TCP packets is known as what kind of attack?

    A. Christmas tree

    B. Teardrop

    C. Stack killer

    D. Frag grenade

48. Angela uses a sniffer to monitor traffic from a RADIUS server configured with default settings. What protocol should she monitor, and what traffic will she be able to read?

    A. UDP, none. All RADIUS traffic is encrypted.

    B. TCP, all traffic but the passwords, which are encrypted

    C. UDP, all traffic but the passwords, which are encrypted

    D. TCP, none. All RADIUS traffic is encrypted.

49. Segmentation, sequencing, and error checking all occur at what layer of the OSI model that is associated with SSL, TLS, and UDP?

    A. The Transport layer

    B. The Network layer

    C. The Session layer

    D. The Presentation layer

50. In what type of attack do attackers manage to insert themselves into a connection between a user and a legitimate website?

    A. Man-in-the-middle

    B. Fraggle

    C. Wardriving

    D. Meet-in-the-middle

51. What type of key does WEP use to encrypt wireless communications?

    A. An asymmetric key

    B. Unique key sets for each host

    C. A predefined shared static key

    D. Unique asymmetric keys for each host

52. What does a bluesnarfing attack target?

    A. Data on IBM systems

    B. An outbound phone call via Bluetooth

    C. 802.11b networks

    D. Data from a Bluetooth-enabled device

53. Susan is writing a best practices statement for her organizational users who need to use Bluetooth. She knows that there are many potential security issues with Bluetooth and wants to provide the best advice she can. Which of the following sets of guidance should Susan include?

    A. Use Bluetooth's built-in strong encryption, change the default PIN on your device, turn off discovery mode, and turn off Bluetooth when it's not in active use.

    B. Use Bluetooth only for those activities that are not confidential, change the default PIN on your device, turn off discovery mode, and turn off Bluetooth when it's not in active use.

    C. Use Bluetooth's built-in strong encryption, use extended (eight digits or longer) Bluetooth PINs, turn off discovery mode, and turn off Bluetooth when it's not in active use.

    D. Use Bluetooth only for those activities that are not confidential, use extended (eight digits or longer) Bluetooth PINs, turn off discovery mode, and turn off Bluetooth when it's not in active use.

54. Lauren uses the ping utility to check whether a remote system is up as part of a penetration testing exercise. If she does not want to see her own ping packets, what protocol should she filter out from her packet sniffer's logs?

    A. UDP

    B. TCP

    C. IP

    D. ICMP

55. During a port scan using nmap, Joseph discovers that a system shows two ports open that cause him immediate worry:

21/open

23/open

What services are likely running on those ports?

A. SSH and FTP

B. FTP and Telnet

C. SMTP and Telnet

D. POP3 and SMTP

56. One of the findings that Jim made when performing a security audit was the use of non-IP protocols in a private network. What issue should Jim point out that may result from the use of these non-IP protocols?

A. They are outdated and cannot be used on modern PCs.

B. They may not be able to be filtered by firewall devices.

C. They may allow Christmas tree attacks.

D. IPX extends on the IP protocol and may not be supported by all TCP stacks.

57. What type of attack is most likely to occur after a successful ARP spoofing attempt?

A. A DoS attack

B. A Trojan

C. A replay attack

D. A man-in-the-middle attack

58. Arnold is receiving reports from end users that their Internet connections are extremely slow. He looks at the firewall and determines that there are thousands of unexpected inbound connections per second arriving from all over the world. What type of attack is most likely occurring?

A. A worm

B. A denial-of-service attack

C. A virus

D. A smurf attack

59. Jim is building a research computing system that benefits from being part of a full mesh topology between systems. In a five-node full mesh topology design, how many connections will an individual node have?

A. Two

B. Three

C. Four

D. Five

60. During a security assessment of a wireless network, Jim discovers that LEAP is in use on a network using WPA. What recommendation should Jim make?

A. Continue to use LEAP. It provides better security than TKIP for WPA networks.

B. Use an alternate protocol like PEAP or EAP-TLS and implement WPA2 if supported.

C. Continue to use LEAP to avoid authentication issues, but move to WPA2.

D. Use an alternate protocol like PEAP or EAP-TLS, and implement Wired Equivalent Privacy to avoid wireless security issues.

61. Which one of the following security tools is not capable of generating an active response to a security event?

A. IPS

B. Firewall

C. IDS

D. Antivirus software

For questions 62–65, please refer to a stateful inspection firewall running the rulebase shown here. The source ports have been omitted from the figure, but you may assume that they are specified correctly for the purposes of answering questions 62–65.

Rule	Action	Source IP	Source Port	Destination IP	Destination Port
1	ALLOW	ANY	_____	10.1.0.50	80
2	DENY	15.246.10.1	_____	10.1.0.50	80
3	ALLOW	ANY	_____	10.1.0.26	25
4	ALOW	ANY	_____	10.1.0.26	465

62. Which one of the following rules is not shown in the rulebase but will be enforced by the firewall?

A. Stealth

B. Implicit deny

C. Connection proxy

D. Egress filter

63. What type of server is running at IP address 10.1.0.26?

A. Email

B. Web

C. FTP

D. Database

64. The system at 15.246.10.1 attempts HTTP and HTTPS connections to the web server running at 10.1.0.50. Which one of the following statements is true about that connection?

    A. Both connections will be allowed.

    B. Both connections will be blocked.

    C. The HTTP connection will be allowed, and the HTTPS connection will be blocked.

    D. The HTTP connection will be blocked, and the HTTPS connection will be allowed.

65. What value should be used to fill in the source port for rule 3?

    A. 25

    B. 465

    C. 80

    D. Any

66. What type of firewall design is shown in the following image?

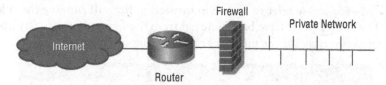

    A. Single-tier

    B. Two-tier

    C. Three-tier

    D. Next generation

67. Ben has configured his network to not broadcast an SSID. Why might Ben disable SSID broadcast, and how could his SSID be discovered?

    A. Disabling SSID broadcast prevents attackers from discovering the encryption key. The SSID can be recovered from decrypted packets.

    B. Disabling SSID broadcast hides networks from unauthorized personnel. The SSID can be discovered using a wireless sniffer.

    C. Disabling SSID broadcast prevents issues with beacon frames. The SSID can be recovered by reconstructing the BSSID.

    D. Disabling SSID broadcast helps avoid SSID conflicts. The SSID can be discovered by attempting to connect to the network.

68. The DARPA TCP/IP model's Application layer matches up to what three OSI model layers?

    A. Application, Presentation, and Transport

    B. Presentation, Session, and Transport

    C. Application, Presentation, and Session

    D. There is not a direct match. The TCP model was created before the OSI model.

69. When a host on an Ethernet network detects a collision and transmits a jam signal, what happens next?

   A. The host that transmitted the jam signal is allowed to retransmit while all other hosts pause until that transmission is received successfully.

   B. All hosts stop transmitting, and each host waits a random period of time before attempting to transmit again.

   C. All hosts stop transmitting, and each host waits a period of time based on how recently it successfully transmitted.

   D. Hosts wait for the token to be passed and then resume transmitting data as they pass the token.

70. Which of the following options includes standards or protocols that exist in layer 6 of the OSI model?

   A. NFS, SQL, and RPC

   B. TCP, UDP, and TLS

   C. JPEG, ASCII, and MIDI

   D. HTTP, FTP, and SMTP

71. WPA2's Counter Mode Cipher Block Chaining Message Authentication Mode Protocol (CCMP) is based on which common encryption scheme?

   A. DES

   B. 3DES

   C. AES

   D. TLS

72. What type of firewall design does the following image show?

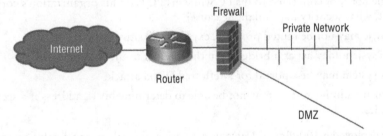

   A. A single-tier firewall

   B. A two-tier firewall

   C. A three-tier firewall

   D. A fully protected DMZ firewall

73. During troubleshooting, Chris uses the `nslookup` command to check the IP address of a host he is attempting to connect to. The IP he sees in the response is not the IP that should resolve when the lookup is done. What type of attack has likely been conducted?

   A. DNS spoofing

   B. DNS poisoning

   C. ARP spoofing

   D. A Cain attack

74. Which of the following does not describe data in motion?

   A. Data on a backup tape that is being shipped to a storage facility

   B. Data in a TCP packet

   C. Data in an e-commerce transaction

   D. Data in files being copied between locations

75. Kim is troubleshooting an application firewall that serves as a supplement to the organization's network and host firewalls and intrusion prevention system, providing added protection against web-based attacks. The issue the organization is experiencing is that the firewall technology suffers somewhat frequent restarts that render it unavailable for 10 minutes at a time. What configuration might Kim consider to maintain availability during that period at the lowest cost to the company?

   A. High availability cluster

   B. Failover device

   C. Fail open

   D. Redundant disks

76. Chris uses a cellular hot spot (modem) to provide Internet access when he is traveling. If he leaves the hot spot connected to his PC while his PC is on his organization's corporate network, what security issue might he cause?

   A. Traffic may not be routed properly, exposing sensitive data.

   B. His system may act as a bridge from the Internet to the local network.

   C. His system may be a portal for a reflected DDoS attack.

   D. Security administrators may not be able to determine his IP address if a security issue occurs.

77. Ben has deployed a 1000BaseT 1 gigabit network and needs to run a cable to another building. If Ben is running his link directly from a switch to another switch in that building, what is the maximum distance Ben can cover according to the 1000BaseT specification?

   A. 2 kilometers

   B. 500 meters

   C. 185 meters

   D. 100 meters

78. Match the following numbered wireless attack terms with their appropriate lettered descriptions:

Wireless attack terms	**Descriptions**
1. Rogue access point	**A.** An attack that relies on an access point to spoof a legitimate access point's SSID and Mandatory Access Control (MAC) address
2. Replay	
3. Evil twin	**B.** An access point intended to attract new connections by using an apparently legitimate SSID
4. War driving	
	C. An attack that retransmits captured communication to attempt to gain access to a targeted system
	D. The process of using detection tools to find wireless networks

79. Lisa is attempting to prevent her network from being targeted by IP spoofing attacks as well as preventing her network from being the source of those attacks. Which one of the following rules is *not* a best practice that Lisa can configure at her network border?

A. Block packets with internal source addresses from entering the network.

B. Block packets with external source addresses from leaving the network.

C. Block packets with private IP addresses from exiting the network.

D. Block packets with public IP addresses from entering the network.

80. Lauren's and Nick's PCs simultaneously send traffic by transmitting at the same time. What network term describes the range of systems on a network that could be affected by this same issue?

A. The subnet

B. The supernet

C. A collision domain

D. A broadcast domain

81. What type of firewall is capable of inspecting traffic at layer 7 and performing protocol-specific analysis for malicious traffic?

A. Application firewall

B. Stateful inspection firewall

C. Packet filtering firewall

D. Bastion host

82. Which of the following sequences properly describes the TCP three-way handshake?

A. SYN, ACK, SYN/ACK

B. PSH, RST, ACK

C. SYN, SYN/ACK, ACK

D. SYN, RST, FIN

83. SMTP, HTTP, and SNMP all occur at what layer of the OSI model?

 A. Layer 4

 B. Layer 5

 C. Layer 6

 D. Layer 7

84. During a forensic investigation, Charles is able to determine the Media Access Control address of a system that was connected to a compromised network. Charles knows that MAC addresses are tied back to a manufacturer or vendor and are part of the fingerprint of the system. To which OSI layer does a MAC address belong?

 A. The Application layer

 B. The Session layer

 C. The Physical layer

 D. The Data Link layer

85. What technology could Lauren's employer implement to help prevent confidential data from being emailed out of the organization?

 A. DLP

 B. IDS

 C. A firewall

 D. UDP

86. Alaina wants to set up WPA2 Enterprise using an EAP-based protocol that uses certificate-based authentication. Which of the following EAP versions should she select?

 A. LEAP

 B. EAP-FAST

 C. EAP-TLS

 D. EAP-PKI

87. Ben wants to control lateral movement between servers in a data center where workloads move dynamically due to virtualization. What technology would be the most effective to implement to accomplish this?

 A. Software-defined networking

 B. OSI-based span control

 C. Hardware-controlled networking

 D. VPN

88. Mikayla's organization uses virtual machines as their primary deployment method for servers and wants to add intrusion prevention capabilities inside their data center. Mikayla wants to be able to deploy the IPS devices to cover each of multiple clusters of machines based on their purpose, hosted in their VMware cluster. What deployment location will minimize latency, maximize network bandwidth, and allow the maximum degree of flexibility through automation for deployments?

    A. The IPSs should be inline with the VMware servers.

    B. The IPSs should be physical devices to handle the throughput required.

    C. The IPSs should be virtual, just like the VMware virtual machines.

    D. The IPSs should be software based and placed on each virtual machine.

89. Charles is reviewing data communications for cellular-enabled devices in his organization's field locations. He wants to ensure that traffic is encrypted between the data collection devices and his company's data logging service. What should he note about the connection if he knows that the devices are connecting via LTE (4G) cellular connections from a commercial carrier?

    A. The connections will be encrypted from end to end between the device and the server.

    B. The connections will be encrypted between the device and the cellular base station.

    C. The connections will not be encrypted by default.

    D. The connections will be encrypted and then decrypted and re-encrypted at each hop in the cellular network.

90. Li wants to create a layer 2 network that spans multiple layer 3 networks. What network virtualization technology can she use to accomplish this task?

    A. VXLAN

    B. VMLAN

    C. 802.2n

    D. 802.1v

91. Henry wants to create a custom rule for his web application firewall that will prevent attackers from deleting data from his database. Which of the following rules is best suited to stop that type of attack?

    A. Block all queries that include the string UNION.

    B. Block all queries that include the string DROP.

    C. Block all queries that contain the string +OR+1=1.

    D. Block all queries that include the string SELECT.

92. Ruchika wants to deploy a WPA2 network that is accessible for her customers. What WPA2 mode should she deploy if she wants to provide a security code to her customers without having to create accounts for them to log in with?

    A. WPA2 PSK

    B. WPA2 Open

    C. WPA2 Enterprise

    D. WPA2 Home

93. Tony's organization has suffered repeated, large-scale distributed denial-of-service attacks against its websites. Tony has been assigned to design a more robust infrastructure than the current design, which uses a cluster of load-balanced physical servers located in a data center at his organization's headquarters. Which of the following solutions is most likely to keep the website online during a distributed denial-of-service attack?

    A. Using a CDN

    B. Using a WAF to filter out all SQL injection attacks

    C. Moving to virtual machines hosted in the data center to allow greater scalability across existing hardware

    D. Moving to a containerized cluster of machines hosted in a third-party data center that can have multiple new systems added during heavy load

94. Yuri wants to protect his organization's IoT devices. They connect to a wireless WiFi network using WPA2, but do not support enterprise mode, so they have to use PSK mode. Which of the following techniques will best help to protect the IoT devices from attacks?

    A. Switch to WEP to ensure that a more secure protocol is used.

    B. Regularly change the preshared key to prevent attackers from brute-forcing it.

    C. Place the IoT devices on a separate wireless VLAN from other users and devices.

    D. Force all traffic from the devices to use TLS so that the traffic remains secure even if the wireless key is compromised.

95. Which of the following capabilities is not common for a software-defined wide area network (SD-WAN) solution?

    A. Traffic classification and optimization

    B. Responding to packet loss and latency issues

    C. Micro-segmentation and zone-based firewalling

    D. Automated malware detection and reporting

Chapter 7

Systems and Application Security (Domain 7)

THE SSCP EXAM TOPICS COVERED IN THIS CHAPTER INCLUDE:

✓ **Domain 7.0: Systems and Application Security**

- **7.1 Identify and analyze malicious code and activity**
    - Malware (e.g., rootkits, spyware, scareware, ransomware, trojans, virus, worms, trapdoors, backdoors, fileless)
    - Malware countermeasures (e.g., scanners, anti-malware, code signing)
    - Malicious activity (e.g., insider threat, data theft, distributed denial of service (DDoS), botnet, zero-day exploits, web-based attacks, advanced persistent threat (APT))
    - Malicious activity countermeasures (e.g., user awareness, system hardening, patching, isolation, data loss prevention (DLP))
    - Social engineering (e.g., phishing, impersonation)
    - Behavior analytics (e.g., machine learning, Artificial Intelligence (AI), data analytics)

- **7.2 Implement and operate endpoint device security**
    - Host-based intrusion prevention system (HIPS)
    - Host-based firewalls
    - Application whitelisting
    - Endpoint encryption (e.g., whole disk encryption)
    - Trusted Platform Module (TPM)
    - Secure browsing
    - Endpoint Detection and Response (EDR)

- **7.3 Administer Mobile Device Management (MDM)**
  - Provisioning techniques (e.g., corporate owned, personally enabled (COPE), Bring Your Own Device (BYOD))
  - Containerization
  - Encryption
  - Mobile application management (MAM)
- **Understand and configure cloud security**
  - Deployment models (e.g., public, private, hybrid, community)
  - Service models (e.g., Infrastructure as a Service (IaaS), Platform as a Service (PaaS), Software as a Service (SaaS))
  - Virtualization (e.g., hypervisor)
  - Legal and regulatory concerns (e.g., privacy, surveillance, data ownership, jurisdiction, eDiscovery)
  - Data storage, processing, and transmission (e.g., archiving, recovery, resilience)
  - Third-party/outsourcing requirements (e.g., service-level agreement (SLA), data portability, data destruction, auditing)
  - Shared responsibility model
- **7.5 Operate and maintain secure virtual environments**
  - Hypervisor
  - Virtual appliances
  - Containers
  - Continuity and resilience
  - Attacks and countermeasures
  - Shared storage

1. Valerie's organization recently fell victim to a scam where an attacker emailed various staff members from an account that appeared to belong to a senior vice president in the organization. The email stated that the vice president was out of the office and needed iTunes gift cards to purchase an application that she needed to accomplish her work. The email asked that the individual immediately purchase an iTunes gift card and send it back via email so that the vice president could continue her work. Valerie wants to prevent this type of attack from succeeding in the future. What should she recommend as an appropriate preventative measure?

   A. Require the organization to use digital signatures for all email.

   B. Require the use of DKIM.

   C. Require the use of SPF and DMARC.

   D. Implement awareness training including simulated phishing attacks.

2. Tiffany needs to assess the patch level of a Windows 2012 server and wants to use a freely available tool to check the system for security issues. Which of the following tools will provide the most detail about specific patches installed or missing from her machine?

   A. Nmap

   B. Nessus

   C. MBSA

   D. Metasploit

3. Maria wants to deploy an anti-malware tool to detect zero-day malware. What type of detection method should she look for in her selected tool?

   A. Signature-based

   B. Heuristic-based

   C. Trend-based

   D. Availability-based

4. Cameron is configuring his organization's Internet router and would like to enable anti-spoofing technology. Which one of the following source IP addresses on an inbound packet should trigger anti-spoofing controls?

   A. 192.168.163.109

   B. 13.5.102.5

   C. 124.70.14.100

   D. 222.222.222.222

5. As part of her malware analysis process, Caitlyn diagrams the high-level functions and processes that the malware uses to accomplish its goals. What is this process known as?

   A. Static analysis

   B. Composition

   C. Dynamic analysis

   D. Decomposition

6. The company that Lauren works for is making significant investments in infrastructure as a service hosting to replace its traditional data center. Members of her organization's management have expressed concerns about data remanence when Lauren's team moves from one virtual host to another in their cloud service provider's environment. What should she instruct her team to do to avoid this concern?

    A. Zero-wipe drives before moving systems.

    B. Use full disk encryption.

    C. Use data masking.

    D. Span multiple virtual disks to fragment data.

7. Lucca wants to prevent workstations on his network from attacking each other. If Lucca's corporate network looks like the network shown here, what technology should he select to prevent laptop A from being able to attack workstation B?

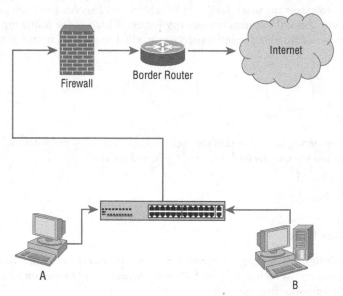

    A. IPS

    B. IDS

    C. HIPS

    D. HIDS

8. The company that Dan works for has recently migrated to a Service as a Service provider for its enterprise resource planning (ERP) software. In its traditional on-site ERP environment, Dan conducted regular port scans to help with security validation for the systems. What will Dan most likely have to do in this new environment?

    A. Use a different scanning tool.

    B. Rely on vendor testing and audits.

    C. Engage a third-party tester.

    D. Use a VPN to scan inside the vendor's security perimeter.

9. While investigating a malware infection, Lauren discovers that the hosts file for the system she is reviewing contains multiple entries as shown here:

```
0.0.0.0          symantec.com
0.0.0.0          mcafee.com
0.0.0.0          microsoft.com
0.0.0.0          kapersky.com
```

Why would the malware make this change?

   A. To redirect 0.0.0.0 to known sites

   B. To prevent antivirus updates

   C. To prevent other attackers from compromising the system

   D. To enable remote access to the system

10. Geoff is responsible for hardening systems on his network and discovers that a number of network appliances have exposed services including telnet, FTP, and web servers. What is his best option to secure these systems?

   A. Enable host firewalls.

   B. Install patches for those services.

   C. Turn off the services for each appliance.

   D. Place a network firewall between the devices and the rest of the network.

11. Tim needs to lock down a Windows workstation that has recently been scanned using nmap with the results shown here. He knows that the workstation needs to access websites and that the system is part of a Windows domain. What ports should he allow through the system's firewall for externally initiated connections?

```
root@kali:~# nmap -sS -P0 -p 0-65535 192.168.1.14

Starting Nmap 7.25BETA2 ( https://nmap.org ) at 2017-05-25 21:08 EDT
Nmap scan report for dynamo (192.168.1.14)
Host is up (0.00023s latency).
Not shown: 65524 filtered ports
PORT        STATE SERVICE
80/tcp      open  http
135/tcp     open  msrpc
139/tcp     open  netbios-ssn
445/tcp     open  microsoft-ds
902/tcp     open  iss-realsecure
912/tcp     open  apex-mesh
2869/tcp    open  icslap
3389/tcp    open  ms-wbt-server
5357/tcp    open  wsdapi
7680/tcp    open  unknown
22350/tcp open  CodeMeter
49677/tcp open  unknown
MAC Address: BC:5F:F4:7B:4B:7D (ASRock Incorporation)

Nmap done: 1 IP address (1 host up) scanned in 105.78 seconds
```

   A. He should allow ports 80, 135, 139, and 445.

   B. He should allow ports 80, 445, and 3389.

   C. He should allow ports 135, 139, and 445.

   D. No ports should be open.

12. What major issue would Charles face if he relied on hashing malware packages to identify malware packages?

    A. Hashing can be spoofed.

    B. Collisions can result in false positives.

    C. Hashing cannot identify unknown malware.

    D. Hashing relies on unencrypted malware samples.

13. As part of her system hardening process for a Windows 10 workstation, Lauren runs the Microsoft Baseline System Analyzer. She sees the following result after MBSA runs. What can she determine from this scan?

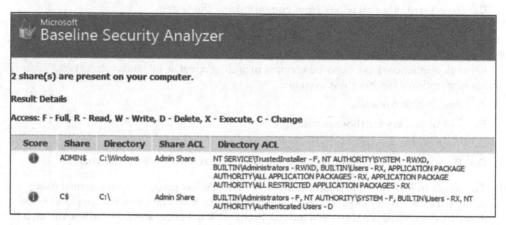

    A. The system has been compromised, and shares allow all users to read and execute administrative files.

    B. The system has default administrative shares enabled.

    C. The system is part of a domain that uses administrative shares to manage systems.

    D. The shares are properly secured and pose no threat to the system.

14. Susan is reviewing files on a Windows workstation and believes that cmd.exe has been replaced with a malware package. Which of the following is the best way to validate her theory?

    A. Submit cmd.exe to VirusTotal.

    B. Compare the hash of cmd.exe to a known good version.

    C. Check the file using the National Software Reference Library.

    D. Run cmd.exe to make sure its behavior is normal.

15. Chris wants to prevent users from running a popular game on Windows workstations he is responsible for. How can Chris accomplish this for Windows 10 Pro workstations?

    A. Using application whitelisting to prevent all unallowed programs from running

    B. Using Windows Defender and adding the game to the blacklist file

    C. By listing in the Blocked Programs list via `secpol.msc`

    D. You cannot blacklist applications in Windows 10 without a third-party application.

16. Ian's company has an internal policy requiring that it perform regular port scans of all of its servers. Ian has been part of a recent effort to move his organization's servers to an infrastructure as a service provider. What change will Ian most likely need to make to his scanning efforts?

    A. Change scanning software.

    B. Follow the service provider's scan policies.

    C. Sign a security contract with the provider.

    D. Discontinue port scanning.

17. Isaac wants to prevent hosts from connecting to known malware distribution domains. What type of solution can he use to do this without deploying endpoint protection software or an IPS?

    A. Route poisoning

    B. Anti-malware router filters

    C. Subdomain whitelisting

    D. DNS blackholing

18. Senior management in Adam's company recently read a number of articles about massive ransomware attacks that successfully targeted organizations like the one that Adam is part of. Adam's organization already uses layered security solutions including a border IPS, firewalls between network zones, local host firewalls, antivirus software, and a configuration management system that applies recommended operating system best practice settings to their workstations. What should Adam recommend to minimize the impact of a similar ransomware outbreak at his organization?

    A. Honeypots

    B. Backups

    C. Anti-malware software

    D. A next-generation firewall appliance

19. Lauren's screenshot shows behavioral analysis of the executed code. From this, we can determine that the tool she used is a dynamic analysis sandbox that runs the malware sample to determine what it does while also analyzing the file.

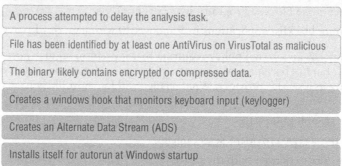

Signatures

> A process attempted to delay the analysis task.

> File has been identified by at least one AntiVirus on VirusTotal as malicious

> The binary likely contains encrypted or compressed data.

> Creates a windows hook that monitors keyboard input (keylogger)

> Creates an Alternate Data Stream (ADS)

> Installs itself for autorun at Windows startup

   A. A reverse engineering tool

   B. A static analysis sandbox

   C. A dynamic analysis sandbox

   D. A decompiler sandbox

Questions 20 through 22 refer to the bare-metal virtualization environment shown here.

A	A	A	A
B			
C			

20. What component is identified by A in the image?

   A. Hypervisor

   B. Host operating system

   C. Guest operating system

   D. Physical hardware

21. What component is identified by B in the image?

   A. Hypervisor

   B. Host operating system

   C. Guest operating system

   D. Physical hardware

22. What component is identified by C in the image?

   A. Hypervisor

   B. Host operating system

   C. Guest operating system

   D. Physical hardware

23. Frank discovers a missing Windows security patch during a vulnerability scan of a server in his organization's data center. Upon further investigation, he discovers that the system is virtualized. Where should he apply the patch?

   A. To the virtualized system

   B. The patch is not necessary.

   C. To the domain controller

   D. To the virtualization platform

24. Mike runs a vulnerability scan against his company's virtualization environment and finds the vulnerability shown here in several of the virtual hosts. What action should Mike take?

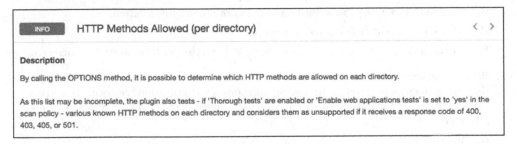

   A. No action is necessary because this is an informational report.

   B. Mike should disable HTTP on the affected devices.

   C. Mike should upgrade the version of OpenSSL on the affected devices.

   D. Mike should immediately upgrade the hypervisor.

25. During a recent vulnerability scan, Ed discovered that a web server running on his network has access to a database server that should be restricted. Both servers are running on his organization's VMware virtualization platform. Where should Ed look first to configure a security control to restrict this access?

   A. VMware

   B. Data center firewall

   C. Perimeter (Internet) firewall

   D. Intrusion prevention system

26. Which one of the following protocols might be used within a virtualization platform for monitoring and managing the network?

    A. SNMP

    B. SMTP

    C. BGP

    D. EIGRP

27. Don completed a vulnerability scan of his organization's virtualization platform from an external host and discovered the vulnerability shown here. How should Don react?

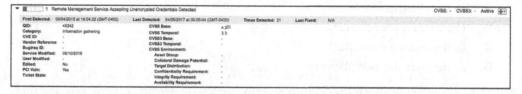

    A. This is a critical issue that requires immediate adjustment of firewall rules.

    B. This issue has a very low severity and does not require remediation.

    C. This issue should be corrected as time permits.

    D. This is a critical issue, and Don should shut down the platform until it is corrected.

28. While conducting a vulnerability scan of his organization's data center, Renee discovers that the management interface for the organization's virtualization platform is exposed to the scanner. In typical operating circumstances, what is the proper exposure for this interface?

    A. Internet

    B. Internal networks

    C. No exposure

    D. Management network

29. Angela wants to understand what a malware package does and executes it in a virtual machine that is instrumented using tools that will track what the program does, what changes it makes, and what network traffic it sends while allowing her to make changes on the system or to click on files as needed. What type of analysis has Angela performed?

    A. Manual code reversing

    B. Interactive behavior analysis

    C. Static property analysis

    D. Dynamic code analysis

30. Derek sets up a series of virtual machines that are automatically created in a completely isolated environment. Once created, the systems are used to run potentially malicious software and files. The actions taken by those files and programs are recorded and then reported. What technique is Derek using?

A. Sandboxing

B. Reverse engineering

C. Malware disassembly

D. Darknet analysis

31. Ian is reviewing the security architecture shown here. This architecture is designed to connect his local data center with an IaaS service provider that his company is using to provide overflow services. What component can be used at the points marked by question marks to provide a secure encrypted network connection?

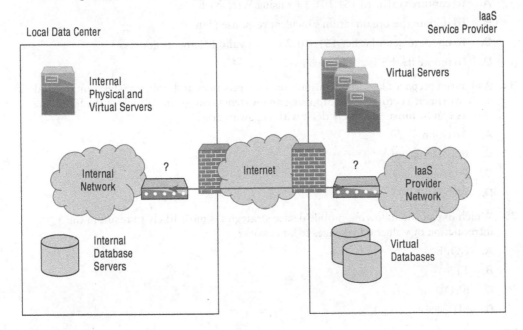

A. Firewall

B. VPN

C. IPS

D. DLP

32. Which one of the following statements is true about virtualized operating systems?

    A. In bare-metal virtualization, all guest operating systems must be the same version.

    B. In bare-metal virtualization, all guest operating systems must be the same platform (e.g., Windows, RedHat, CentOS).

    C. In bare-metal virtualization, the host operating system and guest operating system platforms must be consistent.

    D. None of these statements is correct.

33. While reviewing output from netstat, John sees the following output. What should his next action be?

```
[minesweeper.exe]   TCP     127.0.0.1:62522    dynamo:0              LISTENING
[minesweeper.exe]   TCP     192.168.1.100      151.101.2.69:https    ESTABLISHED
```

    A. To capture traffic to 151.101.2.69 using Wireshark

    B. To initiate the organization's incident response plan

    C. To check to see whether 151.101.2.69 is a valid Microsoft address

    D. To ignore it; this is a false positive.

34. As Lauren prepares her organization's security practices and policies, she wants to address as many threat vectors as she can using an awareness program. Which of the following threats can be most effectively dealt with via awareness?

    A. Attrition

    B. Impersonation

    C. Improper usage

    D. Web

35. Which one of the following mobile device strategies is most likely to result in the introduction of vulnerable devices to a network?

    A. COPE

    B. TLS

    C. BYOD

    D. MDM

36. Jarett needs to protect an application server against resource exhaustion attacks. Which of the following techniques is best suited to surviving a large-scale DDoS attack?

    A. Enable application sharding.

    B. Review each query and implement query optimization.

    C. Implement aggressive aging at the organization's firewall.

    D. Employ a CDN.

37. Jennifer is an Active Directory domain administrator for her company and knows that a quickly spreading botnet relies on a series of domain names for command and control and that preventing access to those domain names will cause the malware infection that connects to the botnet to fail to take further action. Which of the following actions is her best option if she wants to prevent off-site Windows users from connecting to botnet command-and-control systems?

   A. Force a BGP update.

   B. Set up a DNS sinkhole.

   C. Modify the hosts file.

   D. Install an anti-malware application.

38. Several employees will need to travel with sensitive information on their laptops. Martin is concerned that one of those laptops may be lost or stolen. Which one of the following controls would best protect the data on stolen devices?

   A. FDE

   B. Strong passwords

   C. Cable lock

   D. IPS

For questions 39–41, please refer to the following scenario.

Ben is an information security professional at an organization that is replacing its physical servers with virtual machines. As the organization builds its virtual environment, it is decreasing the number of physical servers it uses while purchasing more powerful servers to act as the virtualization platforms.

39. The IDS Ben is responsible for is used to monitor communications in the data center using a mirrored port on the data center switch. What traffic will Ben see once the majority of servers in the data center have been virtualized?

   A. The same traffic he currently sees

   B. All inter-VM traffic

   C. Only traffic sent outside the VM environment

   D. All inter-hypervisor traffic

40. The VM administrators recommend enabling cut and paste between virtual machines. What security concern should Ben raise about this practice?

   A. It can cause a denial-of-service condition.

   B. It can serve as a covert channel.

   C. It can allow viruses to spread.

   D. It can bypass authentication controls.

41. Ben is concerned about exploits that allow VM escape. What option should Ben suggest to help limit the impact of VM escape exploits?

   A. Separate virtual machines onto separate physical hardware based on task or data types.

   B. Use VM escape detection tools on the underlying hypervisor.

   C. Restore machines to their original snapshots on a regular basis.

   D. Use a utility like Tripwire to look for changes in the virtual machines.

42. Michael is responsible for forensic investigations and is investigating a medium-severity security incident that involved the defacement of a corporate website. The web server in question ran on a virtualization platform, and the marketing team would like to get the website up and running as quickly as possible. What would be the most reasonable next step for Michael to take?

    A. Keep the website offline until the investigation is complete.

    B. Take the virtualization platform offline as evidence.

    C. Take a snapshot of the compromised system and use that for the investigation.

    D. Ignore the incident and focus on quickly restoring the website.

43. Sonia recently removed an encrypted hard drive from a laptop and moved it to a new device because of a hardware failure. She is having difficulty accessing encrypted content on the drive despite that she knows the user's password. What hardware security feature is likely causing this problem?

    A. TCB

    B. TPM

    C. NIACAP

    D. RSA

44. In an infrastructure as a service (IaaS) environment where a vendor supplies a customer with access to storage services, who is normally responsible for removing sensitive data from drives that are taken out of service?

    A. Customer's security team

    B. Customer's storage team

    C. Customer's vendor management team

    D. Vendor

45. Gary is concerned about applying consistent security settings to the many mobile devices used throughout his organization. What technology would best assist with this challenge?

    A. MDM

    B. IPS

    C. IDS

    D. SIEM

46. In a software as a service cloud computing environment, who is normally responsible for ensuring that appropriate firewall controls are in place to protect the application?

    A. Customer's security team

    B. Vendor

    C. Customer's networking team

    D. Customer's infrastructure management team

47. Grace would like to implement application control technology in her organization. Users often need to install new applications for research and testing purposes, and she does not want to interfere with that process. At the same time, she would like to block the use of known malicious software. What type of application control would be appropriate in this situation?

- **A.** Blacklisting
- **B.** Graylisting
- **C.** Whitelisting
- **D.** Bluelisting

48. In a virtualized computing environment, what component is responsible for enforcing separation between guest machines?

- **A.** Guest operating system
- **B.** Hypervisor
- **C.** Kernel
- **D.** Protection manager

49. During a third-party vulnerability scan and security test, Danielle's employer recently discovered that the embedded systems that were installed to manage her company's new buildings have a severe remote access vulnerability. The manufacturer has gone out of business, and there is no patch or update for the devices. What should Danielle recommend that her employer do about the hundreds of devices that are vulnerable?

- **A.** Identify a replacement device model and replace every device
- **B.** Turn off all the devices
- **C.** Move the devices to a secured network segment
- **D.** Reverse engineer the devices and build an in-house patch

50. Henry wants to ensure resilience for data that is being actively processed in his organization's cloud environment. Which of the following techniques is best suited to ensuring that transactions will not be lost if a cloud-hosted system or container fails during processing?

- **A.** Building retry operations into applications
- **B.** Using a load balancer
- **C.** Using a cluster
- **D.** Using a CDN

51. Ben's organization has had an issue with unauthorized access to applications and workstations during the lunch hour when employees aren't at their desk. What are the best types of session management solutions for Ben to recommend to help prevent this type of access?

- **A.** Use session IDs for all access and verify system IP addresses of all workstations.
- **B.** Set session timeouts for applications and use password-protected screensavers with inactivity time-outs on workstations.
- **C.** Use session IDs for all applications and use password protected screensavers with inactivity timeouts on workstations.
- **D.** Set session timeouts for applications and verify system IP addresses of all workstations.

52. Harold recently added an input validation routine to a web application that is designed to remove any instances of the <SCRIPT> tag in user input. What type of attack is Harold attempting to mitigate?

   A. SQL injection

   B. CSRF

   C. XSS

   D. Man-in-the-middle

53. Under what virtualization model does the virtualization platform separate the network control plane from the data plane and replace complex network devices with simpler devices that simply receive instructions from the controller?

   A. Virtual machines

   B. VSAN

   C. VLAN

   D. SDN

54. Which one of the following terms is often used to describe a collection of unrelated patches released in a large collection?

   A. Hotfix

   B. Update

   C. Security fix

   D. Service pack

55. Brian recently joined an organization that runs the majority of its services on a virtualization platform located in its own data center but also leverages an IaaS provider for hosting its web services and an SaaS email system. What term best describes the type of cloud environment this organization uses?

   A. Public cloud

   B. Dedicated cloud

   C. Private cloud

   D. Hybrid cloud

56. Mark is considering replacing his organization's customer relationship management (CRM) solution with a new product that is available in the cloud. This new solution is completely managed by the vendor, and Mark's company will not have to write any code or manage any physical resources. What type of cloud solution is Mark considering?

   A. IaaS

   B. CaaS

   C. PaaS

   D. SaaS

57. Which one of the following statements best describes a zero-day vulnerability?

   A. An attacker who is new to the world of hacking

   B. A database attack that places the date 00/00/0000 in data tables in an attempt to exploit flaws in business logic

   C. An attack previously unknown to the security community

   D. An attack that sets the operating system date and time to 00/00/0000 and 00:00:00

58. Melanie suspects that someone is using malicious software to steal computing cycles from her company. Which one of the following security tools would be in the best position to detect this type of incident?

   A. NIDS

   B. Firewall

   C. HIDS

   D. DLP

59. Brandon observes that an authorized user of a system on his network recently misused his account to exploit a system vulnerability against a shared server that allowed him to gain root access to that server. What type of attack took place?

   A. Denial-of-service

   B. Privilege escalation

   C. Reconnaissance

   D. Brute force

60. Roger recently accepted a new position as a security professional at a company that runs its entire IT infrastructure within an IaaS environment. Which one of the following would most likely be the responsibility of Roger's firm?

   A. Configuring the network firewall

   B. Applying hypervisor updates

   C. Patching operating systems

   D. Wiping drives prior to disposal

61. Renee is a software developer who writes code in Node.js for her organization. The company is considering moving from a self-hosted Node.js environment to one where Renee will run her code on application servers managed by a cloud vendor. What type of cloud solution is Renee's company considering?

   A. IaaS

   B. CaaS

   C. PaaS

   D. SaaS

62. Lauren wants to ensure that her users run only the software that her organization has approved. What technology should she deploy?

   A. Blacklisting

   B. Configuration management

   C. Whitelisting

   D. Graylisting

63. Which one of the following files is most likely to contain a macro virus?

   A. `projections.doc`

   B. `command.com`

   C. `command.exe`

   D. `loopmaster.exe`

64. What type of malware is characterized by spreading from system to system under its own power by exploiting vulnerabilities that do not require user intervention?

   A. Trojan horse

   B. Virus

   C. Logic bomb

   D. Worm

65. Martin is inspecting a system where the user reported unusual activity, including disk activity when the system is idle, and abnormal CPU and network usage. He suspects that the machine is infected by a virus but scans come up clean. What malware technique might be in use here that would explain the clean scan results?

   A. File infector virus

   B. MBR virus

   C. Service injection virus

   D. Stealth virus

66. TJ is inspecting a system where the user reported a strange error message and the inability to access files. He sees the window shown here. What type of malware should TJ suspect?

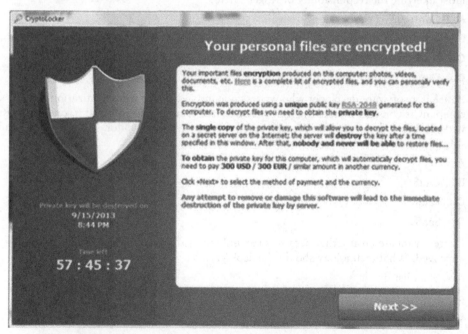

   A. Service injection

   B. Encrypted virus

   C. SQL injection

   D. Ransomware

67. Ghita believes that her organization is having problems with fileless viruses. What Windows component is most likely being leveraged by the malware?

    A. Windows Remote Desktop

    B. Windows Defender

    C. PowerShell

    D. Windows Hello

68. Liu wants to use a publicly available container image to run a service in his cloud-hosted containerization environment. Which of the following best practices will best help him avoid malicious containers?

    A. Validating the container's digital signature

    B. Scanning the container for malicious software

    C. Running only containers that have been published for at least a week so problems can be identified by others

    D. Preventing container updates to avoid the introduction of new malicious code

69. Which of the following is not a common indicator of advanced persistent threat activity?

    A. Unexpected data flows to new or atypical destinations

    B. Remote-access Trojans installed on multiple systems

    C. An increase in spam email

    D. Use of elevated privileges by users who should not have that access

70. Sara has been asked to explain to her organization what an endpoint detection and response (EDR) system could help the organization do. Which of the following functions is not a typical function for an EDR system?

    A. Endpoint data collection and central analysis

    B. Automated responses to threats

    C. Forensic analysis to help with threat response and detection

    D. Cloud and network data collection and central analysis

71. Ian discovers the following URL in a web server log and believes it is some form of web-based attack:

    `http://example.com/ref?file=../../../../etc/passwd`

    What type of attack should Ian identify this as?

    A. A denial-of-service attack

    B. A SQL injection attack

    C. A directory traversal attack

    D. A brute-force attack

72. Murali wants to ensure that if one of his organization's laptops is stolen, the data on it cannot be accessed. If he uses whole-disk encryption, when could data on the drives on his organization's laptops be accessed?

   A. When the systems are off, if the drives are removed and accessed using an external enclosure.

   B. When the laptops are booted and users are logged in.

   C. When the laptops are booted up but users are not logged in.

   D. The data is encrypted both at rest and when the user is logged in.

73. Murali also wants to ensure that data is protected on his organization's mobile devices. His organization uses iPhones and iPads as their corporate devices. When can he expect data to be encrypted on his corporate mobile devices?

   A. When the phone is unlocked

   B. When the phone is locked if he enables encryption on the iPhones and iPads

   C. When the phone is locked, with or without a passcode

   D. When the phone is locked with a passcode, FaceID, or TouchID

74. Olivia wants to use data from systems and devices in her network to identify potential advanced persistent threat activity. What type of analytics should she focus on to provide the best chance of detecting APTs based on indicators of compromise (IoCs) like data exfiltration and privilege misuse?

   A. Signature-based detection

   B. Regression analysis

   C. Behavior analytics

   D. Trend-based analytics

75. Greg's company has selected a bring your own device (BYOD) model for employee mobile devices. Greg has been tasked with recommending how to ensure that corporate data stays secure despite being on personally owned devices. Which of the following techniques is best suited to this in a BYOD environment?

   A. Require the use of a remote desktop environment from the mobile devices.

   B. Use MDM application-based containerization.

   C. Require a SIM swap when switching roles.

   D. Use a SIEM system to control application security.

76. Rosa wants to decrease the chances of both inadvertent data exposure and intentional data exfiltration from her organization. What technology can she implement to help with tagging and protecting data to prevent this scenario?

   A. COPE

   B. APT

   C. DLP

   D. SLA

77. Keisha's organization has begun to purchase mobile devices for use by sales staff who operate outside of the office. Since the devices are in use as their primary phones, the salespeople often have personal applications loaded on them, which has created a security concern for the company since sensitive corporate data, including sales numbers and proprietary customer databases, are stored on or accessed via the phones. What technology should Keisha deploy to control applications on the phones?

A. TPM

B. SCCM

C. MAM

D. MTM

Chapter

8

Practice Test 1

1. Which of the following is not a type of attack used against access controls?

   A. Dictionary attack

   B. Brute-force attack

   C. Teardrop

   D. Man-in-the-middle attack

2. George is assisting a prosecutor with a case against a hacker who attempted to break into the computer systems at George's company. He provides system logs to the prosecutor for use as evidence, but the prosecutor insists that George testify in court about how he gathered the logs. What rule of evidence requires George's testimony?

   A. Testimonial evidence rule

   B. Parol evidence rule

   C. Best evidence rule

   D. Hearsay rule

3. Jim has been asked to individually identify devices that users are bringing to work as part of a new BYOD policy. The devices will not be joined to a central management system like Active Directory, but he still needs to uniquely identify the systems. Which of the following options will provide Jim with the best means of reliably identifying each unique device?

   A. Record the MAC address of each system.

   B. Require users to fill out a form to register each system.

   C. Scan each system using a port scanner.

   D. Use device fingerprinting via a web-based registration system.

4. Greg would like to implement application control technology in his organization. He would like to limit users to installing only approved software on their systems. What type of application control would be appropriate in this situation?

   A. Blacklisting

   B. Graylisting

   C. Whitelisting

   D. Bluelisting

5. Which pair of the following factors is key for user acceptance of biometric identification systems?

   A. The FAR and FRR

   B. The throughput rate and the time required to enroll

   C. The CER and the ERR

   D. How often users must reenroll and the reference profile requirements

6. Sally is wiring a gigabit Ethernet network. What cabling choices should she make to ensure she can use her network at the full 1000 Mbps she wants to provide to her users?

    A. Cat 5 and Cat 6

    B. Cat 5e and Cat 6

    C. Cat 4e and Cat 5e

    D. Cat 6 and Cat 7

For questions 7–9, please refer to the following scenario.

    Alex has been with the university he works at for more than 10 years. During that time, he has been a system administrator and a database administrator, and he has worked in the university's help desk. He is now a manager for the team that runs the university's web applications. Using the provisioning diagram shown here, answer the following questions.

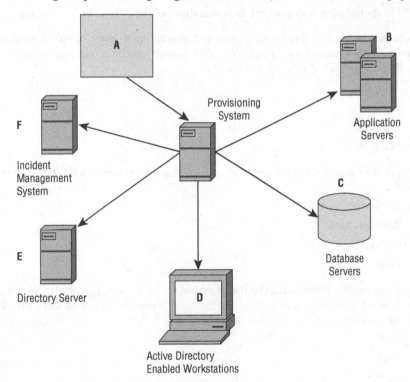

7. If Alex hires a new employee and the employee's account is provisioned after HR manually inputs information into the provisioning system based on data Alex provides via a series of forms, what type of provisioning has occurred?

    A. Discretionary account provisioning

    B. Workflow-based account provisioning

    C. Automated account provisioning

    D. Self-service account provisioning

8. Alex has access to B, C, and D. What concern should he raise to the university's identity management team?

   A. The provisioning process did not give him the rights he needs.

   B. He has excessive privileges.

   C. Privilege creep may be taking place.

   D. Logging is not properly enabled.

9. When Alex changes roles, what should occur?

   A. He should be deprovisioned, and a new account should be created.

   B. He should have his new rights added to his existing account.

   C. He should be provisioned for only the rights that match his role.

   D. He should have his rights set to match those of the person he is replacing.

10. Vivian works for a chain of retail stores and would like to use a software product that restricts the software used on point-of-sale terminals to those packages on a preapproved list. What approach should Vivian use?

    A. Antivirus

    B. Heuristic

    C. Whitelist

    D. Blacklist

11. What type of motion detector senses changes in the electromagnetic fields in monitored areas?

    A. Infrared

    B. Wave pattern

    C. Capacitance

    D. Photoelectric

12. Don's company is considering the use of an object-based storage system where data is placed in a vendor-managed storage environment through the use of API calls. What type of cloud computing service is in use?

    A. IaaS

    B. PaaS

    C. CaaS

    D. SaaS

13. What is the minimum interval at which an organization should conduct business continuity plan refresher training for those with specific business continuity roles?

    A. Weekly

    B. Monthly

    C. Semiannually

    D. Annually

14. What type of log file is shown in this figure?

```
2015-08-09 16:39:01 ALLOW UDP 172.30.0.64 172.30.0.2 62166 53 0 - - - - - - - SEND
2015-08-09 16:39:01 ALLOW UDP 172.30.0.64 172.30.0.2 62167 53 0 - - - - - - - SEND
2015-08-09 16:39:01 ALLOW UDP 172.30.0.64 172.30.0.2 62168 53 0 - - - - - - - SEND
2015-08-09 16:39:01 ALLOW UDP 172.30.0.64 172.30.0.2 62169 53 0 - - - - - - - SEND
2015-08-09 16:39:01 ALLOW UDP 172.30.0.64 172.30.0.2 62170 53 0 - - - - - - - SEND
2015-08-09 16:39:01 ALLOW UDP 172.30.0.64 172.30.0.2 62171 53 0 - - - - - - - SEND
2015-08-09 16:39:01 ALLOW UDP 172.30.0.64 172.30.0.2 62172 53 0 - - - - - - - SEND
2015-08-09 16:39:01 ALLOW UDP 172.30.0.64 172.30.0.2 62173 53 0 - - - - - - - SEND
2015-08-09 16:39:01 ALLOW UDP 172.30.0.64 172.30.0.2 62174 53 0 - - - - - - - SEND
2015-08-09 16:39:01 ALLOW UDP 172.30.0.64 172.30.0.2 62175 53 0 - - - - - - - SEND
2015-08-09 16:39:01 ALLOW UDP 172.30.0.64 172.30.0.2 62176 53 0 - - - - - - - SEND
2015-08-09 16:39:39 ALLOW TCP 54.172.251.189 172.30.0.64 53355 80 0 - 0 0 0 - - - RECEIVE
2015-08-09 16:39:44 ALLOW TCP 54.172.251.189 172.30.0.64 53356 80 0 - 0 0 0 - - - RECEIVE
2015-08-09 16:39:44 ALLOW TCP 127.0.0.1 127.0.0.1 49178 47001 0 - 0 0 0 - - - SEND
2015-08-09 16:39:44 ALLOW TCP 127.0.0.1 127.0.0.1 49178 47001 0 - 0 0 0 - - - RECEIVE
2015-08-09 16:39:47 ALLOW TCP 172.30.0.64 169.254.169.254 49179 80 0 - 0 0 0 - - - SEND
2015-08-09 16:40:37 ALLOW TCP 54.172.251.189 172.30.0.64 53362 80 0 - 0 0 0 - - - RECEIVE
2015-08-09 16:40:47 ALLOW TCP 172.30.0.64 169.254.169.254 49180 80 0 - 0 0 0 - - - SEND
2015-08-09 16:40:55 ALLOW UDP fe80::11ef:7f4f:afb5:7f70 ff02::1:2 546 547 0 - - - - - - - SEND
```

A. Application
B. Web server
C. System
D. Firewall

15. Which one of the following technologies is not normally a capability of mobile device management (MDM) solutions?

A. Remotely wiping the contents of a mobile device
B. Assuming control of a nonregistered BYOD mobile device
C. Enforcing the use of device encryption
D. Managing device backups

16. Alex is preparing to solicit bids for a penetration test of his company's network and systems. He wants to maximize the effectiveness of the testing rather than the realism of the test. What type of penetration test should he require in his bidding process?

A. Black box
B. White box
C. Gray box
D. Zero box

For questions 120–122, please refer to the following scenario:

Ben owns a coffeehouse and wants to provide wireless Internet service for his customers. Ben's network is simple and uses a single consumer-grade wireless router and a cable modem connected via a commercial cable data contract.

17. What RADIUS alternative is commonly used for Cisco network gear and supports two-factor authentication?

A. RADIUS+
B. TACACS+
C. XTACACS
D. Kerberos

18. What type of fire extinguisher is useful against liquid-based fires?
    - **A.** Class A
    - **B.** Class B
    - **C.** Class C
    - **D.** Class D

19. Which one of the following components should be included in an organization's emergency response guidelines?
    - **A.** Immediate response procedures
    - **B.** Long-term business continuity protocols
    - **C.** Activation procedures for the organization's cold sites
    - **D.** Contact information for ordering equipment

20. Which one of the following disaster recovery test types involves the actual activation of the disaster recovery facility?
    - **A.** Simulation test
    - **B.** Tabletop exercise
    - **C.** Parallel test
    - **D.** Checklist review

21. Susan is configuring her network devices to use syslog. What should she set to ensure that she is notified about issues but does not receive normal operational issue messages?
    - **A.** The facility code
    - **B.** The log priority
    - **C.** The security level
    - **D.** The severity level

22. While Lauren is monitoring traffic on two ends of a network connection, she sees traffic that is inbound to a public IP address show up inside the production network bound for an internal host that uses an RFC 1918 reserved address. What technology should she expect is in use at the network border?
    - **A.** NAT
    - **B.** VLANs
    - **C.** S/NAT
    - **D.** BGP

23. Michelle is in charge of her organization's mobile device management efforts and handles lost and stolen devices. Which of the following recommendations will provide the most assurance to her organization that data will not be lost if a device is stolen?
    - **A.** Mandatory passcodes and application management
    - **B.** Full device encryption and mandatory passcodes
    - **C.** Remote wipe and GPS tracking
    - **D.** Enabling GPS tracking and full device encryption

24. Dogs, guards, and fences are all common examples of what type of control?

    A. Detective

    B. Recovery

    C. Administrative

    D. Physical

25. In this diagram of the TCP three-way handshake, what should system A send to system B in step 3?

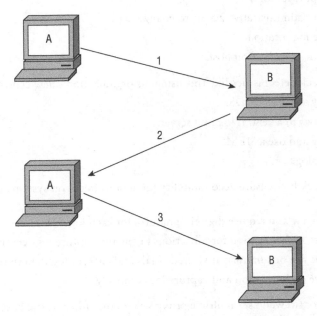

    A. ACK

    B. SYN

    C. FIN

    D. RST

26. In which cloud computing model does a customer share computing infrastructure with other customers of the cloud vendor where one customer may not know the other's identity?

    A. Public cloud

    B. Private cloud

    C. Community cloud

    D. Shared cloud

For questions 27–29, please refer to the following scenario.

The large business that Jack works for has been using noncentralized logging for years. They have recently started to implement centralized logging, however, and as they reviewed logs, they discovered a breach that appeared to have involved a malicious insider.

27. When the breach was discovered and the logs were reviewed, it was discovered that the attacker had purged the logs on the system that they compromised. How can this be prevented in the future?

    A. Encrypt local logs.

    B. Require administrative access to change logs.

    C. Enable log rotation.

    D. Send logs to a bastion host.

28. How can Jack detect issues like this using his organization's new centralized logging?

    A. Deploy and use an IDS.

    B. Send logs to a central logging server.

    C. Deploy and use a SIEM.

    D. Use syslog.

29. How can Jack best ensure accountability for actions taken on systems in his environment?

    A. Log review and require digital signatures for each log.

    B. Require authentication for all actions taken and capture logs centrally.

    C. Log the use of administrative credentials and encrypt log data in transit.

    D. Require authorization and capture logs centrally.

30. What type of firewall uses multiple proxy servers that filter traffic based on analysis of the protocols used for each service?

    A. A static packet filtering firewall

    B. An application-level gateway firewall

    C. A circuit-level gateway firewall

    D. A stateful inspection firewall

31. James is building a disaster recovery plan for his organization and would like to determine the amount of acceptable data loss after an outage. What variable is James determining?

    A. SLA

    B. RTO

    C. MTD

    D. RPO

32. Which one of the following is not one of the canons of the (ISC)² Code of Ethics?

    A. Protect society, the common good, necessary public trust and confidence, and the infrastructure.

    B. Act honorably, honestly, justly, responsibly, and legally.

    C. Provide diligent and competent service to principals.

    D. Maintain competent records of all investigations and assessments.

33. Dave is responsible for password security in his organization and would like to strengthen the security of password files. He would like to defend his organization against the use of rainbow tables. Which one of the following techniques is specifically designed to frustrate the use of rainbow tables?

    A. Password expiration policies

    B. Salting

    C. User education

    D. Password complexity policies

34. What is the process that occurs when the Session layer removes the header from data sent by the Transport layer?

    A. Encapsulation

    B. Packet unwrapping

    C. De-encapsulation

    D. Payloading

35. Which one of the following types of firewalls does not have the ability to track connection status between different packets?

    A. Stateful inspection

    B. Application proxy

    C. Packet filter

    D. Next generation

36. Alice wants to send Bob a message with the confidence that Bob will know the message was not altered while in transit. What goal of cryptography is Alice trying to achieve?

    A. Confidentiality

    B. Nonrepudiation

    C. Authentication

    D. Integrity

37. Chris is troubleshooting an issue with his organization's SIEM reporting. After analyzing the issue, he believes that the timestamps on log entries from different systems are inconsistent. What protocol can he use to resolve this issue?

    A. SSH

    B. FTP

    C. TLS

    D. NTP

38. Alan is installing a fire suppression system that will kick in after a fire breaks out and protect the equipment in the data center from extensive damage. What metric is Alan attempting to lower?

    A. Likelihood

    B. RTO

    C. RPO

    D. Impact

39. Which one of the following technologies is designed to prevent a web server going offline from becoming a single point of failure in a web application architecture?

    A. Load balancing

    B. Dual-power supplies

    C. IPS

    D. RAID

40. Alan is considering the use of new identification cards in his organization that will be used for physical access control. He comes across a sample card and is unsure of the technology. He breaks it open and sees the following internal construction. What type of card is this?

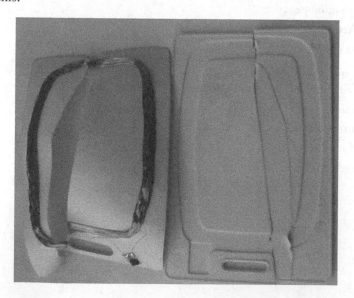

A. Smart card

B. Proximity card

C. Magnetic stripe

D. Phase-two card

41. When an application or system allows a logged-in user to perform specific actions, it is an example of what?

A. Roles

B. Group management

C. Logins

D. Authorization

42. What is the minimum number of cryptographic keys necessary to achieve strong security when using the 3DES algorithm?

A. 1

B. 2

C. 3

D. 4

43. Gina recently took the SSCP certification exam and then wrote a blog post that included the text of many of the exam questions that she experienced. What aspect of the (ISC)² code of ethics is most directly violated in this situation?

A. Advance and protect the profession.

B. Act honorably, honestly, justly, responsibly, and legally.

C. Protect society, the common good, necessary public trust and confidence, and the infrastructure.

D. Provide diligent and competent service to principals.

44. What type of access controls allow the owner of a file to grant other users access to it using an access control list?

A. Role-based

B. Nondiscretionary

C. Rule-based

D. Discretionary

45. Which one of the following components is used to assign classifications to objects in a mandatory access control system?

A. Security label

B. Security token

C. Security descriptor

D. Security capability

46. Tommy handles access control requests for his organization. A user approaches him and explains that he needs access to the human resources database to complete a headcount analysis requested by the CFO. What has the user demonstrated successfully to Tommy?

    A. Clearance

    B. Separation of duties

    C. Need to know

    D. Isolation

47. Which one of the following is not a mode of operation for the Data Encryption Standard?

    A. CBC

    B. CFB

    C. OFB

    D. AES

48. Voice pattern recognition is what type of authentication factor?

    A. Something you know

    B. Something you have

    C. Something you are

    D. Somewhere you are

49. Which of the following is not a single sign-on implementation?

    A. Kerberos

    B. ADFS

    C. CAS

    D. RADIUS

50. Chris is conducting a risk assessment for his organization and has determined the amount of damage that a single flood could be expected to cause to his facilities. What metric has Chris identified?

    A. ALE

    B. SLE

    C. ARO

    D. AV

For questions 51–55, please refer to the following scenario.

Concho Controls is a midsize business focusing on building automation systems. They host a set of local file servers in their on-premises data center that store customer proposals, building plans, product information, and other data that is critical to their business operations.

Tara works in the Concho Controls IT department and is responsible for designing and implementing the organization's backup strategy, among other tasks. She currently conducts full backups every Sunday evening at 8 p.m. and differential backups on Monday through Friday at noon.

Concho experiences a server failure at 3 p.m. on Wednesday. Tara rebuilds the server and wants to restore data from the backups.

51. What backup should Tara apply to the server first?

 A. Sunday's full backup

 B. Monday's differential backup

 C. Tuesday's differential backup

 D. Wednesday's differential backup

52. How many backups in total must Tara apply to the system to make the data it contains as current as possible?

 A. 1

 B. 2

 C. 3

 D. 4

53. In this backup approach, some data may be irretrievably lost. How long is the time period where any changes made will have been lost?

 A. 3 hours

 B. 5 hours

 C. 8 hours

 D. No data will be lost.

54. If Tara followed the same schedule but switched the differential backups to incremental backups, how many backups in total would she need to apply to the system to make the data it contains as current as possible?

 A. 1

 B. 2

 C. 3

 D. 4

55. If Tara made the change from differential to incremental backups and we assume that the same amount of information changes each day, which one of the following files would be the largest?

   A. Monday's incremental backup

   B. Tuesday's incremental backup

   C. Wednesday's incremental backup

   D. All three will be the same size.

56. Susan has discovered that the smart card–based locks used to keep the facility she works at secure are not effective because staff members are propping the doors open. She places signs on the doors reminding staff that leaving the door open creates a security issue, and she adds alarms that will sound if the doors are left open for more than five minutes. What type of controls has she put into place?

   A. Physical

   B. Administrative

   C. Compensation

   D. Recovery

57. During what phase of the electronic discovery reference model does an organization ensure that potentially discoverable information is protected against alteration or deletion?

   A. Identification

   B. Preservation

   C. Collection

   D. Production

58. Marty discovers that the access restrictions in his organization allow any user to log into the workstation assigned to any other user, even if they are from completely different departments. This type of access most directly violates which information security principle?

   A. Separation of duties

   B. Two-person control

   C. Need to know

   D. Least privilege

59. Which of the following tools is best suited to testing known exploits against a system?

   A. Nikto

   B. Ettercap

   C. Metasploit

   D. THC Hydra

60. Denise is preparing for a trial relating to a contract dispute between her company and a software vendor. The vendor is claiming that Denise made a verbal agreement that amended their written contract. What rule of evidence should Denise raise in her defense?

   A. Real evidence rule

   B. Best evidence rule

   C. Parol evidence rule

   D. Testimonial evidence rule

61. During which phase of the incident response process would an organization determine whether it is required to notify law enforcement officials or other regulators of the incident?

    A. Detection

    B. Recovery

    C. Remediation

    D. Reporting

62. Gordon is conducting a risk assessment for his organization and determined the amount of damage that flooding is expected to cause to his facilities each year. What metric has Gordon identified?

    A. ALE

    B. ARO

    C. SLE

    D. EF

63. Data is sent as bits at what layer of the OSI model?

    A. Transport

    B. Network

    C. Data Link

    D. Physical

64. Angie is configuring egress monitoring on her network to provide added security. Which one of the following packet types should Angie allow to leave the network headed for the Internet?

    A. Packets with a source address from Angie's public IP address block

    B. Packets with a destination address from Angie's public IP address block

    C. Packets with a source address outside Angie's address block

    D. Packets with a source address from Angie's private address block

65. Harry would like to access a document owned by Sally stored on a file server. Applying the subject/object model to this scenario, who or what is the object of the resource request?

    A. Harry

    B. Sally

    C. File server

    D. Document

66. Information about an individual like their name, Social Security number, date and place of birth, or their mother's maiden name is an example of what type of protected information?

    A. PHI

    B. Proprietary data

    C. PII

    D. EDI

67. Greg is building a disaster recovery plan for his organization and would like to determine the amount of time that it should take to restore a particular IT service after an outage. What variable is Greg calculating?

    A. MTD

    B. RTO

    C. RPO

    D. SLA

68. What type of access control is intended to discover unwanted or unauthorized activity by providing information after the event has occurred?

    A. Preventive

    B. Corrective

    C. Detective

    D. Directive

69. What business process typically requires sign-off from a manager before modifications are made to a system?

    A. SDN

    B. Release management

    C. Change management

    D. Versioning

70. Gordon is developing a business continuity plan for a manufacturing company's IT operations. The company is located in North Dakota and currently evaluating the risk of earthquake. They choose to pursue a risk acceptance strategy. Which one of the following actions is consistent with that strategy?

    A. Purchasing earthquake insurance

    B. Relocating the data center to a safer area

    C. Documenting the decision-making process

    D. Reengineering the facility to withstand the shock of an earthquake

For questions 71–74, please refer to the following scenario.

Matthew and Richard are friends located in different physical locations who would like to begin communicating with each other using cryptography to protect the confidentiality of their communications. They exchange digital certificates to begin this process and plan to use an asymmetric encryption algorithm for the secure exchange of email messages.

71. When Matthew sends Richard a message, what key should he use to encrypt the message?

    A. Matthew's public key

    B. Matthew's private key

    C. Richard's public key

    D. Richard's private key

72. When Richard receives the message from Matthew, what key should he use to decrypt the message?

   A. Matthew's public key

   B. Matthew's private key

   C. Richard's public key

   D. Richard's private key

73. Matthew would like to enhance the security of his communication by adding a digital signature to the message. What goal of cryptography are digital signatures intended to enforce?

   A. Secrecy

   B. Availability

   C. Confidentiality

   D. Nonrepudiation

74. When Matthew goes to add the digital signature to the message, what encryption key does he use to create the digital signature?

   A. Matthew's public key

   B. Matthew's private key

   C. Richard's public key

   D. Richard's private key

75. What type of motion detector uses high microwave frequency signal transmissions to identify potential intruders?

   A. Infrared

   B. Heat-based

   C. Wave pattern

   D. Capacitance

76. Bert is considering the use of an infrastructure as a service cloud computing partner to provide virtual servers. Which one of the following would be a vendor responsibility in this scenario?

   A. Maintaining the hypervisor

   B. Managing operating system security settings

   C. Maintaining the host firewall

   D. Configuring server access control

77. Callback to a landline phone number is an example of what type of factor?

   A. Something you know

   B. Somewhere you are

   C. Something you have

   D. Something you are

78. Renee is using encryption to safeguard sensitive business secrets when in transit over the Internet. What risk metric is she attempting to lower?

    A. Likelihood

    B. RTO

    C. MTO

    D. Impact

79. Kim is the system administrator for a small business network that is experiencing security problems. She is in the office in the evening working on the problem, and nobody else is there. As she is watching, she can see that systems on the other side of the office that were previously behaving normally are now exhibiting signs of infection. What type of malware is Kim likely dealing with?

    A. Virus

    B. Worm

    C. Trojan horse

    D. Logic bomb

80. What two logical network topologies can be physically implemented as a star topology?

    A. A bus and a mesh

    B. A ring and a mesh

    C. A bus and a ring

    D. It is not possible to implement other topologies as a star.

81. Jim has worked in human relations, payroll, and customer service roles in his company over the past few years. What type of process should his company perform to ensure that he has appropriate rights?

    A. Re-provisioning

    B. Account review

    C. Privilege creep

    D. Account revocation

82. What type of inbound packet is characteristic of a ping flood attack?

    A. ICMP echo request

    B. ICMP echo reply

    C. ICMP destination unreachable

    D. ICMP route changed

83. What penetration testing technique can best help assess training and awareness issues?

    A. Port scanning

    B. Discovery

    C. Social engineering

    D. Vulnerability scanning

84. GAD Systems is concerned about the risk of hackers stealing sensitive information stored on a file server. They choose to pursue a risk mitigation strategy. Which one of the following actions would support that strategy?

    A. Encrypting the files

    B. Deleting the files

    C. Purchasing cyber-liability insurance

    D. Taking no action

85. Sally's organization needs to be able to prove that certain staff members sent emails, and she wants to adopt a technology that will provide that capability without changing their existing email system. What is the technical term for the capability Sally needs to implement as the owner of the email system, and what tool could she use to do it?

    A. Integrity; IMAP

    B. Repudiation; encryption

    C. Nonrepudiation; digital signatures

    D. Authentication; DKIM

86. What type of virus is characterized by the use of two or more different propagation mechanisms to improve its likelihood of spreading between systems?

    A. Stealth virus

    B. Polymorphic virus

    C. Multipartite virus

    D. Encrypted virus

87. Which one of the following provides an authentication mechanism that would be appropriate for pairing with a password to achieve multifactor authentication?

    A. Username

    B. Personal identification number (PIN)

    C. Security question

    D. Fingerprint scan

88. Colleen is conducting a business impact assessment for her organization. What metric provides important information about the amount of time that the organization may be without a service before causing irreparable harm?

    A. MTD

    B. ALE

    C. RPO

    D. RTO

89. The separation of network infrastructure from the control layer, combined with the ability to centrally program a network design in a vendor-neutral, standards-based implementation, is an example of what important concept?

    A. MPLS, a way to replace long network addresses with shorter labels and support a wide range of protocols

    B. FCoE, a converged protocol that allows common applications over Ethernet

    C. SDN, a converged protocol that allows network virtualization

    D. CDN, a converged protocol that makes common network designs accessible

90. Ben is selecting an encryption algorithm for use in an organization with 10,000 employees. He must facilitate communication between any two employees within the organization. Which one of the following algorithms would allow him to meet this goal with the least time dedicated to key management?

    A. RSA

    B. IDEA

    C. 3DES

    D. Skipjack

91. Which of the following is used only to encrypt data in transit over a network and cannot be used to encrypt data at rest?

    A. TKIP

    B. AES

    C. 3DES

    D. RSA

92. Which one of the following tools may be used to achieve the goal of nonrepudiation?

    A. Digital signature

    B. Symmetric encryption

    C. Firewall

    D. IDS

93. When should an organization conduct a review of the privileged access that a user has to sensitive systems?

    A. On a periodic basis

    B. When a user leaves the organization

    C. When a user changes roles

    D. All of the above

94. Nessus, OpenVAS, and SAINT are all examples of what type of tool?

    A. Port scanners

    B. Patch management suites

    C. Port mappers

    D. Vulnerability scanners

95. Kolin is searching for a network security solution that will allow him to help reduce zero-day attacks while using identities to enforce a security policy on systems before they connect to the network. What type of solution should Kolin implement?

    A. A firewall

    B. A NAC system

    C. An intrusion detection system

    D. Port security

96. How many possible keys exist when using a cryptographic algorithm that has an 8-bit binary encryption key?

    A. 16

    B. 128

    C. 256

    D. 512

97. In what cloud computing model does the customer build a cloud computing environment in his or her own data center or build an environment in another data center that is for the customer's exclusive use?

    A. Public cloud

    B. Private cloud

    C. Hybrid cloud

    D. Shared cloud

98. What major issue often results from decentralized access control?

    A. Access outages may occur.

    B. Control is not consistent.

    C. Control is too granular.

    D. Training costs are high.

99. In what model of cloud computing do two or more organizations collaborate to build a shared cloud computing environment that is for their own use?

    A. Public cloud

    B. Private cloud

    C. Community cloud

    D. Shared cloud

100. Susan's organization is updating its password policy and wants to use the strongest possible passwords. What password requirement will have the highest impact in preventing brute-force attacks?

    A. Change maximum age from 1 year to 180 days.

    B. Increase the minimum password length from 8 characters to 16 characters.

    C. Increase the password complexity so that at least three character classes (such as uppercase, lowercase, numbers, and symbols) are required.

    D. Retain a password history of at least four passwords to prevent reuse.

101. Which of the following statements is true about heuristic-based anti-malware software?

   A. It has a lower false positive rate than signature detection.

   B. It requires frequent definition updates to detect new malware.

   C. It has a higher likelihood of detecting zero-day exploits than signature detection.

   D. It monitors systems for files with content known to be viruses.

102. Which one of the following malware types uses built-in propagation mechanisms that exploit system vulnerabilities to spread?

   A. Trojan horse

   B. Worm

   C. Logic bomb

   D. Virus

103. When Chris verifies an individual's identity and adds a unique identifier like a user ID to an identity system, what process has occurred?

   A. Identity proofing

   B. Registration

   C. Directory management

   D. Session management

104. Fred needs to deploy a network device that can connect his network to other networks while controlling traffic on his network. What type of device is Fred's best choice?

   A. A switch

   B. A bridge

   C. A gateway

   D. A router

105. Match the following numbered types of testing methodologies with the lettered correct level of knowledge:

Testing methodologies	Level of knowledge
1. Black box	A. Full knowledge of the system
2. White box	B. Partial or incomplete knowledge
3. Gray box	C. No prior knowledge of the system

106. Cloud computing uses a shared responsibility model for security, where the vendor and customer each bears some responsibility for security. The division of responsibility depends upon the type of service used. Place the cloud service offerings listed here in order from the case where the customer bears the *least* responsibility to where the customer bears the *most* responsibility.

   A. IaaS

   B. SaaS

   C. PaaS

   D. TaaS

107. Bill implemented RAID level 5 on a server that he operates using a total of three disks. How many disks may fail without the loss of data?

    A. 0

    B. 1

    C. 2

    D. 3

108. What network topology is shown here?

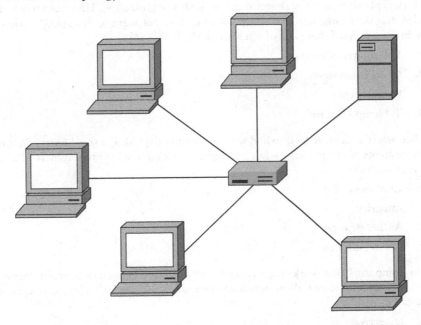

    A. A ring

    B. A bus

    C. A star

    D. A mesh

109. Which one of the following is normally used as an authorization tool?

    A. ACL

    B. Token

    C. Username

    D. Password

110. Ben is concerned about password cracking attacks against his system. He would like to implement controls that prevent an attacker who has obtained those hashes from easily cracking them. What two controls would best meet this objective?

   A. Longer passwords and salting

   B. Over-the-wire encryption and use of SHA1 instead of MD5

   C. Salting and use of MD5

   D. Using shadow passwords and salting

111. Mark is planning a disaster recovery test for his organization. He would like to perform a live test of the disaster recovery facility but does not want to disrupt operations at the primary facility. What type of test should Mark choose?

   A. Full interruption test

   B. Checklist review

   C. Parallel test

   D. Tabletop exercise

112. Alice sends a message to Bob and wants to ensure that Mal, a third party, does not read the contents of the message while in transit. What goal of cryptography is Alice attempting to achieve?

   A. Confidentiality

   B. Integrity

   C. Authentication

   D. Nonrepudiation

113. The company Chris works for has notifications posted at each door reminding employees to be careful to not allow people to enter when they do. Which type of controls best describes this?

   A. Detective

   B. Physical

   C. Preventive

   D. Directive

114. Jim is implementing an IDaaS solution for his organization. What type of technology is he putting in place?

   A. Identity as a service

   B. Employee ID as a service

   C. Intrusion detection as a service

   D. OAuth

115. How many possible keys exist in a cryptographic algorithm that uses 6-bit encryption keys?

    A. 12

    B. 16

    C. 32

    D. 64

116. When an attacker calls an organization's help desk and persuades them to reset a password for them because of the help desk employee's trust and willingness to help, what type of attack succeeded?

    A. A human Trojan

    B. Social engineering

    C. Phishing

    D. Whaling

117. Which one of the following is typically considered a business continuity task?

    A. Business impact assessment

    B. Alternate facility selection

    C. Activation of cold sites

    D. Restoration of data from backup

118. What type of log is shown here?

```
217.69.133.190 - - [11/Apr/2016:09:41:48 -0400] "GET /forum/viewtopic.php?f=4&t=25630 HTTP/1.1" 503 2009 "-
" "Mozilla/5.0 (compatible; Linux x86_64; Mail.RU_Bot/2.0; +http://go.mail.ru/help/robots)"
217.69.133.190 - - [11/Apr/2016:09:41:50 -0400] "GET /forum/viewtopic.php?f=7&t=28513 HTTP/1.1" 503 2009 "-
" "Mozilla/5.0 (compatible; Linux x86_64; Mail.RU_Bot/2.0; +http://go.mail.ru/help/robots)"
188.143.234.155 - - [11/Apr/2016:09:41:50 -0400] "GET /ask-a-pci-dss-question/ HTTP/1.1" 200 6501 "-"
"Mozilla/5.0 (Windows NT 6.1; WOW64; rv:41.0) Gecko/20100101 Firefox/41.0"
217.69.133.242 - - [11/Apr/2016:09:41:51 -0400] "GET /forum/viewtopic.php?f=5&t=27086 HTTP/1.1" 503 2009 "-
" "Mozilla/5.0 (compatible; Linux x86_64; Mail.RU_Bot/2.0; +http://go.mail.ru/help/robots)"
217.69.133.245 - - [11/Apr/2016:09:41:52 -0400] "GET /forum/viewtopic.php?f=6&t=28548 HTTP/1.1" 503 2009 "-
" "Mozilla/5.0 (compatible; Linux x86_64; Mail.RU_Bot/2.0; +http://go.mail.ru/help/robots)"
217.69.133.247 - - [11/Apr/2016:09:41:54 -0400] "GET /forum/viewtopic.php?f=3&t=26497 HTTP/1.1" 503 2009 "-
" "Mozilla/5.0 (compatible; Linux x86_64; Mail.RU_Bot/2.0; +http://go.mail.ru/help/robots)"
217.69.133.247 - - [11/Apr/2016:09:41:55 -0400] "GET /forum/viewtopic.php?f=3&t=27282 HTTP/1.1" 503 2009 "-
" "Mozilla/5.0 (compatible; Linux x86_64; Mail.RU_Bot/2.0; +http://go.mail.ru/help/robots)"
217.69.133.246 - - [11/Apr/2016:09:41:56 -0400] "GET /forum/viewtopic.php?f=6&t=33830 HTTP/1.1" 503 2009 "-
" "Mozilla/5.0 (compatible; Linux x86_64; Mail.RU_Bot/2.0; +http://go.mail.ru/help/robots)"
217.69.133.190 - - [11/Apr/2016:09:41:58 -0400] "GET /forum/viewtopic.php?f=6&t=26425 HTTP/1.1" 503 2009 "-
" "Mozilla/5.0 (compatible; Linux x86_64; Mail.RU_Bot/2.0; +http://go.mail.ru/help/robots)"
217.69.133.245 - - [11/Apr/2016:09:41:59 -0400] "GET /pci-dss/pci-dss-vulnerability-scanning-requirements/
HTTP/1.1" 301 - "-" "Mozilla/5.0 (compatible; Linux x86_64; Mail.RU_Bot/2.0;
+http://go.mail.ru/help/robots)"
217.69.133.247 - - [11/Apr/2016:09:42:01 -0400] "GET /forum/viewtopic.php?f=4&t=26035 HTTP/1.1" 503 2009 "-
" "Mozilla/5.0 (compatible; Linux x86_64; Mail.RU_Bot/2.0; +http://go.mail.ru/help/robots)"
217.69.133.190 - - [11/Apr/2016:09:42:02 -0400] "GET /vulnerability-scanning/pci-dss-vulnerability-
scanning-requirements/ HTTP/1.1" 200 11007 "http://www.pcidssguru.com/pci-dss/pci-dss-vulnerability-
scanning-requirements/" "Mozilla/5.0 (compatible; Linux x86_64; Mail.RU_Bot/2.0;
+http://go.mail.ru/help/robots)"
207.46.13.18 - - [11/Apr/2016:09:42:17 -0400] "GET /category/articles/page/3/ HTTP/1.1" 200 7583 "-"
"Mozilla/5.0 (compatible; bingbot/2.0; +http://www.bing.com/bingbot.htm)"
```

    A. Firewall log

    B. Change log

    C. Application log

    D. System log

119. Kathleen needs to set up an Active Directory trust to allow authentication with an existing Kerberos K5 domain. What type of trust does she need to create?

  A. A shortcut trust

  B. A forest trust

  C. An external trust

  D. A realm trust

For questions 120–122, please refer to the following scenario.

Ben owns a coffeehouse and wants to provide wireless Internet service for his customers. Ben's network is simple and uses a single consumer-grade wireless router and a cable modem connected via a commercial cable data contract.

120. How can Ben provide access control for his customers without having to provision user IDs before they connect while also gathering useful contact information for his business purposes?

  A. WPA3 PSK

  B. A captive portal

  C. Require customers to use a publicly posted password like "BensCoffee."

  D. Port security

121. Ben intends to run an open (unencrypted) wireless network for guests to his organization's facilities. What approach should he take to connect his business devices to a wireless network?

  A. Run WPA3 on the same SSID.

  B. Set up a separate SSID using WPA3.

  C. Run the open network in Enterprise mode.

  D. Set up a separate wireless network using WEP.

122. After implementing the solution from the first question, Ben receives a complaint about users in his cafe hijacking other customers' web traffic, including using their usernames and passwords. How is this possible?

  A. The password is shared by all users, making traffic vulnerable.

  B. A malicious user has installed a Trojan on the router.

  C. A user has ARP spoofed the router, making all traffic broadcast to all users.

  D. Open networks are unencrypted, making traffic easily sniffable.

123. Frank is the security administrator for a web server that provides news and information to people located around the world. His server received an unusually high volume of traffic that it could not handle and was forced to reject requests. Frank traced the source of the traffic back to a botnet. What type of attack took place?

  A. Denial-of-service

  B. Reconnaissance

  C. Compromise

  D. Malicious insider

124. SYN floods rely on implementations of what protocol to cause denial-of-service conditions?

    A. IGMP

    B. UDP

    C. TCP

    D. ICMP

125. What is the longest encryption key supported by the Advanced Encryption Standard (AES) algorithm?

    A. 256 bits

    B. 512 bits

    C. 1,024 bits

    D. 2,048 bits

Chapter

9

Practice Test 2

1. During a system audit, Casey notices that the private key for her organization's web server has been stored in a public Amazon S3 storage bucket for more than a year. What should she do?

    A. Remove the key from the bucket.

    B. Notify all customers that their data may have been exposed.

    C. Request a new certificate using a new key.

    D. Nothing, because the private key should be accessible for validation

2. Which of the following is not a common threat to access control mechanisms?

    A. Fake login pages

    B. Phishing

    C. Dictionary attacks

    D. Man-in-the-middle attacks

3. Which one of the following would be considered an example of infrastructure as a service cloud computing?

    A. Payroll system managed by a vendor and delivered over the web

    B. Application platform managed by a vendor that runs customer code

    C. Servers provisioned by customers on a vendor-managed virtualization platform

    D. Web-based email service provided by a vendor

4. Referring to the fire triangle shown here, which one of the following suppression materials attacks a fire by removing the fuel source?

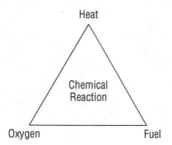

Image reprinted from CISSP (ISC)² Certified Information Systems Security Professional Official Study Guide, 7th Edition © John Wiley & Sons 2015. Reprinted with permission.

    A. Water

    B. Soda acid

    C. Carbon dioxide

    D. Halon

5. What type of alternate processing facility contains the hardware necessary to restore operations but does not have a current copy of data?

    A. Hot site

    B. Warm site

    C. Cold site

    D. Mobile site

6. The IP address 201.19.7.45 is what type of address?

    A. A public IP address

    B. An RFC 1918 address

    C. An APIPA address

    D. A loopback address

7. James has opted to implement a NAC solution that uses a post-admission philosophy for its control of network connectivity. What type of issues can't a strictly post-admission policy handle?

    A. Out-of-band monitoring

    B. Preventing an unpatched laptop from being exploited immediately after connecting to the network

    C. Denying access when user behavior doesn't match an authorization matrix

    D. Allowing user access when user behavior is allowed based on an authorization matrix

8. What process adds a header and a footer to data received at each layer of the OSI model?

    A. Attribution

    B. Encapsulation

    C. TCP wrapping

    D. Data hiding

9. Which of the following is not one of the four canons of the (ISC)² code of ethics?

    A. Avoid conflicts of interest that may jeopardize impartiality.

    B. Protect society, the common good, necessary public trust and confidence, and the infrastructure.

    C. Act honorably, honestly, justly, responsibly, and legally.

    D. Provide diligent and competent service to principals.

For questions 10–13, please refer to the following scenario.

Mike and Renee would like to use an asymmetric cryptosystem to communicate with each other. They are located in different parts of the country but have exchanged encryption keys by using digital certificates signed by a mutually trusted certificate authority.

10. When the certificate authority (CA) created Renee's digital certificate, what key was contained within the body of the certificate?

    A. Renee's public key

    B. Renee's private key

    C. CA's public key

    D. CA's private key

11. When the certificate authority created Renee's digital certificate, what key did it use to digitally sign the completed certificate?

    A. Renee's public key

    B. Renee's private key

    C. CA's public key

    D. CA's private key

12. When Mike receives Renee's digital certificate, what key does he use to verify the authenticity of the certificate?

    A. Renee's public key

    B. Renee's private key

    C. CA's public key

    D. CA's private key

13. Mike would like to send Renee a private message using the information gained during this exchange. What key should he use to encrypt the message?

    A. Renee's public key

    B. Renee's private key

    C. CA's public key

    D. CA's private key

14. Jim starts a new job as a system engineer, and his boss provides him with a document entitled "Forensic Response Guidelines." Which one of the following statements is not true?

    A. Jim must comply with the information in this document.

    B. The document contains information about forensic examinations.

    C. Jim should read the document thoroughly.

    D. The document is likely based on industry best practices.

15. Alex has been employed by his company for more than a decade and has held a number of positions in the company. During an audit, it is discovered that he has access to shared folders and applications because of his former roles. What issue has Alex's company encountered?

    A. Excessive provisioning

    B. Unauthorized access

    C. Privilege creep

    D. Account review

16. RIP, OSPF, and BGP are all examples of protocols associated with what type of network device?

    A. Switches

    B. Bridges

    C. Routers

    D. Gateways

17. If Susan's organization requires her to log in with her username, a PIN, a password, and a retina scan, how many distinct authentication factor types has she used?

    A. One

    B. Two

    C. Three

    D. Four

18. What process makes TCP a connection-oriented protocol?

    A. It works via network connections.

    B. It uses a handshake.

    C. It monitors for dropped connections.

    D. It uses a complex header.

19. What is the goal of the BCP process?

    A. RTO < MTD

    B. MTD < RTO

    C. RPO < MTD

    D. MTD < RPO

20. Which one of the following is an example of an administrative control?

    A. Intrusion detection system

    B. Security awareness training

    C. Firewalls

    D. Security guards

21. What level of RAID is also known as disk mirroring?
    A. RAID 0
    B. RAID 1
    C. RAID 5
    D. RAID 10

22. Lauren needs to send information about services she is provisioning to a third-party organization. What standards-based markup language should she choose to build the interface?
    A. SAML
    B. SOAP
    C. SPML
    D. XACML

23. TCP and UDP both operate at what layer of the OSI model?
    A. Layer 2
    B. Layer 3
    C. Layer 4
    D. Layer 5

24. Linda is selecting a disaster recovery facility for her organization, and she wants to retain independence from other organizations as much as possible. She would like to choose a facility that balances cost and recovery time, allowing activation in about one week after a disaster is declared. What type of facility should she choose?
    A. Cold site
    B. Warm site
    C. Mutual assistance agreement
    D. Hot site

25. Which one of the following backup types does not alter the status of the archive bit on a file?
    A. Full backup
    B. Incremental backup
    C. Partial backup
    D. Differential backup

26. During which phase of the incident response process would administrators design new security controls intended to prevent a recurrence of the incident?
    A. Reporting
    B. Recovery
    C. Remediation
    D. Lessons Learned

27. Match each of the numbered services with the lettered network port commonly used by that service. Each item should be used exactly once.

Service

1. DNS
2. HTTPS
3. SSH
4. RDP
5. MSSQL

Network port

A. TCP port 443
B. TCP port 3389
C. TCP port 1433
D. UDP port 53
E. TCP port 22

28. What type of Windows audit record describes events like an OS shutdown or a service being stopped?

A. An application log

B. A security log

C. A system log

D. A setup log

29. During a log review, Karen discovers that the system she needs to gather logs from has the log setting shown here. What problem is Karen likely to encounter?

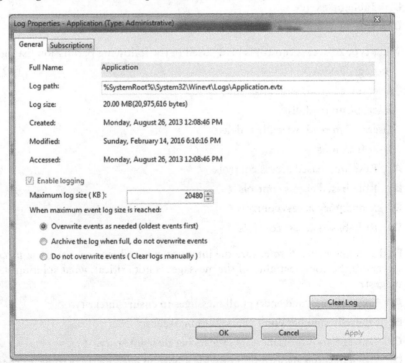

A. Too much log data will be stored on the system.

B. The system is automatically purging archived logs.

C. The logs will not contain the information needed.

D. The logs will contain only the most recent 20 MB of log data.

30. Microsoft's STRIDE threat assessment framework uses six categories for threats: Spoofing, Tampering, Repudiation, Information Disclosure, Denial of Service, and Elevation of Privilege. If a penetration tester is able to modify audit logs, what STRIDE categories best describe this issue?

A. Tampering and information disclosure

B. Elevation of privilege and tampering

C. Repudiation and denial of service

D. Repudiation and tampering

31. Place the list of disaster recovery test types in order of their potential impact on the business, starting with the least impactful and progressing through the most impactful.

A. Checklist review

B. Parallel test

C. Tabletop exercise

D. Full interruption test

32. What type of access control is being used in the following permission listing?

Storage Device X

User1: Can read, write, list

User2: Can read, list

User3: Can read, write, list, delete

User4: Can list

A. Resource-based access controls

B. Role-based access controls

C. Mandatory access controls

D. Rule-based access controls

33. Fred's company wants to ensure the integrity of email messages sent via its central email servers. If the confidentiality of the messages is not critical, what solution should Fred suggest?

A. Digitally sign and encrypt all messages to ensure integrity.

B. Digitally sign but don't encrypt all messages.

C. Use TLS to protect messages, ensuring their integrity.

D. Use a hashing algorithm to provide a hash in each message to prove that it hasn't changed.

34. Which one of the following goals of physical security environments occurs first in the functional order of controls?

A. Delay

B. Detection

C. Deterrence

D. Denial

35. Cameron is responsible for backing up his company's primary file server. He configured a backup schedule that performs full backups every Monday evening at 9 p.m. and incremental backups on other days of the week at that same time. How many files will be copied in Wednesday's backup?

```
File Modifications
Monday 8AM - File 1 created
Monday 10AM - File 2 created
Monday 11AM - File 3 created
Monday 4PM - File 1 modified
Monday 5PM - File 4 created
Tuesday 8AM - File 1 modified
Tuesday 9AM - File 2 modified
Tuesday 10AM - File 5 created
Wednesday 8AM - File 3 modified
Wednesday 9AM - File 6 created
```

A. 1

B. 2

C. 5

D. 6

36. Lauren is responsible for building a banking website. She needs proof of the identity of the users who register for the site. How should she validate user identities?

A. Require users to create unique questions that only they will know.

B. Require new users to bring their driver's license or passport in person to the bank.

C. Use information that both the bank and the user have such as questions pulled from their credit report.

D. Call the user on their registered phone number to verify that they are who they claim to be.

37. Surveys, interviews, and audits are all examples of ways to measure what important part of an organization's security posture?

A. Code quality

B. Service vulnerabilities

C. Awareness

D. Attack surface

38. In the image shown here, what does system B send to system A at `step` 2 of the three-way TCP handshake?

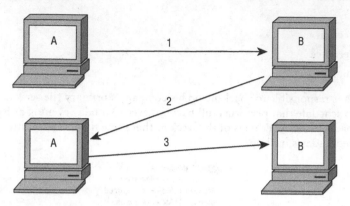

   A. SYN

   B. ACK

   C. FIN/ACK

   D. SYN/ACK

39. Which one of the following is not a valid key length for the Advanced Encryption Standard?

   A. 128 bits

   B. 192 bits

   C. 256 bits

   D. 384 bits

40. Which one of the following is not a technique used by virus authors to hide the existence of their virus from anti-malware software?

   A. Stealth

   B. Multipartitism

   C. Polymorphism

   D. Encryption

For questions 41–43, please refer to the following scenario.

The company that Fred works for is reviewing the security of its company-issued cell phones. They issue 4G-capable smartphones running Android and iOS and use a mobile device management solution to deploy company software to the phones. The mobile device management software also allows the company to remotely wipe the phones if they are lost.

41. What security considerations should Fred's company require for sending sensitive data over the cellular network?

    A. They should use the same requirements as data over any public network.

    B. Cellular provider networks are private networks and should not require special consideration.

    C. Encrypt all traffic to ensure confidentiality.

    D. Require the use of WAP for all data sent from the phone.

42. Fred intends to attend a major hacker conference this year. What should he do if he needs to conduct business activities when connecting to his cellular provider's 5G network while at the conference?

    A. Continue normal usage.

    B. Discontinue all usage; towers can be spoofed.

    C. Only use trusted Wi-Fi networks.

    D. Connect to his company's encrypted VPN service.

43. What are the most likely circumstances that would cause a remote wipe of a mobile phone to fail?

    A. The phone has a passcode on it.

    B. The phone cannot contact a network.

    C. The provider has not unlocked the phone.

    D. The phone is in use.

44. Which one of the following is an example of risk transference?

    A. Building a guard shack

    B. Purchasing insurance

    C. Erecting fences

    D. Relocating facilities

45. Kyle is being granted access to a military computer system that uses System High mode. What is not true about Kyle's security clearance requirements?

    A. Kyle must have a clearance for the highest level of classification processed by the system, regardless of his access.

    B. Kyle must have access approval for all information processed by the system.

    C. Kyle must have a valid need to know for all information processed by the system.

    D. Kyle must have a valid security clearance.

46. Tom is conducting a business continuity planning effort for Orange Blossoms, a fruit orchard located in Central Florida. During the assessment process, the committee determined that there is a small risk of snow in the region but that the cost of implementing controls to reduce the impact of that risk is not warranted. They elect to not take any specific action in response to the risk. What risk management strategy is Orange Blossoms pursuing?

     A. Risk mitigation

     B. Risk transference

     C. Risk avoidance

     D. Risk acceptance

47. Carla has worked for her company for 15 years and has held a variety of different positions. Each time she changed positions, she gained new privileges associated with that position, but no privileges were ever taken away. What concept describes the sets of privileges she has accumulated?

     A. Entitlement

     B. Aggregation

     C. Transitivity

     D. Isolation

48. Which one of the following types of agreements is the most formal document that contains expectations about availability and other performance parameters between a service provider and a customer?

     A. Service-level agreement (SLA)

     B. Operational-level agreement (OLA)

     C. Memorandum of understanding (MOU)

     D. Statement of work (SOW)

49. Chris has been assigned to scan a system on all of its possible TCP and UDP ports. How many ports of each type must he scan to complete his assignment?

     A. 65,536 TCP ports and 32,768 UDP ports

     B. 1,024 common TCP ports and 32,768 ephemeral UDP ports

     C. 65,536 TCP and 65,536 UDP ports

     D. 16,384 TCP ports and 16,384 UDP ports

50. Lauren starts at her new job and finds that she has access to a variety of systems that she does not need to accomplish her job. What problem has she encountered?

     A. Privilege creep

     B. Rights collision

     C. Least privilege

     D. Excessive privileges

51. Jim has been contracted to perform a penetration test of a bank's primary branch. To make the test as real as possible, he has not been given any information about the bank other than its name and address. What type of penetration test has Jim agreed to perform?

    A. A crystal-box penetration test

    B. A gray-box penetration test

    C. A black-box penetration test

    D. A white-box penetration test

52. Lauren builds a table that includes assigned privileges, objects, and subjects to manage access control for the systems she is responsible for. Each time a subject attempts to access an object, the systems check the table to ensure that the subject has the appropriate rights to the objects. What type of access control system is Lauren using?

    A. A capability table

    B. An access control list

    C. An access control matrix

    D. A subject/object rights management system

53. A cloud-based service that provides account provisioning, management, authentication, authorization, reporting, and monitoring capabilities is known as what type of service?

    A. PaaS

    B. IDaaS

    C. IaaS

    D. SaaS

54. What is the maximum penalty that may be imposed by an (ISC)² peer review board when considering a potential ethics violation?

    A. Revocation of certification

    B. Termination of employment

    C. Financial penalty

    D. Suspension of certification

55. Matthew, Richard, and Christopher would like to exchange messages with each other using symmetric cryptography. They want to ensure that each individual can privately send a message to another individual without the third person being able to read the message. How many keys do they need?

    A. 1

    B. 2

    C. 3

    D. 6

56. What UDP port is typically used by the syslog service?
    A. 443
    B. 514
    C. 515
    D. 445

57. During which of the following disaster recovery tests does the team sit together and discuss the response to a scenario but not actually activate any disaster recovery controls?
    A. Checklist review
    B. Full interruption test
    C. Parallel test
    D. Tabletop exercise

58. Which one of the following is a detailed, step-by-step document that describes the exact actions that individuals must complete?
    A. Policy
    B. Standard
    C. Guideline
    D. Procedure

59. Tammy is selecting a disaster recovery facility for her organization. She would like to choose a facility that balances the time required to recover operations with the cost involved. What type of facility should she choose?
    A. Hot site
    B. Warm site
    C. Cold site
    D. Red site

60. Which one of the following statements about malware is correct?
    A. Malware authors do not target Macintosh or Linux systems.
    B. The most reliable way to detect known malware is watching for unusual system activity.
    C. Signature detection is the most effective technique to combat known malware.
    D. APT attackers typically use malware designed to exploit vulnerabilities identified in security bulletins.

61. Ben needs to verify that the most recent patch for his organization's critical application did not introduce issues elsewhere. What type of testing does Ben need to conduct to ensure this?
    A. Unit testing
    B. White box
    C. Regression testing
    D. Black box

62. Warren is designing a physical intrusion detection system for his data center and wants to include technology that issues an alert if the communications lines for the alarm system are unexpectedly cut. What technology would meet this requirement?

    A. Heartbeat sensor

    B. Emanation security

    C. Motion detector

    D. Faraday cage

63. Greg is battling a malware outbreak in his organization. He used specialized malware analysis tools to capture samples of the malware from three different systems and noticed that the code is changing slightly from infection to infection. Greg believes that this is the reason that antivirus software is having a tough time defeating the outbreak. What type of malware should Greg suspect is responsible for this security incident?

    A. Stealth virus

    B. Polymorphic virus

    C. Multipartite virus

    D. Encrypted virus

64. Which group is best suited to evaluate and report on the effectiveness of administrative controls an organization has put in place to a third party?

    A. Internal auditors

    B. Penetration testers

    C. External auditors

    D. Employees who design, implement, and monitor the controls

65. In virtualization platforms, what name is given to the module that is responsible for controlling access to physical resources by virtual resources?

    A. Guest machine

    B. SDN

    C. Kernel

    D. Hypervisor

66. Google's identity integration with a variety of organizations and applications across domains is an example of which of the following?

    A. PKI

    B. Federation

    C. Single sign-on

    D. Provisioning

67. Joe wants to test a program he suspects may contain malware. What technology can he use to isolate the program while it runs?

  A. ASLR

  B. Sandboxing

  C. Clipping

  D. Process isolation

68. What type of attack would the following precautions help prevent?

  ▪ Requesting proof of identity

  ▪ Requiring callback authorizations on voice-only requests

  ▪ Not changing passwords via voice communications

  A. DoS attacks

  B. Worms

  C. Social engineering

  D. Shoulder surfing

69. Mike has been tasked with preventing an outbreak of malware like Mirai. What type of systems should be protected in his organization?

  A. Servers

  B. SCADA

  C. Mobile devices

  D. Internet of Things (IoT) devices

70. What type of risk assessment uses tools such as the one shown here?

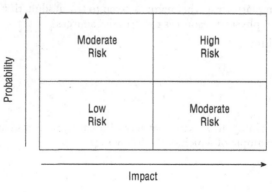

  A. Quantitative

  B. Loss expectancy

  C. Financial

  D. Qualitative

71. Ben has written the password hashing system for the web application he is building. His hashing code function for passwords results in the following process for a series of passwords:

```
hash (password1 + 07C98BFE4CF67B0BFE2643B5B22E2D7D) =
10B222970537B97919DB36EC757370D2
hash (password2 + 07C98BFE4CF67B0BFE2643B5B22E2D7D) =
F1F16683F3E0208131B46D37A79C8921
```

What flaw has Ben introduced with his hashing implementation?

   A. Plaintext salting

   B. Salt reuse

   C. Use of a short salt

   D. Poor salt algorithm selection

72. Which one of the following tools is most often used for identification purposes and is not suitable for use as an authenticator?

   A. Password

   B. Retinal scan

   C. Username

   D. Token

73. Theresa is implementing a new access control system and wants to ensure that developers do not have the ability to move code from development systems into the production environment. What information security principle is she most directly enforcing?

   A. Separation of duties

   B. Two-person control

   C. Least privilege

   D. Job rotation

74. NIST Special Publication 800-92, the Guide to Computer Security Log Management, describes four types of common challenges to log management:

   ▪ Many log sources

   ▪ Inconsistent log content

   ▪ Inconsistent timestamps

   ▪ Inconsistent log formats

Which of the following solutions is best suited to solving these issues?

   A. Implement SNMP for all logging devices.

   B. Implement a SIEM.

   C. Standardize on the Windows event log format for all devices and use NTP.

   D. Ensure that logging is enabled on all endpoints using their native logging formats and set their local time correctly.

75. Which one of the following components should be included in an organization's emergency response guidelines?

   A. Secondary response procedures for first responders

   B. Long-term business continuity protocols

   C. Activation procedures for the organization's cold sites

   D. Contact information for ordering equipment

76. Grace is considering the use of new identification cards in her organization that will be used for physical access control. She comes across the sample card shown here and is unsure of the technology it uses. What type of card is this?

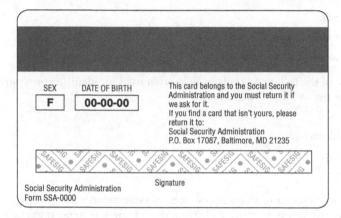

   A. Smart card

   B. Phase-two card

   C. Proximity card

   D. Magnetic stripe card

77. Gary is analyzing a security incident and, during his investigation, encounters a user who denies having performed an action that Gary believes he did perform. What type of threat has taken place under the STRIDE model?

   A. Repudiation

   B. Information disclosure

   C. Tampering

   D. Elevation of privilege

78. After scanning all the systems on his wireless network, Mike notices that one system is identified as an iOS device running a massively out-of-date version of Apple's mobile operating system. When he investigates further, he discovers that the device is an original iPad and that it cannot be updated to a current secure version of the operating system. What should Mike recommend?

   A. Retire or replace the device.

   B. Isolate the device on a dedicated wireless network.

   C. Install a firewall on the tablet.

   D. Reinstall the OS.

79. What type of access control scheme is shown in the following table?

Highly Sensitive	Red	Blue	Green
Confidential	Purple	Orange	Yellow
Internal Use	Black	Gray	White
Public	Clear	Clear	Clear

   A. RBAC

   B. DAC

   C. MAC

   D. TBAC

80. Rick is an application developer who works primarily in Python. He recently decided to evaluate a new service where he provides his Python code to a vendor who then executes it on their server environment. What type of cloud computing environment is this service?

   A. SaaS

   B. PaaS

   C. IaaS

   D. CaaS

81. During a penetration test, Chris recovers a file containing hashed passwords for the system he is attempting to access. What type of attack is most likely to succeed against the hashed passwords?

   A. A brute-force attack

   B. A pass-the-hash attack

   C. A rainbow table attack

   D. A salt recovery attack

82. Kay is selecting an application management approach for her organization. Employees need the flexibility to install software on their systems, but Kay wants to prevent them from installing certain prohibited packages. What type of approach should she use?

   A. Antivirus

   B. Whitelist

   C. Blacklist

   D. Heuristic

83. Owen recently designed a security access control structure that prevents a single user from simultaneously holding the role required to create a new vendor and the role required to issue a check. What principle is Owen enforcing?

   A. Two-person control

   B. Least privilege

   C. Separation of duties

   D. Job rotation

84. IP addresses like 10.10.10.10 and 172.19.24.21 are both examples of what type of IP address?

   A. Public IP addresses

   B. Prohibited IP addresses

   C. Private IP addresses

   D. Class B IP ranges

85. Fran's company is considering purchasing a web-based email service from a vendor and eliminating its own email server environment as a cost-saving measure. What type of cloud computing environment is Fran's company considering?

   A. SaaS

   B. IaaS

   C. CaaS

   D. PaaS

86. Match each of the numbered cable types with exactly one of the lettered maximum cable lengths.

Cable type	**Maximum length**
1. Category 5e	**A.** 500 feet
2. Coaxial (RG-58)	**B.** 300 feet
3. Fiber optic	**C.** 1+ kilometers

87. Which component of IPsec provides authentication, integrity, and nonrepudiation?

   A. L2TP

   B. Encapsulating Security Payload

   C. Encryption Security Header

   D. Authentication Header

88. Alex's job requires him to see protected health information (PHI) to ensure proper treatment of patients. His access to their medical records does not provide access to patient addresses or billing information. What access control concept best describes this control?

   A. Separation of duties

   B. Constrained interfaces

   C. Context-dependent control

   D. Need to know

89. Which one of the following investigation types has the loosest standards for collecting and preserving information?

   A. Civil investigation

   B. Operational investigation

   C. Criminal investigation

   D. Regulatory investigation

90. Susan is working to improve the strength of her organization's passwords by changing the password policy. The password system that she is using allows uppercase and low-ercase letters as well as numbers but no other characters. It has a minimum password length of eight characters and does not have password expiration dates. What would be the best change she could make to improve the password policy?

   A. Set a 90-day password expiration policy.

   B. Allow the use of symbols.

   C. Change the minimum password length to nine characters.

   D. No changes are necessary.

91. Purchasing insurance is a form of what type of risk response?

   A. Transfer

   B. Avoid

   C. Mitigate

   D. Accept

92. Which one of the following metrics specifies the amount of time that business continuity planners find acceptable for the restoration of service after a disaster?

   A. MTD

   B. RTO

   C. RPO

   D. MTO

93. Jacob is planning his organization's biometric authentication system and is considering retina scans. What concern may be raised about retina scans by others in his organization?

   A. Retina scans can reveal information about medical conditions.

   B. Retina scans are painful because they require a puff of air in the user's eye.

   C. Retina scanners are the most expensive type of biometric device.

   D. Retina scanners have a high false positive rate and will cause support issues.

94. What is the best way to ensure email confidentiality in motion?

   A. Use TLS between the client and server.

   B. Use SSL between the client and server.

   C. Encrypt the email content.

   D. Use a digital signature.

95. What layer of the OSI model is associated with datagrams?

    A. Session

    B. Transport

    C. Network

    D. Data Link

96. What type of vulnerability scan accesses configuration information from the systems it is run against as well as information that can be accessed via services available via the network?

    A. Authenticated scans

    B. Web application scans

    C. Unauthenticated scans

    D. Port scans

97. What term is used to describe a starting point for a minimum security standard?

    A. Outline

    B. Baseline

    C. Policy

    D. Configuration guide

98. Full disk encryption like Microsoft's BitLocker is used to protect data in what state?

    A. Data in transit

    B. Data at rest

    C. Unlabeled data

    D. Labeled data

99. Gwen comes across an application that is running under a service account on a web server. The service account has full administrative rights to the server. What principle of information security does this violate?

    A. Need to know

    B. Separation of duties

    C. Least privilege

    D. Job rotation

100. Using the OSI model, what format does the Data Link layer use to format messages received from higher up the stack?

    A. A data stream

    B. A frame

    C. A segment

    D. A datagram

101. What type of forensic investigation typically has the highest evidentiary standards?

    A. Administrative

    B. Criminal

    C. Civil

    D. Industry

102. Lauren's healthcare provider maintains such data as details about her health, treatments, and medical billing. What type of data is this?

    A. Protected health information

    B. Personally identifiable information

    C. Protected health insurance

    D. Individual protected data

103. In Jen's job as the network administrator for an industrial production facility, she is tasked with ensuring that the network is not susceptible to electromagnetic interference due to the large motors and other devices running on the production floor. What type of network cabling should she choose if this concern is more important than cost and difficulty of installation?

    A. 10Base2

    B. 100BaseT

    C. 1000BaseT

    D. Fiber-optic

104. What type of penetration testing provides detail on the scope of a penetration test—including items like what systems would be targeted—but does not provide full visibility into the configuration or other details of the systems or networks the penetration tester must test?

    A. Crystal box

    B. White box

    C. Black box

    D. Gray box

105. You are the CISO for a major hospital system and are preparing to sign a contract with a software as a service (SaaS) email vendor and want to ensure that its business continuity planning measures are reasonable. What type of audit might you request to meet this goal?

    A. SOC 1

    B. FISMA

    C. PCI DSS

    D. SOC 2

106. Which of the following types of controls does not describe a mantrap?

    A. Deterrent

    B. Preventive

    C. Compensating

    D. Physical

107. Match each one of the numbered protocols with the most accurate lettered description. Use each answer exactly once.

Protocol	Description
1. TCP	**A.** Performs translations between MAC addresses and IP addresses
2. UDP	**B.** Performs translations between FQDNs and IP addresses
3. DNS	**C.** Transports data over a network in a connection-oriented fashion
4. ARP	**D.** Transports data over a network in a connectionless fashion

108. What should be true for salts used in password hashes?

    A. A single salt should be set so passwords can be de-hashed as needed.

    B. A single salt should be used so the original salt can be used to check passwords against their hash.

    C. Unique salts should be stored for each user.

    D. Unique salts should be created every time a user logs in.

109. STRIDE, which stands for Spoofing, Tampering, Repudiation, Information Disclosure, Denial of Service, Elevation of Privilege, is useful in what part of application threat modeling?

    A. Vulnerability assessment

    B. Misuse case testing

    C. Threat categorization

    D. Penetration test planning

110. Which one of the following is not a basic preventative measure that you can take to protect your systems and applications against attack?

    A. Implement intrusion detection and prevention systems.

    B. Maintain current patch levels on all operating systems and applications.

    C. Remove unnecessary accounts and services.

    D. Conduct forensic imaging of all systems.

111. You are conducting a qualitative risk assessment for your organization. The two important risk elements that should weigh most heavily in your analysis of risk are probability and _____ .

    A. Likelihood

    B. History

    C. Impact

    D. Cost

112. Fred needs to transfer files between two servers on an untrusted network. Since he knows the network isn't trusted, he needs to select an encrypted protocol that can ensure that his data remains secure. What protocol should he choose?

    A. SSH

    B. TCP

    C. SFTP

    D. IPsec

113. Which one of the following investigation types always uses the beyond-a-reasonable-doubt standard of proof?

    A. Civil investigation

    B. Criminal investigation

    C. Operational investigation

    D. Regulatory investigation

114. Norm would like to conduct a disaster recovery test for his organization and wants to choose the most thorough type of test, recognizing that it may be quite disruptive. What type of test should Norm choose?

    A. Full interruption test

    B. Parallel test

    C. Tabletop exercise

    D. Checklist review

115. Ed is tasked with protecting information about his organization's customers, including their name, Social Security number, birthdate, and place of birth, as well as a variety of other information. What is this information known as?

    A. PHI

    B. PII

    C. Personal protected data

    D. PID

116. Susan is conducting a STRIDE threat assessment by placing threats into one or more of the following categories: Spoofing, Tampering, Repudiation, Information Disclosure, Denial of Service, and Elevation of Privilege. As part of her assessment, she has discovered an issue that allows transactions to be modified between a web browser and the application server that it accesses. What STRIDE categorization(s) best fit this issue?

    A. Tampering and Information Disclosure

    B. Spoofing and Tampering

    C. Tampering and Repudiation

    D. Information Disclosure and Elevation of Privilege

117. Tamara recently decided to purchase cyber-liability insurance to cover her company's costs in the event of a data breach. What risk management strategy is she pursuing?

    A. Risk acceptance

    B. Risk mitigation

    C. Risk transference

    D. Risk avoidance

118. Referring to the figure shown here, what is the name of the security control indicated by the arrow?

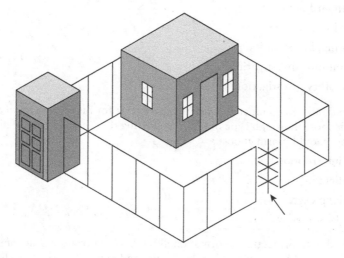

    A. Mantrap

    B. Intrusion prevention system

    C. Turnstile

    D. Portal

119. Elaine is developing a business continuity plan for her organization. What value should she seek to minimize?

    A. AV

    B. SSL

    C. RTO

    D. MTO

120. Chris is deploying a gigabit Ethernet network using Category 6 cable between two buildings. What is the maximum distance he can run the cable according to the Category 6 standard?

    A. 50 meters

    B. 100 meters

    C. 200 meters

    D. 300 meters

121. What type of alternate processing facility includes all of the hardware and data necessary to restore operations in a matter of minutes or seconds?

 A. Hot site

 B. Warm site

 C. Cold site

 D. Mobile site

For questions 122–124, please refer to the following scenario.

The organization that Ben works for has a traditional on-site Active Directory environment that uses a manual provisioning process for each addition to their 350-employee company. As the company adopts new technologies, they are increasingly using software as a service applications to replace their internally developed software stack.

Ben has been tasked with designing an identity management implementation that will allow his company to use cloud services while supporting their existing systems. Using the logical diagram shown here, answer the following questions about the identity recommendations Ben should make.

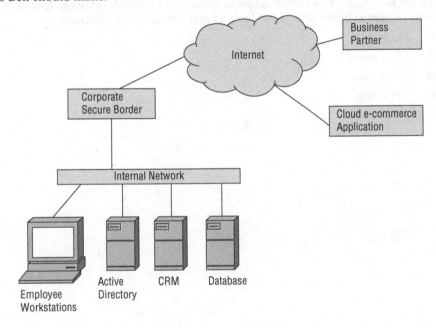

122. If availability of authentication services is the organization's biggest priority, what type of identity platform should Ben recommend?

 A. On-site

 B. Cloud-based

 C. Hybrid

 D. Outsourced

123. If Ben needs to share identity information with the business partner shown, what should he investigate?

    A. Single sign-on

    B. Multifactor authentication

    C. Federation

    D. IDaaS

124. What technology is likely to be involved when Ben's organization needs to provide authentication and authorization assertions to their cloud e-commerce application?

    A. Active Directory

    B. SAML

    C. RADIUS

    D. SPML

125. Norm is configuring an RSA cryptosystem for use within his organization and is selecting the key lengths that he will support. Which one of the following key lengths is not both supported by the RSA algorithm and generally considered secure?

    A. 512 bits

    B. 1,024 bits

    C. 2,048 bits

    D. 4,096 bits

Appendix

Answers to Review Questions

Chapter 1: Security Operations and Administration (Domain 1)

1. B. Privacy is of the utmost concern when handling personally identifiable information (PII). PII includes any information that may be reasonably tied to a specific person. This would include street addresses, telephone numbers, and national ID numbers (such as Social Security numbers). Item codes, when not tied to a name or other identifier, would not constitute PII.

2. D. While all of the items listed are components of a strong security program, periodic audits would provide Carl with the assurance that controls continue to operate effectively over the long term.

3. A. The situation Darlene finds herself in is an ethical dilemma, and a code of ethics would be the best place to look for guidance. This situation is specific to her employer, so she should turn to her organization's code of ethics, rather than the more general (ISC)² Code of Ethics.

4. B. Nondisclosure agreements (NDAs) protect the confidentiality of sensitive information by requiring that employees and affiliates not share confidential information with third parties. NDAs normally remain in force after an employee leaves the company.

5. A. Supply chain management can help ensure the security of hardware, software, and services that an organization acquires. Chris should focus on each step that his laptops take from the original equipment manufacturer to delivery.

6. B. The (ISC)² code of ethics also includes "Act honorably, honestly, justly, responsibly, and legally" but does not specifically require credential holders to disclose all breaches of privacy, trust, or ethics.

7. B. A fence does not have the ability to detect intrusions. It does, however, have the ability to prevent and deter an intrusion. Fences are an example of a physical control.

8. B. RAID technology provides fault tolerance for hard drive failures and is an example of a business continuity action. Restoring from backup tapes, relocating to a cold site, and restarting business operations are all disaster recovery actions.

9. D. Fire suppression systems protect infrastructure from physical damage. Along with uninterruptible power supplies, fire suppression systems are good examples of technology used to harden physical infrastructure. Antivirus software, hardware firewalls, and two-factor authentication are all examples of logical controls.

10. A. The message displayed is an example of ransomware, which encrypts the contents of a user's computer to prevent legitimate use. This is an example of an availability attack.

11. B. When following the separation of duties principle, organizations divide critical tasks into discrete components and ensure that no one individual has the ability to perform both actions. This prevents a single rogue individual from performing that task in an unauthorized manner.

12. **A.** Integrity controls, such as the one Beth is implementing in this example, are designed to prevent the unauthorized modification of information.

13. **B.** Virtual private networks (VPNs) provide secure communications channels over otherwise insecure networks (such as the Internet) using encryption. If you establish a VPN connection between the two offices, users in one office could securely access content located on the other office's server over the Internet. Digital signatures are used to provide nonrepudiation, not confidentiality. Virtual LANs (VLANs) provide network segmentation on local networks but do not cross the Internet. Digital content management solutions are designed to manage web content, not access shared files located on a file server.

14. **C.** RAID uses additional hard drives to protect the server against the failure of a single device. Load balancing and server clustering do add robustness but require the addition of a server. Scheduled backups protect against data loss but do not provide immediate access to data in the event of a hard drive failure.

15. **A.** Hashing allows you to computationally verify that a file has not been modified between hash evaluations. ACLs and read-only attributes are useful controls that may help you prevent unauthorized modification, but they cannot verify that files were not modified. Firewalls are network security controls and do not verify file integrity.

16. **D.** Mandatory vacation programs require that employees take continuous periods of time off each year and revoke their system privileges during that time. This will ideally disrupt any attempt to engage in the cover-up actions necessary to hide fraud and result in exposing the threat. Separation of duties, least privilege, and defense in depth controls all may help prevent the fraud in the first place but are unlikely to speed the detection of fraud that has already occurred.

17. **B.** Baselines provide the minimum level of security that every system throughout the organization must meet.

18. **A.** Keyloggers monitor the keystrokes of an individual and report them back to an attacker. They are designed to steal sensitive information, a disruption of the goal of confidentiality.

19. **C.** Confidentiality controls prevent the disclosure of sensitive information to unauthorized individuals. Limiting the likelihood of a data breach is an attempt to prevent unauthorized disclosure.

20. **D.** Keeping a server up and running is an example of an availability control because it increases the likelihood that a server will remain available to answer user requests.

21. **D.** Session timeouts, password aging, and encryption are all examples of technical controls. Data classification is an administrative control.

22. **C.** The change control board (CCB) has primary responsibility for reviewing the impact of a proposed change and coordinating the review and approval processes.

23. **B.** During the Analysis/Impact Assessment phase, the organization subjects the change to peer review. In the peer review, technologists verify the accuracy and completeness of the change request and attempt to uncover any impact on other systems that might occur as a result of the change.

24. B. Organizations adopting change management practices should appoint a change manager who will be responsible for managing policies and procedures. The change manager is also responsible for developing and maintaining the processes for requesting, approving, testing, and controlling changes.

25. D. An organization's incident response plan may be invoked as a result of a change gone awry, but the incident response plan itself is a stand-alone process and does not need to be included in a change request. The change request should definitely include a description of the change, an implementation plan, and a backout plan, among other components.

26. D. Nonrepudiation allows a recipient to prove to a third party that a message came from a purported source. Authentication would provide proof to Ben that the sender was authentic, but Ben would not be able to prove this to a third party.

27. C. Defense in depth states that organizations should have overlapping security controls designed to meet the same security objectives whenever possible. This approach provides security in the event of a single control failure.

28. D. Stakeholders should be informed of changes before, not after, they occur. The other items listed are goals of change management programs.

29. B. Ben should encrypt the data to provide an additional layer of protection as a compensating control. The organization has already made a policy exception, so he should not react by objecting to the exception or removing the data without authorization. Purchasing insurance may transfer some of the risk but is not a mitigating control.

30. D. Wireshark is a protocol analyzer and may be used to eavesdrop on network connections. Eavesdropping is an attack against confidentiality.

31. A. An organization pursuing a vital records management program should begin by identifying all of the documentation that qualifies as a vital business record. This should include all of the records necessary to restart the business in a new location should the organization invoke its business continuity plan.

32. B. Security training is designed to provide employees with the specific knowledge they need to fulfill their job functions. It is usually designed for individuals with similar job functions.

33. D. Awareness establishes a minimum standard of information security understanding. It is designed to accommodate all personnel in an organization, regardless of their assigned tasks.

34. C. Sanitization is a combination of processes that ensure that data from a system cannot be recovered by any means. Erasing and clearing are both prone to mistakes and technical problems that can result in remnant data and don't make sense for systems that handled proprietary information. Destruction is the most complete method of ensuring that data cannot be exposed, and some organizations opt to destroy the entire workstation, but that is not a typical solution because of the cost involved.

35.   B. A baseline is a set of security configurations that can be adopted and modified to fit an organization's security needs. A security policy is written to describe an organization's approach to security, while DSS is the second half of the Payment Card Industry Data Security Standard. The NIST SP-800 series of documents address computer security in a variety of areas.

36.   A. The need to protect sensitive data drives information classification. This allows organizations to focus on data that needs to be protected rather than spending effort on less important data. Remanence describes data left on media after an attempt is made to remove the data. Transmitting data isn't a driver for an administrative process to protect sensitive data, and clearing is a technical process for removing data from media.

37.   D. The NIST SP 800-88 process for sanitization and disposition shows that media that will be reused and was classified at a moderate level should be purged and then that purge should be validated. Finally, it should be documented.

38.   C. Security baselines provide a starting point to scope and tailor security controls to your organization's needs. They aren't always appropriate to specific organizational needs, they cannot ensure that systems are always in a secure state, and they do not prevent liability.

39.   D. Record retention is the process of retaining and maintaining information for as long as it is needed. A data storage policy describes how and why data is stored, while data storage is the process of actually keeping the data. Asset maintenance is a process for maintaining physical assets that is not related to information security.

40.   A. Fires may be detected as early as the incipient stage. During this stage, air ionization takes place, and specialized incipient fire detection systems can identify these changes to provide early warning of a fire.

41.   D. A preaction fire suppression system activates in two steps. The pipes fill with water once the early signs of a fire are detected. The system does not dispense water until heat sensors on the sprinkler heads trigger the second phase.

42.   A. Closed-circuit television (CCTV) systems act as a secondary verification mechanism for physical presence because they allow security officials to view the interior of the facility when a motion alarm sounds to determine the current occupants and their activities.

43.   A. Mantraps use a double set of doors to prevent piggybacking by allowing only a single individual to enter a facility at a time.

44.   A. While it would be ideal to have wiring closets in a location where they are monitored by security staff, this is not feasible in most environments. Wiring closets must be distributed geographically in multiple locations across each building used by an organization.

45.   C. Parameter checking, or input validation, is used to ensure that input provided by users to an application matches the expected parameters for the application. Developers may use parameter checking to ensure that input does not exceed the expected length, preventing a buffer overflow attack.

46. C. A magnetic lock may usually be retrofitted to an existing door with a minimum of effort. Installing an electric lock usually requires replacing the entire door. Mantraps and turnstiles will require significant renovation projects.

47. A. The card shown in the image has a smart chip underneath the American flag. Therefore, it is an example of a smart card. This is the most secure type of identification card technology.

48. C. Sensitive compartmented information facilities (SCIFs) are highly secure government facilities designed for processing classified information. They would have stricter physical security requirements than any other type of facility.

49. D. In this case, the organization used the data that they collected for a purpose other than the one that they obtained consent for from the data subjects. This is a violation of purpose limitations. There is no evidence presented that the organization collected more data than was necessary, which would violate data minimization. They disposed of the data promptly, so there was no violation of storage limitations. There is also no indication that any of the data was inaccurate.

50. D. Administrative access controls are procedures and the policies from which they derive. They are based on regulations, requirements, and the organization's own policies. Corrective access controls return an environment to its original status after an issue, while logical controls are technical access controls that rely on hardware or software to protect systems and data. Compensating controls are used in addition to or as an alternative to other controls.

51. The security controls match with the categories as follows:

1. Password: B. Technical

2. Account reviews: A. Administrative

3. Badge readers: C. Physical

4. MFA: B. Technical

5. IDP: B. Technical

Passwords, multifactor authentication (MFA) techniques, and intrusion prevention systems (IPS) are all examples of technical controls. Account reviews are an administrative control, while using badges to control access is a physical control.

52. B. Locks can be preventative access controls by stopping unwanted access, and are physical access controls because they secure access to physical facilities. They are not corrective controls because they do not act to restore normal conditions after an incident occurs.

53. B. Gary should follow the least privilege principle and assign users only the permissions they need to perform their job responsibilities. Aggregation is a term used to describe the unintentional accumulation of privileges over time, also known as privilege creep. Separation of duties and separation of privileges are principles used to secure sensitive processes.

54. A. The matrix shown in the figure is known as a segregation of duties matrix. It is used to ensure that one person does not obtain two privileges that would create a potential conflict. Aggregation describes the unintentional accumulation of privileges over time, also known as privilege creep. Two-person control is used when two people must work together to perform a sensitive action. Defense in depth is a general security principle used to describe a philosophy of overlapping security controls.

55. A. Lydia is following the need-to-know principle. While the user may have the appropriate security clearance to access this information, there is no business justification provided, so she does not know that the user has an appropriate need to know the information.

56. B. In this scenario, Helen designed a process that requires the concurrence of two people to perform a sensitive action. This is an example of two-person control.

57. C. The (ISC)² code of ethics applies only to information security professionals who are members of (ISC)². Adherence to the code is a condition of certification, and individuals found in violation of the code may have their certifications revoked. (ISC)² members who observe a breach of the code are required to report the possible violation by following the ethics complaint procedures.

58. B. The principle of least privilege says that an individual should only have the privileges necessary to complete their job functions. Removing administrative privileges from nonadministrative users is an example of least privilege.

59. C. An attack committed against an organization by an insider, such as an employee, is known as sabotage. Espionage and confidentiality breaches involve the theft of sensitive information, which is not alleged to have occurred in this case. Integrity breaches involve the unauthorized modification of information, which is not described in this scenario.

60. B. The four canons of the (ISC)² code of ethics are to protect society, the common good, necessary public trust and confidence and the infrastructure; act honorably, honestly, justly, responsibly and legally; provide diligent and competent service to principals; and advance and protect the profession.

61. B. Hilda's design follows the principle of separation of duties. Giving one user the ability to both create new accounts and grant administrative privileges combines two actions that would result in a significant security change that should be divided among two users.

62. C. Baseline configurations serve as the starting point for configuring secure systems and applications. They contain the security settings necessary to comply with an organization's security policy and may then be customized to meet the specific needs of an implementation. While security policies and guidelines may contain information needed to secure a system, they do not contain a set of configuration settings that may be applied to a system. The running configuration of a system is the set of currently applied settings, which may or may not be secure.

63. C. Regression testing is software testing that runs a set of known inputs against an application and then compares the results to those produced by an earlier version of the software. It is designed to capture unanticipated consequences of deploying new code versions prior to introducing them into a production environment.

64. A. The defense-in-depth principle states that an organization should prepare for the failure of a single security control by ensuring that each security objective is covered by two or more overlapping controls.

65. C. Configuration management practices ensure that an organization manages the configuration of systems in an organized and automated fashion. This would include ensuring that systems remain in compliance with the baseline requirements of the organization's security standards.

66. B. Requiring authentication can help provide accountability by ensuring that any action taken can be tracked back to a specific user. Storing logs centrally ensures that users can't erase the evidence of actions that they have taken. Reviewing the logs can be useful when identifying issues, but digital signatures are not a typical part of a logging environment. Logging the use of administrative credentials helps for users with privileged access but won't cover all users, and encrypting the logs doesn't help with accountability. Authorization helps, but being able to specifically identify users through authentication is more important.

67. D. Selecting security controls is a design task, so it should be done during the design phase of the program's development. The selected controls would later be implemented/assessed and operated/maintained during the appropriate phases. The inventory and licensing phase would track the assets used in her organization.

68. D. If software is released into the public domain, anyone may use it for any purpose, without restriction. All other license types may contain at least some level of restriction.

69. B. Social engineering exploits humans to allow attacks to succeed. Since help desk employees are specifically tasked with being helpful, they may be targeted by attackers posing as legitimate employees. Trojans are a type of malware, whereas phishing is an attack via electronic communication methods intended to capture passwords or other sensitive data. Whaling is a type of phishing aimed at high-profile or important targets.

Chapter 2: Access Controls (Domain 2)

1. B. Device authentication allows the venue to restrict network access to authorized scanners but does not require individual ushers to sign in to the device. This seems an acceptable level of security for this environment, as the scanners are carefully controlled. Moving to any authentication scheme that requires user authentication would be unwieldy.

2. D. The purpose of an extranet is to allow outside organizations that are business partners to access limited resources on the corporate network. That describes the situation in this scenario, so Norma is building an extranet.

3. B. A mandatory access control (MAC) scheme is an example of a nondiscretionary approach to access control, as the owner of objects does not have the ability to set permissions on those objects. It is possible for a visitor list or file ACLs to be configured using a nondiscretionary scheme, but these approaches can also be configured as discretionary access control (DAC) implementations.

4. C. Digital certificates are the strongest device-based access control mechanism listed in this scenario. Administrators may create certificates for each device and tie them to the physical device. Passwords are easily transferred to other devices and are not as strong an approach. IP addresses are easily changed and should not be used. MAC addresses theoretically identify devices uniquely, but it is possible to alter a MAC address, so they should not be relied upon for authentication.

5. A. Kaiden should use a virtual private network (VPN) for all remote connections to the extranet. The VPN will encrypt traffic sent over public networks and protect it from eavesdropping.

6. B. The permissions granted on files in Linux designate what authorized users can do with those files—read, write, or execute. In the image shown, all users can read, write, and execute index.html, whereas the owner can read, write, and execute example.txt, the group cannot, and everyone can write and execute it.

7. C. Usernames are an identification tool. They are not secret, so they are not suitable for use as a password.

8. B. Before granting access, Gary should verify that the user has a valid security clearance and a business need to know the information. Gary is performing an authorization task, so he does not need to verify the user's credentials, such as a password or biometric scan.

9. C. The crossover error rate is the point where false acceptance rate and false rejection rate cross over and is a standard assessment used to compare the accuracy of biometric devices.

10. A. At point B, the false acceptance rate, or FAR, is quite high, while the false rejection rate, or FRR, is relatively low. This may be acceptable in some circumstances, but in organizations where a false acceptance can cause a major problem, it is likely that they should instead choose a point to the right of point A.

11. B. CER is a standard used to assess biometric devices. If the CER for this device does not fit the needs of the organization, Ben should assess other biometric systems to find one with a lower CER. Sensitivity is already accounted for in CER charts, and moving the CER isn't something Ben can do. FRR is not a setting in software, so Ben can't use that as an option either.

12. B. The process of a subject claiming or professing an identity is known as *identification*. Authorization verifies the identity of a subject by checking a factor such as a password. Logins typically include both identification and authorization, and token presentation is a type of authentication.

13. B. All of these are objects. Although some of these items can be subjects, files, databases, and storage media can't be. Processes and programs aren't file stores, and of course none of these is a user.

14. B. Mandatory access control systems can be hierarchical, where each domain is ordered and related to other domains above and below it; compartmentalized, where there is no relationship between each domain; or hybrid, where both hierarchy and compartments are used. There is no concept of bracketing in mandatory access control design.

15. B. All of the controls listed here, if properly implemented, have the potential to improve the organization's security posture. However, only single sign-on is likely to improve the user experience by eliminating barriers to authentication across multiple systems. Mandatory access control and multifactor authentication will likely be seen as inconveniences by users, while automated deprovisioning will improve the experience of identity and access management administrators but not affect the end user experience.

16. A. An attribute-based access control (ABAC) system will allow Susan to specify details about subjects, objects, and access, allowing granular control. Although a rule-based access control system (RBAC) might allow this, the attribute-based access control system can be more specific and thus is more flexible. Discretionary access control (DAC) would allow object owners to make decisions, and mandatory access controls (MACs) would use classifications; neither of these capabilities was described in the requirements.

17. B. Decentralized access control empowers people closer to the resources to control access but does not provide consistent control. It does not provide redundancy, since it merely moves control points, the cost of access control depends on its implementation and methods, and granularity can be achieved in both centralized and decentralized models.

18. C. Capability tables list the privileges assigned to subjects and identify the objects that subjects can access. Access control lists are object-focused rather than subject-focused. Implicit deny is a principle that states that anything that is not explicitly allowed is denied, and a rights management matrix is not an access control model.

19. The security controls match with the categories as follows:
   1. Password: B. Something you know
   2. ID card: A. Something you have
   3. Retinal scan: C. Something you are
   4. Smartphone token: A. Something you have
   5. Fingerprint analysis: C. Something you are

20. C. OpenID is a widely supported standard that allows a user to use a single account to log into multiple sites, and Google accounts are frequently used with OpenID.

21. C. Synchronous soft tokens, such as Google Authenticator, use a time-based algorithm that generates a constantly changing series of codes. Asynchronous tokens typically require a challenge to be entered on the token to allow it to calculate a response, which the server compares to the response it expects. Smartcards typically present a certificate but may have other token capabilities built in. Static tokens are physical devices that can contain credentials and include smart cards and memory cards.

22. B. Studies consistently show that users are more likely to write down passwords if they have more accounts. Central control of a single account is also easier to shut off if something does go wrong. Simply decreasing the number of accounts required for a subject doesn't increase security by itself, and SSO does not guarantee individual system logging, although it should provide central logging of SSO activity. Since an SSO system was not specified, there is no way of determining whether a given SSO system provides better or worse encryption for authentication data.

23. B. Software tokens are flexible, with delivery options including mobile applications, SMS, and phone delivery. They have a relatively low administrative overhead, as users can typically self-manage. Biometrics require significant effort to register users and to deploy and maintain infrastructure, and they require hardware at each authentication location. Both types of hardware tokens can require additional overhead for distribution and maintenance, and token failure can cause support challenges.

24. D. Electronic access to company resources must be carefully coordinated. An employee who retains access after being terminated may use that access to take retaliatory action. On the other hand, if access is terminated too early, the employee may figure out that he or she is about to be terminated.

25. C. A trust that allows one forest to access another's resources without the reverse being possible is an example of a one-way trust. Since Jim doesn't want the trust path to flow as the domain tree is formed, this trust has to be nontransitive.

26. A. Verifying information that an individual should know about themselves using third-party factual information (a Type 1 authentication factor) is sometimes known as dynamic knowledge-based authentication and is a type of identity proofing. Out-of-band identity proofing would use another means of contacting the user, such as a text message or phone call, and password verification requires a password.

27. A. Lauren's team would benefit from a credential management system. Credential management systems offer features such as password management, multifactor authentication to retrieve passwords, logging, audit, and password rotation capabilities. A strong password policy would only make maintenance of passwords for many systems a more difficult task if done manually. Single sign-on would help if all of the systems had the same sensitivity levels, but different credentials are normally required for higher-sensitivity systems.

28. A. Transitive trusts go beyond the two domains directly involved in the trust relationship and extend to their subdomains. Nontransitive trusts are not inheritable to other domains. The terms *inheritable trust* and *noninheritable trust* are not normally used.

29. B. We know that both Adam and the server administrator have the username and password, but this is information used for identification and authentication, not authorization. We do not know what information Adam's supervisor might have. The server is a standalone file server, so it must have information about the activities that Adam is authorized to perform.

30. B. Privilege creep is a common problem when employees change roles over time and their privileges and permissions are not properly modified to reflect their new roles. Least privilege issues are a design or implementation problem, and switching roles isn't

typically what causes them to occur. Account creep is not a common industry term, and account termination would imply that someone has removed her account instead of switching her to new groups or new roles.

31. A. Adam created a list of individual users that may access the file. This is an access control list, which consists of multiple access control entries. It includes the names of users, so it is not role-based, and Adam was able to modify the list, so it is not mandatory access control.

32. A. Knowledge-based authentication relies on preset questions such as "What is your pet's name?" and the answers. It can be susceptible to attacks because of the availability of the answers on social media or other sites. Dynamic knowledge-based authentication relies on facts or data that the user already knows that can be used to create questions they can answer on an as-needed basis (for example, a previous address, or a school they attended). Out-of-band identity proofing relies on an alternate channel like a phone call or text message. Finally, Type 3 authentication factors are biometric, or "something you are," rather than knowledge-based.

33. C. Authorization defines what a subject can or can't do. Identification occurs when a subject claims an identity, accountability is provided by the logs and audit trail that track what occurs on a system, and authorization occurs when that identity is validated.

34. B. Discretionary access control (DAC) can provide greater scalability by leveraging many administrators, and those administrators can add flexibility by making decisions about access to their objects without fitting into an inflexible mandatory access control (MAC) system. MAC is more secure because of the strong set of controls it provides, but it does not scale as well as DAC and is relatively inflexible in comparison.

35. C. While signature-based detection is used to detect attacks, review of provisioning processes typically involves checking logs, reviewing the audit trail, or performing a manual review of permissions granted during the provisioning process.

36. D. The principle of least privilege should guide Joe in this case. He should apply no access permissions by default and then give each user the necessary permissions to perform their job responsibilities. Read-only, editor, and administrator permissions may be necessary for one or more of these users, but those permissions should be assigned based upon business need and not by default.

37. C. Type 2 errors occur in biometric systems when an invalid subject is incorrectly authenticated as a valid user. In this case, nobody except the actual customer should be validated when fingerprints are scanned. Type 2 errors are also known as false positive errors. Type 1 (or false negative) errors occur when a valid subject is not authenticated; if the existing customer was rejected, it would be a Type 1 error. Registration is the process of adding users, but registration errors and time-of-use, method-of-use errors are not specific biometric authentication terms.

38. A. Entering a password is an act that proves a user's identity and, therefore, is an authentication step. Laura likely already identified herself by providing her username or performing a similar identification function. Authorization occurs after authentication when the system determines what actions Laura is allowed to take. Accounting occurs when the system logs Laura's activity.

39.   D. Current best practice guidance from NIST, published in NIST Special Publication 800-63b, suggests that organizations should not impose password expiration requirements on end users.

40.   C. Security Assertion Markup Language (SAML) is the best choice for providing authentication and authorization information, particularly for browser-based SSO. HTML is primarily used for web pages, SPML is used to exchange user information for SSO, and XACML is used for access control policy markup.

41.   B. Mandatory access control (MAC) applies labels to subjects and objects and allows subjects to access objects when their labels match. Discretionary access control (DAC) is controlled by the owner of objects, rule-based access control applies rules throughout a system, and role-based access control bases rights on roles, which are often handled as groups of users.

42.   C. Mandatory access control systems are based on a lattice-based model. Lattice-based models use a matrix of classification labels to compartmentalize data. Discretionary access models allow object owners to determine access to the objects they control, role-based access controls are often group-based, and rule-based access controls like firewall ACLs apply rules to all subjects they apply to.

43.   A. In the subject/object model of access control, the user or process making the request for a resource is the subject of that request. In this example, Ricky is requesting access to the VPN (the object of the request) and is, therefore, the subject.

44.   B. Firewalls use rule-based access control in their access control lists and apply rules created by administrators to all traffic that passes through them. DAC, or discretionary access control, allows owners to determine who can access objects they control, while task-based access control lists tasks for users. MAC, or mandatory access control, uses classifications to determine access.

45.   C. While all of the listed controls would improve authentication security, most simply strengthen the use of knowledge-based authentication. The best way to improve the authentication process would be to add a factor not based on knowledge through the use of multifactor authentication. This may include the use of biometric controls or token-based authentication.

46.   C. Self-service password reset tools typically have a significant impact on the number of password reset contacts that a help desk has. Two-factor and biometric authentication both add additional complexity and may actually increase the number of contacts. Passphrases can be easier to remember than traditional complex passwords and may decrease calls, but they don't have the same impact that a self-service system does.

47.   B. OAuth provides the ability to access resources from another service and would meet Jim's needs. OpenID would allow him to use an account from another service with his application, and Kerberos and LDAP are used more frequently for in-house services.

48.   D. Authorization occurs when a system determines whether an authenticated user is permitted to perform an activity, such as by consulting an access control list. Authentication occurs when a user proves his or her identity to a system, such as by providing a password or completing a facial recognition scan. When a system logs user activity, this is an example of accounting.

49. A. This type of authentication, where one domain trusts users from another domain, is called federation. Federation may involve transitive trusts, where the trusts may be followed through a series of domains, but this scenario only describes the use of two domains. The scenario only describes use of credentials for a single system and does not describe a multiple-system scenario where single sign-on would be relevant. There is no requirement described for the use of multifactor authentication, which would require the use of two or more diverse authentication techniques.

50. D. Role-based access control would be an excellent solution for Luke's requirements. Administrators would assign permissions to roles and then simply adjust the role of a user when he or she changes jobs, rather than changing all of the individual permissions.

51. C. When you input a username and password, you are authenticating yourself by providing a unique identifier and a verification that you are the person who should have that identifier (the password). Authorization is the process of determining what a user is allowed to do. Validation and login both describe elements of what is happening in the process; however, they aren't the most important identity and access management activity.

52. D. Kerberos is an authentication protocol that uses tickets and provides secure communications between the client, key distribution center (KDC), ticket-granting service (TGS), authentication server (AS), and endpoint services. RADIUS does not provide the same level of security by default, SAML is a markup language, and OAuth is designed to allow third-party websites to rely on credentials from other sites like Google or Microsoft.

53. C. Palm scans compare the vein patterns in the palm to a database to authenticate a user. Vein patterns are unique, and this method is a better single-factor authentication method than voice pattern recognition, hand geometry, and pulse patterns, each of which can be more difficult to uniquely identify between individuals or can be fooled more easily.

54. A. Asynchronous tokens use a challenge/response process in which the system sends a challenge and the user responds with a PIN and a calculated response to the challenge. The server performs the same calculations, and if both match, it authenticates the user. Synchronous tokens use a time-based calculation to generate codes. Smart cards are paired with readers and don't need to have challenges entered, and RFID devices are not used for challenge/response tokens.

55. B. Provisioning includes the creation, maintenance, and removal of user objects from applications, systems, and directories. Registration occurs when users are enrolled in a biometric system; population and authenticator loading are not common industry terms.

56. C. Discretionary access control gives owners the right to decide who has access to the objects they own. Role-based access control uses administrators to make that decision for roles or groups of people with a role, task-based access control uses lists of tasks for each user, and rule-based access control applies a set of rules to all subjects.

57. D. The Linux filesystem allows the owners of objects to determine the access rights that subjects have to them. This means that it is a discretionary access control. If the system enforced a role-based access control, Alex wouldn't set the controls; they would be set based on the roles assigned to each subject. A rule-based access control system would apply rules throughout the system, and a mandatory access control system uses classification labels.

58. C. The U.S. government's Common Access Card is a smart card. The U.S. government also issues PIV cards, or personal identity verification cards.

59. B. Privilege creep is the term used to describe the security issue that arises when users move between jobs in an organization and accumulate privileges that are never revoked when no longer necessary. This is a violation of the principle of least privilege.

60. C. In a mandatory access control system, all subjects and objects have a label. Compartments may or may not be used, but there is not a specific requirement for either subjects or objects to be compartmentalized. The specific labels of Confidential, Secret, and Top Secret are not required by MAC.

61. B. Mandatory access control systems allow an administrator to configure access permissions but do not allow users to delegate permission to others. Discretionary access control systems do allow this delegation. The scenario does not provide information to indicate whether a decentralized or rule-based approach is appropriate.

62. C. Kathleen should implement a biometric factor. The cards and keys are an example of a Type 2 factor, or "something you have." Using a smart card replaces this with another Type 2 factor, but the cards could still be loaned out or stolen. Adding a PIN suffers from the same problem: A PIN can be stolen. Adding cameras doesn't prevent access to the facility and thus doesn't solve the immediate problem (but it is a good idea!).

63. D. Entitlement refers to the privileges granted to users when an account is first provisioned. Aggregation is the accumulation of privileges over time. Transitivity is the inheritance of privileges and trust through relationships. Baselines are snapshots of a system or application's security that allow analysts to detect future modifications.

64. A. Role-based access control gives each user an array of permissions based on their position in the organization, such as the scheme shown here. Task-based access control is not a standard approach. Rule-based access controls use rules that apply to all subjects, which isn't something we see in the list. Discretionary access control gives object owners rights to choose how the objects they own are accessed, which is not what this list shows.

65. C. Identity proofing that relies on a type of verification outside the initial environment that required the verification is out-of-band identity proofing. This type of verification relies on the owner of the phone or phone number having control of it but removes the ability for attackers to use only Internet-based resources to compromise an account. Knowledge-based authentication relies on answers to preselected information, whereas dynamic knowledge–based authentication builds questions using facts or data about the user. Risk-based identity proofing uses risk-based metrics to determine whether identities should be permitted or denied access. It is used to limit fraud in financial transactions, such as credit card purchases. This is a valid form of proofing but does not necessarily use an out-of-band channel, such as SMS.

66. A. Zero-trust network architectures make trust decisions based upon the identity of the user or device making the request. They do not make trust decisions based upon network location characteristics, such as an IP address, VLAN assignment, or network segment.

Chapter 3: Risk Identification, Monitoring, and Analysis (Domain 3)

1. D. HAL Systems decided to stop offering the service because of the risk. This is an example of a risk avoidance strategy. The company altered its operations in a manner that eliminates the risk of NTP misuse.

2. A. The change log contains information about approved changes and the change management process. While other logs may contain details about the change's effect, the audit trail for change management would be found in the change log.

3. C. Fuzzers are tools that are designed to provide invalid or unexpected input to applications, testing for vulnerabilities like format string vulnerabilities, buffer overflow issues, and other problems. A static analysis relies on examining code without running the application or code and thus would not fill forms as part of a web application. Brute-force tools attempt to bypass security by trying every possible combination for passwords or other values. A black box is a type of penetration test where the testers do not know anything about the environment.

4. C. The exposure factor is the percentage of the facility that risk managers expect will be damaged if a risk materializes. It is calculated by dividing the amount of damage by the asset value. In this case, that is $5 million in damage divided by the $10 million facility value, or 50 percent.

5. B. The annualized rate of occurrence is the number of times that risk analysts expect a risk to happen in any given year. In this case, the analysts expect tornados once every 200 years, or 0.005 times per year.

6. A. The annualized loss expectancy is calculated by multiplying the single loss expectancy (SLE) by the annualized rate of occurrence (ARO). In this case, the SLE is $5,000,000, and the ARO is 0.005. Multiplying these numbers together gives you the ALE of $25,000.

7. B. Jim should ask the information security team to flag the issue as resolved if he is sure the patch was installed. Many vulnerability scanners rely on version information or banner information and may flag patched versions if the software provider does not update the information they see. Uninstalling and reinstalling the patch will not change this. Changing the version information may not change all of the details that are being flagged by the scanner and may cause issues at a later date. Reviewing the vulnerability information for a workaround may be a good idea but should not be necessary if the proper patch is installed; it can create maintenance issues later.

8. B. NIST SP 800-53A is titled "Assessing Security and Privacy Controls in Federal Information Systems and Organizations: Building Effective Assessment Plans" and covers methods for assessing and measuring controls.

   NIST 800-12 is an introduction to computer security, 800-34 covers contingency planning, and 800-86 is the "Guide to Integrating Forensic Techniques into Incident Response."

9. C. Zero knowledge, sometimes called black-box tests, are the closest to actual attacks because an attacker would not have internal knowledge prior to their attack. Full and partial knowledge attacks both rely on pre-existing information, and specific knowledge is not a commonly used term for this.

10. D. Installing a device that will block attacks is an attempt to lower risk by reducing the likelihood of a successful application attack.

11. C. Vulnerability scanners that do not have administrative rights to access a machine or that are not using an agent scan remote machines to gather information, including fingerprints from responses to queries and connections, banner information from services, and related data. CVE information is Common Vulnerabilities and Exposures information, or vulnerability information. A port scanner gathers information about what service ports are open, although some port scanners blur the line between port and vulnerability scanners. Patch management tools typically run as an agent on a system to allow them to both monitor patch levels and update the system as needed. Service validation typically involves testing the functionality of a service, not its banner and response patterns.

12. D. Regression testing, which is a type of functional or unit testing, tests to ensure that changes have not introduced new issues. Nonregression testing checks to see whether a change has had the effect it was supposed to, smoke testing focuses on simple problems with impact on critical functionality, and evolution testing is not a software testing technique.

13. C. Risk mitigation strategies attempt to lower the probability and/or impact of a risk occurring. Intrusion prevention systems attempt to reduce the probability of a successful attack and are, therefore, examples of risk mitigation.

14. B. TCP port 443 normally indicates an HTTPS server. Nikto is useful for vulnerability scanning web servers and applications and is the best choice listed for a web server. Metasploit includes some scanning functionality but is not a purpose-built tool for vulnerability scanning. zzuf is a fuzzing tool and isn't relevant for vulnerability scans, whereas sqlmap is a SQL injection testing tool.

15. C. After developing a list of assets, the business impact analysis team should assign values to each asset.

16. D. The menu shown will archive logs when they reach the maximum size allowed (20 MB). These archives will be retained, which could fill the disk. Log data will not be overwritten, and log data should not be lost when the data is archived. The question does not include enough information to determine if needed information may not be logged.

17. A. Syslog is a widely used protocol for event and message logging. Eventlog, netlog, and Remote Log Protocol are all made-up terms.

18. C. Risks are the combination of a threat and a vulnerability. Threats are the external forces seeking to undermine security, such as the malicious hacker in this case. Vulnerabilities are the internal weaknesses that might allow a threat to succeed. In this case, the missing patch is the vulnerability. In this scenario, if the malicious hacker (threat) attempts a SQL injection attack against the unpatched server (vulnerability), the result is website defacement.

19. B. Group Policy provides the ability to monitor and apply settings in a security baseline. Manual checks by users and using startup scripts provide fewer reviews and may be prone to failure, while periodic review of the baseline won't result in compliance being checked.

20. B. Group Policy enforced by Active Directory can ensure consistent logging settings and can provide regular enforcement of policy on systems. Periodic configuration audits won't catch changes made between audits, and local policies can drift because of local changes or differences in deployments. A Windows syslog client will enable the Windows systems to send syslog to the SIEM appliance but won't ensure consistent logging of events.

21. B. Windows systems generate logs in the Windows native logging format. To send syslog events, Windows systems require a helper application or tool. Enterprise wireless access points, firewalls, and Linux systems all typically support syslog.

22. B. Network Time Protocol (NTP) can ensure that systems are using the same time, allowing time sequencing for logs throughout a centralized logging infrastructure. Syslog is a way for systems to send logs to a logging server and won't address time sequencing. Neither logsync nor SNAP is an industry term.

23. C. Key risk indicators are used to tell those in charge of risk management how risky an activity is and how much impact changes are having on that risk profile. Identifying key risk indicators and monitoring them can help to identify high-risk areas earlier in their lifecycle. Yearly risk assessments may be a good idea but only provide a point-in-time view, whereas penetration tests may miss out on risks that are not directly security related. Monitoring logs and events using a SIEM device can help detect issues as they occur but won't necessarily show trends in risk.

24. D. The annualized rate of occurrence (ARO) is the frequency at which you should expect a risk to materialize each year. In a 100-year flood plain, risk analysts expect a flood to occur once every 100 years, or 0.01 times per year.

25. C. Simply updating the version that an application provides may stop the vulnerability scanner from flagging it, but it won't fix the underlying issue. Patching, using workarounds, or installing an application layer firewall or IPS can all help to remediate or limit the impact of the vulnerability.

26. C. SSH uses TCP port 22, so this attack is likely an attempt to scan for open or weakly secured SSH servers. FTP uses ports 20 and 21. Telnet uses port 23, and HTTP uses port 80.

27. A. Netflow records contain an entry for every network communication session that took place on a network and can be compared to a list of known malicious hosts. IDS logs may contain a relevant record, but it is less likely because they would create log entries only if the traffic triggers the IDS, as opposed to netflow records, which encompass all communications. Authentication logs and RFC logs would not have records of any network traffic.

28. B. OpenVAS is an open source vulnerability scanning tool that will provide Susan with a report of the vulnerabilities that it can identify from a remote, network-based scan. Nmap is an open source port scanner. Both the Microsoft Baseline Security Analyzer (MBSA) and Nessus are closed source tools, although Nessus was originally open source.

29. B. Not having enough log sources is not a key consideration in log management system design, although it may be a worry for security managers who can't capture the data they need. Log management system designs must take into account the volume of log data and the network bandwidth it consumes, the security of the data, and the amount of effort required to analyze the data.

30. B. Port 80 is used by the HTTP protocol for unencrypted web communications. If Kara wants to protect against eavesdropping, she should block this port and restrict web access to encrypted HTTPS connections on port 443.

31. A. Port 22 is used by the Secure Shell (SSH) protocol for administrative connections. If Kara wants to restrict administrative connections, she should block access on this port.

32. B. TCP and UDP ports 137–139 are used for NetBIOS services, whereas 445 is used for Active Directory. TCP 1433 is the default port for Microsoft SQL, indicating that this is probably a Windows server providing SQL services.

33. B. Purchasing insurance is a means of transferring risk. If Sally had worked to decrease the likelihood of the events occurring, she would have been using a reduce or risk mitigation strategy, while simply continuing to function as the organization has would be an example of an acceptance strategy. Rejection, or denial of the risk, is not a valid strategy, even though it occurs!

34. A. Logging systems can provide accountability for identity systems by tracking the actions, changes, and other activities a user or account performs.

35. D. Once a vulnerability scanner identifies a potential problem, validation is necessary to verify that the issue exists. Reporting, patching, or other remediation actions can be conducted once the vulnerability has been confirmed.

36. D. In a risk acceptance strategy, the organization decides that taking no action is the most beneficial route to managing a risk.

37. B. Brute-force attacks try every possible password. In this attack, the password is changing by one letter at each attempt, which indicates that it is a brute-force attack. A dictionary attack would use dictionary words for the attack, whereas a man-in-the-middle or pass-the-hash attack would most likely not be visible in an authentication log except as a successful login.

38. C. The audit finding indicates that the backup administrator may not be monitoring backup logs and taking appropriate action based on what they report, thus resulting in potentially unusable backups. Issues with review, logging, or being aware of the success or failure of backups are less important than not having usable backups.

39. B. Microsoft's STRIDE threat assessment model places threats into one of six categories:

Spoofing—threats that involve user credentials and authentication, or falsifying legitimate communications

Tampering—threats that involve the malicious modification of data

Repudiation—threats that cause actions to occur that cannot be denied by a user

Information disclosure—threats that involve exposure of data to unauthorized individuals

Denial of service—threats that deny service to legitimate users

Elevation of privilege—threats that provide higher privileges to unauthorized users

Using role-based access controls (RBACs) for specific operations will help to ensure that users cannot perform actions that they should not be able to. Auditing and logging can help detect abuse but won't prevent it, and data type, format checks, and whitelisting are all useful for preventing attacks like SQL injection and buffer overflow attacks but are not as directly aimed at authorization issues.

40. D. Since a shared symmetric key could be used by any of the servers, transaction identification problems caused by a shared key are likely to involve a repudiation issue. If encrypted transactions cannot be uniquely identified by server, they cannot be proved to have come from a specific server.

41. C. Filtering is useful for preventing denial-of-service attacks but won't prevent tampering with data. Hashes and digital signatures can both be used to verify the integrity of data, and authorization controls can help ensure that only those with the proper rights can modify the data.

42. D. Network-enabled printers often provide services via TCP 515 and 9100 and have both nonsecure and secure web-enabled management interfaces on TCP 80 and 443. Web servers, access points, and file servers would not typically provide service on the LPR and LPD ports (515 and 9100).

43. C. In reduction analysis, the security professional breaks the system down into five key elements: trust boundaries, data flow paths, input points, privileged operations, and details about security controls.

44. C. Penetration tests are intended to help identify vulnerabilities, and exploiting them is part of the process rather than a hazard. Application crashes; denial of service due to system, network, or application failures; and even data corruption can all be hazards of penetration tests.

45. D. Nmap is a popular open source port scanner. Nmap is not a vulnerability scanner, nor is it a web application fuzzer. While port scanners can be used to partially map a network and its name stands for Network Mapper, it is not a network design tool.

46. D. Mutation testing modifies a program in small ways and then tests that mutant to determine whether it behaves as it should or whether it fails. This technique is used to design and test software tests through mutation. Static code analysis and regression testing are both means of testing code, whereas code auditing is an analysis of source code rather than a means of designing and testing software tests.

47. C. Rebooting a Windows machine results in an information log entry. Windows defines five types of events: errors, which indicate a significant problem; warnings, which may indicate future problems; information, which describes successful operation; success audits, which record successful security accesses; and failure audits, which record failed security access attempts.

48. C. The most important first step for a penetration test is getting permission. Once permission has been received, planning, data gathering, and then elements of the actual test like port scanning can commence.

49. D. In an elevation of privilege attack, the attacker transforms a limited user account into an account with greater privileges, powers, and/or access to the system. Spoofing attacks falsify an identity, while repudiation attacks attempt to deny accountability for an action. Tampering attacks attempt to violate the integrity of information or resources.

50. C. At this point in the process, Ann has no reason to believe that any actual security compromise or policy violation took place, so this situation does not meet the criteria for a security incident or intrusion. Rather, the alert generated by the intrusion detection system is simply a security event requiring further investigation. Security occurrence is not a term commonly used in incident handling.

51. A. DNS traffic commonly uses port 53 for both TCP and UDP communications. SSH and SCP use TCP port 22. SSL and TLS do not have ports assigned to them but are commonly used for HTTPS traffic on port 443. Unencrypted web traffic over HTTP often uses port 80.

52. D. The attack described in this scenario has all of the hallmarks of a denial-of-service attack. More specifically, Ann's organization is likely experiencing a DNS amplification attack where an attacker sends false requests to third-party DNS servers with a forged source IP address belonging to the targeted system. Because the attack uses UDP requests, there is no three-way handshake. The attack packets are carefully crafted to elicit a lengthy response from a short query. The purpose of these queries is to generate responses headed to the target system that are sufficiently large and numerous enough to overwhelm the targeted network or system.

53. B. Now that Ann suspects an attack against her organization, she has sufficient evidence to declare a security incident. The attack underway seems to have undermined the availability of her network, meeting one of the criteria for a security incident. This is an escalation beyond a security event but does not reach the level of an intrusion because there is no evidence that the attacker has even attempted to gain access to systems on Ann's network. Security occurrence is not a term commonly used in incident handling.

54. C. Dictionary attacks use a dictionary or list of common passwords as well as variations of those words to attempt to log in as an authorized user. This attack shows a variety of passwords based on a similar base word, which is often a good indicator of a dictionary attack. A brute-force attack will typically show simple iteration of passwords, while a man-in-the-middle attack would not be visible in the authentication log. A rainbow table attack is used when attackers already have password hashes in their possession and would also not show up in logs.

55. B. ISO 27002 is an international standard focused on information security and titled "Information technology—Security techniques—Code of practice for information security management." The Information Technology Infrastructure Library (ITIL) does contain security management practices, but it is not the sole focus of the document, and the ITIL security section is derived from ISO 27002. The Capability Maturity Model (CMM) is focused on software development, and the Project Management Body of Knowledge (PMBOK) Guide focuses on project management.

56. The status messages match with the descriptions as follows:

1. Open: C. The port is accessible on the remote system and an application is accepting connections on that port.

2. Closed: A. The port is accessible on the remote system, but no application is accepting connections on that port.

3. Filtered: B. The port is not accessible on the remote system.

57. D. Tony would see the best results by combining elements of quantitative and qualitative risk assessment. Quantitative risk assessment excels at analyzing financial risk, while qualitative risk assessment is a good tool for intangible risks. Combining the two techniques provides a well-rounded risk picture.

58. B. zzuf is the only fuzzer on the list, and zzuf is specifically designed to work with tools like web browsers, image viewers, and similar software by modifying network and file input to application. Nmap is a port scanner, Nessus is a vulnerability scanner, and Nikto is a web server scanner.

59. B. Flows, also often called network flows, are captured to provide insight into network traffic for security, troubleshooting, and performance management. Audit logging provides information about events on the routers, route logging is not a common network logging function, and trace logs are used in troubleshooting specific software packages as they perform their functions.

60. B. Metasploit is an exploitation package that is designed to assist penetration testers. A tester using Metasploit can exploit known vulnerabilities for which an exploit has been created or can create their own exploits using the tool. While Metasploit provides built-in access to some vulnerability scanning functionality, a tester using Metasploit should primarily be expected to perform actual tests of exploitable vulnerabilities. Similarly, Metasploit supports creating buffer overflow attacks, but it is not a purpose-built buffer overflow testing tool, and of course testing systems for zero-day exploits doesn't work unless they have been released.

61. D. Whenever you choose to accept a risk, you should maintain detailed documentation of the risk acceptance process to satisfy auditors in the future. This should happen before implementing security controls, designing a disaster recovery plan, or repeating the business impact analysis (BIA).

62. C. After scanning for open ports using a port scanning tool like nmap, penetration testers will identify interesting ports and then conduct vulnerability scans to determine what services may be vulnerable. This will perform many of the same activities as connecting to a web server. It will also typically be more useful than trying to manually test for vulnerable accounts via Telnet. sqlmap would typically be used after a vulnerability scanner identifies additional information about services, and the vulnerability scanner will normally provide a wider range of useful information.

63. B. The system is likely a Linux system. The system shows X11, as well as login, shell, and nfs ports, all of which are more commonly found on Linux systems than Windows systems or network devices. This system is also very poorly secured; many of the services running on it should not be exposed in a modern secure network.

64. D. Nmap only scans 1000 TCP and UDP ports by default, including ports outside the 0–1024 range of "well-known" ports. By using the defaults for nmap, Ben missed 64,535 ports. OS fingerprinting won't cover more ports but would have provided a best guess of the OS running on the scanned system.

65. A. Risks exist when there is an intersection of a threat and a vulnerability. This is described using the equation Risk = Threat * Vulnerability.

66. D. In many cases when an exploit is initially reported, there are no prebuilt signatures or detections for vulnerability scanners, and the CVE database may not immediately have information about the attack. Jacob's best option is to quickly gather information and review potentially vulnerable servers based on their current configuration. As more information becomes available, signatures and CVE information are likely to be published. Unfortunately for Jacob, IDS and IPS signatures will only detect attacks and won't detect whether systems are vulnerable unless he sees the systems being exploited.

67. C. Inconsistent time stamps are a common problem, often caused by improperly set time zones or because of differences in how system clocks are set. In this case, a consistent time difference often indicates that one system uses local time, and the other is using Greenwich mean time (GMT). Logs from multiple sources tend to cause problems with centralization and collection, whereas different log formats can create challenges in parsing log data. Finally, modified logs are often a sign of intrusion or malicious intent.

68. D. The final step of a quantitative risk analysis is conducting a cost-benefit analysis to determine whether the organization should implement proposed countermeasure(s).

69. C. The string shown in the logs is characteristic of a directory traversal attack where the attacker attempts to force the web application to navigate up the file hierarchy and retrieve a file that should not normally be provided to a web user, such as the password file. The series of "double dots" is indicative of a directory traversal attack because it is the character string used to reference the directory one level up in a hierarchy.

70. C. The two main methods of choosing records from a large pool for further analysis are sampling and clipping. Sampling uses statistical techniques to choose a sample that is representative of the entire pool, while clipping uses threshold values to select those records that exceed a predefined threshold because they may be of most interest to analysts.

71. A. Isaac could use the Common Vulnerability Scoring System (CVSS) to calculate an appropriate score that will help him compare and contrast vulnerabilities for his organization in a standard and widely used format. Mitre's ATT&CK is a framework for describing adversary tactics, and SAML is the Security Assertion Markup Language.

72. B. Qualitative tools are often used in business impact assessment to capture the impact on intangible factors such as customer confidence, employee morale, and reputation.

73. C. Vulnerability scanners cannot detect vulnerabilities for which they do not have a test, plug-in, or signature. Signatures often include version numbers, service fingerprints, or configuration data. They can detect local vulnerabilities as well as those that require authentication if they are provided with credentials, and of course, they can detect service vulnerabilities.

74. C. Path disclosures, local file inclusions, and buffer overflows are all vulnerabilities that may be found by a web vulnerability scanner, but race conditions that take advantage of timing issues tend to be found either by code analysis or using automated tools that specifically test for race conditions as part of software testing.

75. D. The IP addresses that his clients have provided are RFC 1918 nonroutable IP addresses, and Jim will not be able to scan them from off-site. To succeed in his penetration test, he will have to either first penetrate their network border or place a machine inside their network to scan from the inside. IP addresses overlapping is not a real concern for scanning, and the ranges can easily be handled by current scanning systems.

76. C. A security orchestration, automation, and response (SOAR) system is designed to do just what Naomi wants. SOAR systems extend the capabilities of SIEM systems beyond aggregation and correlation into response and workflows. A network-attached storage (NAS) device is used to store data, not for security purposes. An IPS would allow her to detect attacks, but does not aggregate and correlate event data from other devices. An MDR is a managed detection and response system and is a third-party solution. Since Naomi wants to have the tasks performed by her team, rather than outsourcing, an MDR is not an appropriate solution.

77. C. SQL injection attack details can typically be found in application logs like those found on a web server where the query will be logged. They can also be found in web application firewall (WAF) logs and in the logs from the database itself when actions are taken. Network switches, however, are unlikely to contain useful detail in their logs about SQL injection attacks.

78. A. Once a discovery process is complete, assets are typically prioritized. Once that is complete, baseline risk profiles are created as part of the assessment process, and then reporting, remediation, and verification are conducted.

79. D. While it may be tempting to ignore the risks, even residual risks need to be accepted rather than being ignored. Thus, Diego should document the risks and ensure that an appropriate owner accepts them. Transferring or mitigating the risks was noted as not cost effective, so Diego already knows that those two answers would not work for his organization.

80. B. Kathleen's organization is likely to spend more resources to mitigate risks due to their low risk tolerance combined with strong executive support. They are unlikely to avoid or accept risks if they have a low risk tolerance, and they are also unlikely to avoid spending resources if they have strong executive support and risk assessment processes.

81. B. Megan should note this as an architecture risk. Her organization may want to seek an additional backup path to the Internet and should ensure that it uses a physically distinct path as well as a different Internet service provider to be a fully effective backup link. A supplier risk would involve a third party, and no third party is mentioned in the question. Similarly, no contract is specified. Finally, intrinsic risk is not a commonly used term in information security risk practice.

82. C. Indicators of compromise (IoCs) are data that is likely to indicate a compromise has occurred or is being attempted. Unusual traffic, logins, service ports or traffic, and use of privileges are all common IoCs. While some of these might be caused by vulnerability scans, not all of them are likely to be caused by such scans. SQL injection log data is often found in server logs, and key performance indicators (KPIs) are metrics used to determine if an organization or service is performing well.

83. D. One of the most common reasons for notifications to be ignored is receiving too many due to improperly set thresholds. Susan should work with responders and administrators to ensure that thresholds are set to effectively detect incidents without generating undue numbers of notifications. Automated email is useful to ensure that recipients get information, but won't meet the need for real-time notification for actual issues. Requiring logins when notifications are sent can help to ensure data is not exposed, but this does not help with preventing staff from ignoring them; adding another step may cause fewer staff to read them. Finally, timelines are useful, but they won't prevent notifications from being ignored.

Chapter 4: Incident Response and Recovery (Domain 4)

1. C. Tara's highest priority should be containing the damage to prevent the spread of the incident to other systems and networks. She has already detected the incident, so detection is not a priority. Eradication and recovery should occur only after the incident has been contained.

2. C. Alan should request that the organization provide him with a securely generated hash value that was created when the evidence was originally collected. Alan can then compare the hash value of the current drive contents with that value to verify that the evidence was not altered.

3. C. Photo metadata commonly includes the GPS location, the type of camera used to capture the photo, and the timestamp when the photo was taken. It does not include the number of times that the file was copied.

4. D. John the Ripper is a password cracking tool. Using it on a Linux system requires copies of both the /etc/passwd and /etc/shadow files.

5. C. NIST describes this type of event as a security incident because it is a violation or imminent threat of violation of security policies and practices. An adverse event is any event with negative consequences, and an event is any observable occurrence on a system or network.

6. B. In cases where an advanced persistent threat (APT) has been present for an unknown period of time, backups should be assumed to be compromised. Since APTs often have tools that cannot be detected by normal anti-malware techniques, the best option that Charles has is to carefully rebuild the systems from the ground up and then ensure that they are fully patched and secured before returning them to service.

7. A. Purging requires complete removal of data, and cryptographic erase is the only option that will fully destroy the contents of a drive from this list. Reformatting will leave the original data in place, overwriting leaves the potential for file remnants in slack space, and repartitioning will also leave data intact in the new partitions.

8. B. Unless she already knows the protocol that a particular beacon uses, filtering out beacons by protocol may cause her to miss beaconing behavior. Attackers want to dodge common analytical tools and will use protocols that are less likely to attract attention. Filtering network traffic for beacons based on the intervals and frequency they are sent at, if the beacon persists over time, and removing known traffic are common means of filtering traffic to identify beacons.

9. C. Local scans often provide more information than remote scans because of network or host firewalls that block access to services. This is the most likely problem. The second most likely answer is that Scott or Joanna used different settings when they scanned.

10. B. A hardware write blocker can ensure that connecting or mounting the drive does not cause any changes to occur on the drive. Mika should create one or more forensic images of the original drive and then work with the copy or copies as needed. She may then opt to use forensic software, possibly including a software write blocker.

11. A. This form is a chain of custody form. It includes information about the case, copies of drives that were created, and who was in possession of drives, devices, and copies during the investigation.

12. B. SNMP, packet sniffing, and Netflow are commonly used when monitoring bandwidth consumption. Portmon is an aging Windows tool used to monitor serial ports, not exactly the sort of tool that you'd use to monitor network bandwidth!

13. B. Conducting a lessons-learned review after using an incident response plan can help to identify improvements and to ensure that the plan is up-to-date and ready to handle future events.

14. B. If Kathleen's company uses a management system or inventory process to capture the MAC addresses of known systems, then a MAC address report from her routers and switches will show her devices that are connected to the network but not in the inventory. She can then track down where the devices are physically connected to a switch port and investigate the device.

15. B. If business concerns override his ability to suspend the system, the best option that Charles has is to copy the virtual disk files and then use a live memory imaging tool. This will give him the best forensic copy achievable under the circumstances. Snapshotting the system and booting it will result in a loss of live memory artifacts. Escalating may be possible in some circumstances, but the scenario specifies that the system must remain online. Finally, Volatility can capture memory artifacts, but is not designed to capture a full virtual machine.

16. D. A CSIRT leader must have authority to direct the incident response process and should be able to act as a liaison with organizational management. While Lauren may not have deep incident response experience, she is in the right role to provide those connections and leadership. She should look at retaining third-party experts for incidents if she needs additional skills or expertise on her IR team.

17. A. A logical acquisition focuses on specific files of interest, such as a specific type of file, or files from a specific location. In Eric's case, a logical acquisition meets his needs. A sparse acquisition also collects data from unallocated space. A bit-by-bit acquisition is typically performed for a full drive and will take longer.

18. C. An organization's incident response communications plan should include details of appropriate contacts with all entities who may be involved in incident response. This likely includes law enforcement agencies, the media, and security vendors. It is less likely that an organization would need to contact utility providers during a cybersecurity incident response effort.

19. B. Disclosure based on regulatory or legislative requirements is commonly part of an incident response process; however, public feedback is typically a guiding element of information release. Limiting communication to trusted parties and ensuring that data and communications about the incident are properly secured are both critical to the security of the incident response process. This also means that responders should work to limit the potential for accidental release of incident related information.

20. C. NIST describes events with negative consequences as adverse events. It might be tempting to immediately call this a security incident; however, this wouldn't be classified that way until an investigation was conducted. If the user accidentally accessed the file, it would typically not change classification. Intentional or malicious access would cause the adverse event to become a security incident.

21. B. When forensic evidence or information is produced for a civil case, it is called eDiscovery. This type of discovery often involves massive amounts of data including email, files, text messages, and any other electronic evidence that is relevant to the case.

22. C. RAID level 5, disk striping with parity, requires a minimum of three physical hard disks to operate.

23. A. Senior managers play several business continuity planning roles. These include setting priorities, obtaining resources, and arbitrating disputes among team members.

24. A. Business continuity plan documentation normally includes the continuity planning goals, a statement of importance, statement of priorities, statement of organizational responsibility, statement of urgency and timing, risk assessment and risk acceptance and mitigation documentation, a vital records program, emergency response guidelines, and documentation for maintaining and testing the plan.

25. C. Electronic vaulting is a data backup task that is part of disaster recovery, not business continuity, efforts.

26. C. Everyone in the organization should receive a basic awareness training for the business continuity program. Those with specific roles, such as first responders and senior executives, should also receive detailed, role-specific training.

27. A. The emergency response guidelines should include the immediate steps an organization should follow in response to an emergency situation. These include immediate response procedures, a list of individuals who should be notified of the emergency and secondary response procedures for first responders. They do not include long-term actions such as activating business continuity protocols, ordering equipment, or activating DR sites.

28. A. Alejandro is in the first stage of the incident response process, detection. During this stage, the intrusion detection system provides the initial alert, and Alejandro performs preliminary triaging to determine whether an intrusion is actually taking place and whether the scenario fits the criteria for activating further steps of the incident response process (which include response, mitigation, reporting, recovery, remediation, and lessons learned).

29. C. After detection of a security incident, the next step in the process is response, which should follow the organization's formal incident response procedure. The first step of this procedure is activating the appropriate teams, including the organization's computer security incident response team (CSIRT).

30. C. The root-cause analysis examines the incident to determine what allowed it to happen and provides critical information for repairing systems so that the incident does not recur. This is a component of the remediation step of the incident response process because the root cause analysis output is necessary to fully remediate affected systems and processes.

31. A. The risk assessment team should pay the most immediate attention to those risks that appear in quadrant I. These are the risks with a high probability of occurring and a high impact on the organization if they do occur.

32. C. While senior management should be represented on the BCP team, it would be highly unusual for the CEO to fill this role personally.

33. D. Of the states listed, Florida is the only one that is not shaded to indicate a serious risk of a major earthquake.

34. D. The system Charles is remediating may have a firmware or BIOS infection, with malware resident on the system board. While uncommon, this type of malware can be difficult to find and remove. Since he used original media, it is unlikely that the malware came from the software vendor. Charles wiped the system partition, and the system would have been rebooted before being rebuilt, thus clearing system memory.

35. B. Matt is helping to maintain the chain of custody documentation for his electronic evidence. This can be important if his organization needs to prove that the digital evidence they handled has not been tampered with. A better process would involve more than one person to ensure that no tampering was possible.

36. B. Karen can't use MTD verification because MTD is the maximum tolerable downtime. Verifying it will only tell her how long systems can be offline without significant business impact. Reviewing logs, using hashing to verify that the logs are intact, and performing periodic tests are all valid ways to verify that the backups are working properly.

37. A. The illustration shows an example of a failover cluster, where DB1 and DB2 are both configured as database servers. At any given time, only one will function as the active database server, while the other remains ready to assume responsibility if the first one fails. While the environment may use UPS, tape backup, and cold sites as disaster recovery and business continuity controls, they are not shown in the diagram.

38. B. Testimony should not be favorable; ethics demands that professionals offer true, accurate, and complete testimony. All the other answers are common ethical standards. Civil law covers behavior that could cause injury to a corporation, individual, or other party. Criminal law covers behavior that could cause harm to society or the state. Administrative law regulates government agencies. Ethical standards are not a type of law.

39. D. The checklist review is the least disruptive type of disaster recovery test. During a checklist review, team members each review the contents of their disaster recovery checklists on their own and suggest any necessary changes. During a tabletop exercise, team members come together and walk through a scenario without making any changes to information systems. During a parallel test, the team actually activates the disaster recovery site for testing, but the primary site remains operational. During a full interruption test, the team takes down the primary site and confirms that the disaster recovery site is capable of handling regular operations. The full interruption test is the most thorough test but also the most disruptive.

40. B. The Grandfather/Father/Son, Tower of Hanoi, and Six Cartridge Weekly schemes are all different approaches to rotating backup media that balance reuse of media with data retention concerns. Meet-in-the-middle is a cryptographic attack against 2DES encryption.

41. C. Evidence provided in court must be relevant to determining a fact in question, material to the case at hand, and competently obtained. Evidence does not need to be tangible. Witness testimony is an example of intangible evidence that may be offered in court.

42. C. In this scenario, all of the files on the server will be backed up on Monday evening during the full backup. The differential backup on Wednesday will then copy all files modified since the last full backup. These include files 1, 2, 3, 5, and 6: a total of five files.

```
File Modifications
Monday 8AM - File 1 created
Monday 10AM - File 2 created
Monday 11AM - File 3 created
Monday 4PM - File 1 modified
Monday 5PM - File 4 created
Tuesday 8AM - File 1 modified
Tuesday 9AM - File 2 modified
Tuesday 10AM - File 5 created
Wednesday 8AM - File 3 modified
Wednesday 9AM - File 6 created
```

43. B. The scrutiny of hard drives for forensic purposes is an example of media analysis. Embedded device analysis looks at the computers included in other large systems, such as automobiles or security systems. Software analysis analyzes applications and their logs. Network analysis looks at network traffic and logs.

44. C. Security incidents negatively affect the confidentiality, integrity, or availability of information or assets and/or violate a security policy. The unauthorized vulnerability scan of a server does violate security policy and may negatively affect the security of that system, so it qualifies as a security incident. The completion of a backup schedule, logging of system access, and update of antivirus signatures are all routine actions that do not violate policy or jeopardize security, so they are all events rather than incidents.

45. B. The maximum tolerable downtime (MTD) is the longest amount of time that an IT service or component may be unavailable without causing serious damage to the organization. The recovery time objective (RTO) is the amount of time expected to return an IT service or component to operation after a failure. The recovery point objective (RPO) identifies the maximum amount of data, measured in time, that may be lost during a recovery effort. Service-level agreements (SLAs) are written contracts that document service expectations.

46. A. Interviews occur when investigators meet with an individual who may have information relevant to their investigation but is not a suspect. If the individual is a suspect, then the meeting is an interrogation.

47. The terms match with the definitions as follows:

1. Hot site: B. A site with dedicated storage and real-time data replication, often with shared equipment that allows restoration of service in a very short time

2. Cold site: D. A rented space with power, cooling, and connectivity that can accept equipment as part of a recovery effort

3. Warm site: C. A site that relies on shared storage and backups for recovery

4. Service bureau: A. An organization that can provide on-site or off-site IT services in the event of a disaster

48. C. In an electronic vaulting approach, automated technology moves database backups from the primary database server to a remote site on a scheduled basis, typically daily. Transaction logging is not a recovery technique alone; it is a process for generating the logs used in remote journaling. Remote journaling transfers transaction logs to a remote site on a more frequent basis than electronic vaulting, typically hourly. Remote mirroring maintains a live database server at the backup site and mirrors all transactions at the primary site on the server at the backup site.

49. C. The end goal of the disaster recovery process is restoring normal business operations in the primary facility. All of the other actions listed may take place during the disaster recovery process, but the process is not complete until the organization is once again functioning normally in its primary facilities.

50. C. The Mitigation phase of incident response focuses on actions that can contain the damage incurred during an incident. This includes limiting the scope and or effectiveness of the incident.

51. C. The National Institute for Standards and Technologies recommends that organizations implement a mentoring program for incident response team members and provide team members with the opportunity to work on other tasks. They also recommend periodic exercises to evaluate the team's effectiveness. Rather than assigning all members of the team on a permanent basis, NIST recommends rotating members on and off the team periodically.

52. C. Gordon may conduct his investigation as he wants and use any information that is legally available to him, including information and systems belonging to his employer. There is no obligation to contact law enforcement. However, Gordon may not perform "hack back" activities because those may constitute violations of the law and/or (ISC)[2] Code of Ethics.

53. B. Netflow data contains information on the source, destination, and size of all network communications and is routinely saved as a matter of normal activity. Packet capture data would provide relevant information, but it must be captured during the suspicious activity and cannot be re-created after the fact unless the organization is already conducting 100 percent packet capture, which is rare. Additionally, the use of encryption limits the effectiveness of packet capture. Intrusion detection system logs would not likely contain relevant information because the encrypted traffic would probably not match intrusion signatures. Centralized authentication records would not contain information about network traffic.

54. B. During a parallel test, the team actually activates the disaster recovery site for testing, but the primary site remains operational. During a full interruption test, the team takes down the primary site and confirms that the disaster recovery site is capable of handling regular operations. The full interruption test is the most thorough test but also the most disruptive. The checklist review is the least disruptive type of disaster recovery test. During a checklist review, team members each review the contents of their disaster recovery checklists on their own and suggest any necessary changes. During a tabletop exercise, team members come together and walk through a scenario without making any changes to information systems.

55. C. Both the receipt of alerts and the verification of their accuracy occur during the Detection phase of the incident response process.

56. A. Virtual machines run full guest operating systems on top of a host platform known as the hypervisor.

57. A. During the lessons learned phase, analysts close out an incident by conducting a review of the entire incident response process. This may include making recommendations for improvements to the process that will streamline the efficiency and effectiveness of future incident response efforts.

58. C. In this case, the person perpretrating the security incident is an employee. This person is likely able to bypass many of the organization's security controls and the activity would not likely be identified by an intrusion detection system or firewall logs. There is no mention of malicious software, so antivirus software would also be unlikely to detect the issue. However, file integrity monitoring systems would likely detect the unauthorized data modification.

59. B. During the containment phase, the incident response team's goal is to limit the damage caused by an incident. They do this by isolating impacted systems and restricting access to resources to prevent the spread of the incident.

60. A. Expert opinion evidence allows individuals to offer their opinion based upon the facts in evidence and their personal knowledge. Expert opinion evidence may be offered only if the court accepts the witness as an expert in a particular field. Direct evidence is when witnesses testify about their direct observations. Real evidence consists of tangible items brought into court as evidence. Documentary evidence consists of written records used as evidence in court.

61. B. The analysis of application logs is one of the core tasks of software analysis. This is the correct answer because SQL injection attacks are application attacks.

62. A. A lessons learned document is often created and distributed to involved parties after a postmortem review to ensure that those who were involved in the incident and others who may benefit from the knowledge are aware of what they can do to prevent future issues and to improve response in the event that one occurs.

63. B. A content distribution network (CDN) is designed to provide reliable, low-latency, geographically distributed content distribution. In this scenario, a CDN is an ideal solution. A P2P CDN like BitTorrent isn't a typical choice for a commercial entity, whereas redundant servers or a hot site can provide high availability but won't provide the remaining requirements.

64.   B. Although the CEO will not normally serve on a BCP team, it is best to obtain top-level management approval for your plan to increase the likelihood of successful adoption.

65.   D. The project scope and planning phase includes four actions: a structured analysis of the organization, the creation of a BCP team, an assessment of available resources, and an analysis of the legal and regulatory landscape.

66.   A. Civil law covers behavior that could cause injury to a corporation, individual, or other party. Criminal law covers behavior that could cause harm to society or the state. Administrative law regulates government agencies. Ethical standards are not a type of law.

67.   D. When a forensic investigation is complete and the materials may be needed for legal or administrative actions, they should be secured and preserved. Since this case involves a human resources action, Joanna should preserve them. Notifying the subject of a forensic investigation is not a typical process when the investigation is done, nor is notifying law enforcement without a specific need to do so.

68.   A. Supply chain disruptions are not typically considered in emergency response plans. They're more likely to be handled through procurement processes and supplier management practices. Man-made and natural disasters as well as pandemics are all commonly addressed in emergency response plans.

69.   B. Crisis management is much like other forms of incident response, and once a crisis has occurred, response and then recovery must occur. Once recovery has happened, mitigation and preparation for the next event can begin.

70.   C. The most important factor when selecting backup site locations is to identify a location that is unlikely to be impacted by the same natural disaster. In many cases, this is a location 50 to 90 miles away, but other factors can come into play when selecting a site. Examples include placing backup facilities for a site that may be impacted by a hurricane inland so that a single weather event is unlikely to impact both locations. Network bandwidth, availability of backup power, and the risk of natural disasters are all factors, but geographic dispersion is the most important element to consider.

Chapter 5: Cryptography (Domain 5)

1.   C. Protecting the sensitive information with either full disk encryption or file encryption would render it unreadable to anyone finding the device. Data minimization would involve the removal of sensitive information from the device. File integrity monitoring would detect any changes in information stored on the device but would not protect against data loss.

2.   B. Self-signed certificates are functionally equivalent to those purchased from a trusted certificate authority. The fundamental difference is that they don't carry the trusted signature of a CA and, therefore, won't be trusted by web browsers by default. They are generally only appropriate for internal use.

3. D. Phil Zimmerman's Pretty Good Privacy (PGP) software is an encryption technology based upon the Web of Trust (WoT). This approach extends the social trust relationship to encryption keys.

4. A. Kevin can take a cryptographic hash of the log files when they are created and then later repeat the use of the same hash function and compare the two hash values. If the hash values are identical, Kevin can be confident that the file was not altered.

5. C. Secure Sockets Layer (SSL), Transport Layer Security (TLS), and virtual private networks (VPNs) are all used to protect data in motion. AES cryptography may be used to protect data at rest. SSL is no longer considered secure, so it is not a good choice for Greg. The only answer choice that matches each tool with the appropriate type of information and does not use SSL is using TLS for data in motion and AES for data at rest.

6. A. Unfortunately, the RADIUS protocol only supports the weak MD5 hash function. This is the major criticism of the RADIUS protocol. Most organizations require that RADIUS be protected with additional encryption to compensate for this vulnerability.

7. C. Encryption is often used to protect traffic like bank transactions from sniffing. While packet injection and man-in-the-middle attacks are possible, they are far less likely to occur, and if a VPN were used, it would be used to provide encryption. TEMPEST is a specification for techniques used to prevent spying using electromagnetic emissions and wouldn't be used to stop attacks at any normal bank.

8. C. Information shared with customers is public, internal business could be sensitive or private, and trade secrets are proprietary. Thus, public, sensitive, proprietary matches this most closely. Confidential is a military classification, which removes two of the remaining options, and trade secrets are more damaging to lose than a private classification would allow.

9. C. A watermark is used to digitally label data and can be used to indicate ownership. Encryption would have prevented the data from being accessed if it was lost, while classification is part of the set of security practices that can help make sure the right controls are in place. Finally, metadata is used to label data and might help a data loss prevention system flag it before it leaves your organization.

10. B. AES is a strong modern symmetric encryption algorithm that is appropriate for encrypting data at rest. TLS is frequently used to secure data when it is in transit. A virtual private network is not necessarily an encrypted connection and would be used for data in motion, while DES is an outdated algorithm and should not be used for data that needs strong security.

11. C. A and E can both be expected to have data at rest. C, the Internet, is an unknown, and the data can't be guaranteed to be at rest. B, D, and F are all data in transit across network links.

12. C. B, D, and F all show network links. Of the answers provided, Transport Layer Security (TLS) provides the best security for data in motion. AES-256 and 3DES are both symmetric ciphers and are more likely to be used for data at rest. SSL has been replaced with TLS and should not be a preferred solution.

13. B. Sending a file that is encrypted before it leaves means that exposure of the file in transit will not result in a confidentiality breach, and the file will remain secure until decrypted at location E. Since answers A, C, and D do not provide any information about what happens at point C, they should be considered insecure, as the file may be at rest at point C in an unencrypted form.

14. C. Data at rest is inactive data that is physically stored. Data in an IPsec tunnel or part of an e-commerce transaction is data in motion. Data in RAM is ephemeral and is not inactive.

15. B. FTP and Telnet do not provide encryption for the data they transmit and should not be used if they can be avoided. SFTP and SSH provide encryption to protect both the data they send and the credentials that are used to log in via both utilities.

16. A. NIST Special Publication 800-122 defines PII as any information that can be used to distinguish or trace an individual's identity, such as name, Social Security number, date and place of birth, mother's maiden name, biometric records, and other information that is linked or linkable to an individual such as medical, educational, financial, and employment information. PHI is health-related information about a specific person, Social Security numbers are issued to individuals in the United States, and SII is a made-up term.

17. The data elements match with the categories as follows:

Data elements

1. Medical records: B. PHI

2. Credit card numbers: A. PCI DSS

3. Social Security numbers: C. PII

4. Driver's license numbers: C. PII

Medical records are an example of protected health information (PHI). Credit card numbers are personally identifiable information (PII), but they are also covered by the Payment Card Industry Data Security Standard (PCI DSS), which is a more specific category governing only credit card information and is a better answer. Social Security numbers and driver's license numbers are examples of PII.

18. C. TLS is a modern encryption method used to encrypt and protect data in transit. BitLocker is a full disk encryption technology used for data at rest. DES and SSL are both outdated encryption methods and should not be used for data that requires high levels of security.

19. C. ISO 27001 provides guidance on implementing an information security management system (ISMS). The very similarly numbered ISO 27701 covers privacy, rather than cybersecurity, controls. ISO 9000 covers quality management, while ISO 22301 covers business continuity.

20. B. It is possible that any of these technologies could play a role in this system, but the relevant words in this question are that Maria is seeking a distributed, immutable ledger. This is the core function of blockchain solutions, making blockchain the best possible answer.

21. D. Using strong encryption, like AES-256, can help ensure that loss of removable media like tapes doesn't result in a data breach. Security labels may help with handling processes, but they won't help once the media is stolen or lost. Having multiple copies will ensure that you can still access the data but won't increase the security of the media. Finally, using hard drives instead of tape only changes the media type and not the risk from theft or loss.

22. D. Electronic signatures, as used in this rule, prove that the signature was provided by the intended signer. Electronic signatures as part of the FDA code are intended to ensure that electronic records are "trustworthy, reliable, and generally equivalent to paper records and handwritten signatures executed on paper." Signatures cannot provide confidentiality or integrity and don't ensure that someone has reviewed the data.

23. D. Secure Shell (SSH) is an encrypted protocol for remote login and command-line access. SCP and SFTP are both secure file transfer protocols, while WDS is the acronym for Windows Deployment Services, which provides remote installation capabilities for Windows operating systems.

24. D. Data in transit is data that is traversing a network or is otherwise in motion. TLS, VPNs, and IPsec tunnels are all techniques used to protect data in transit. AES, Serpent, and IDEA are all symmetric algorithms, while Telnet, ISDN, and UDP are all protocols. BitLocker and FileVault are both used to encrypt data, but they protect only stored data, not data in transit.

25. D. Bcrypt is based on Blowfish (the b is a key hint here). AES and 3DES are both replacements for DES, while Diffie–Hellman is a protocol for key exchange.

26. D. Personally identifiable information includes any information that can uniquely identify an individual. This would include name, Social Security number, and any other unique identifier (including a student ID number). ZIP code, by itself, does not uniquely identify an individual.

27. C. AES is a strong symmetric cipher that is appropriate for use with data at rest. SHA1 is a cryptographic hash, while TLS is appropriate for data in motion. DES is an outdated and insecure symmetric encryption method.

28. B. Symmetric encryption like AES is typically used for data at rest. Asymmetric encryption is often used during transactions or communications when the ability to have public and private keys is necessary. DES is an outdated encryption standard, and OTP is the acronym for onetime password.

29. A. Tapes are frequently exposed because of theft or loss in transit. That means that tapes that are leaving their normal storage facility should be handled according to the organization's classification schemes and handling requirements. Purging the tapes would cause the loss of data, while increasing the classification level of the tapes. The tapes should be encrypted rather than decrypted.

30. C. PGP, or Pretty Good Privacy (or its open source alternative, GPG), provides strong encryption of files, which can then be sent via email. Email traverses multiple servers and will be unencrypted at rest at multiple points along its path as it is stored and forwarded to its destination.

31. D. Intentional collisions have been created with MD5, and a real-world collision attack against SHA 1 was announced in early 2017. 3DES is not a hashing tool, leaving SHA 256 (sometimes called SHA 2) as the only real choice that Chris has in this list.

32. B. The salt is a random value added to a password before it is hashed by the operating system. The salt is then stored in a password file with the hashed password. This increases the complexity of cryptanalytic attacks by negating the usefulness of attacks that use precomputed hash values, such as rainbow tables.

33. A. Hash functions do not include any element of secrecy and, therefore, do not require a cryptographic key.

34. B. The Encapsulating Security Payload (ESP) protocol provides confidentiality and integrity for packet contents. It encrypts packet payloads and provides limited authentication and protection against replay attacks.

35. C. In an asymmetric cryptosystem, the sender of a message always encrypts the message using the recipient's public key.

36. D. When Bob receives the message, he uses his own private key to decrypt it. Since he is the only one with his private key, he is the only one who should be able to decrypt it, thus preserving confidentiality.

37. B. Each user retains their private key as secret information. In this scenario, Bob would only have access to his own private key and would not have access to the private key of Alice or any other user.

38. B. Alice creates the digital signature using her own private key. Then Bob, or any other user, can verify the digital signature using Alice's public key.

39. D. The greatest risk when a device is lost or stolen is that sensitive data contained on the device will fall into the wrong hands. Confidentiality protects against this risk.

40. C. The Payment Card Industry Data Security Standard (PCI DSS) contains specific technical requirements for credit card processing, including the use of encryption. The Gramm-Leach-Bliley Act (GLBA) does also regulate the financial industry, but it does not contain technical requirements. The Health Insurance Portability and Accountability Act (HIPAA) applies to healthcare providers, insurance companies, and their service providers. The Family Educational Rights and Privacy Act (FERPA) applies to student educational records.

41. B. The Diffie–Hellman algorithm allows for the secure exchange of symmetric encryption keys over a public network.

42. A. Hash functions must be able to work on any variable-length input and produce a fixed-length output from that input, regardless of the length of the input.

43.   C. Binary keyspaces contain a number of keys equal to two raised to the power of the number of bits. Two to the fifth power is 32, so a 5-bit keyspace contains 32 possible keys.

44.   B. Kerckhoff's principle says that a cryptographic system should be secure even if everything about the system, except the key, is public knowledge.

45.   C. Nonrepudiation occurs when the recipient of a message is able to demonstrate to a third party that the message came from the purported sender.

46.   A. The MD5 hash algorithm has known collisions and, as of 2005, is no longer considered secure for use in modern environments.

47.   C. In a known plaintext attack, the attacker has a copy of the encrypted message along with the plaintext message used to generate that ciphertext.

48.   A. The X.509 standard, developed by the International Telecommunications Union, contains the specification for digital certificates.

49.   C. This message was most likely encrypted with a transposition cipher. The use of a substitution cipher, a category that includes AES and 3DES, would change the frequency distribution so that it did not mirror that of the English language.

50.   A. Answering this question requires combining information about different types of cryptographic flaws. First, symmetric algorithms are thought to be resistant to future quantum attacks, while asymmetric algorithms are likely vulnerable to these attacks. Therefore, we can eliminate the two asymmetric algorithms as options: RSA and ECC. Next, the DES algorithm is weak and should no longer be used. That leaves us with the Advanced Encryption Standard (AES) as the only viable answer.

51.   A. Blowfish allows the user to select any key length between 32 and 448 bits.

52.   A. Digital signatures are possible only when using an asymmetric encryption algorithm. Of the algorithms listed, only RSA is asymmetric and supports digital signature capabilities.

53.   A. In TLS, both the server and the client first communicate using an ephemeral symmetric session key. They exchange this key using asymmetric cryptography, but all encrypted content is protected using symmetric cryptography.

54.   C. Asymmetric cryptosystems use a pair of keys for each user. In this case, with 1,000 users, the system will require 2,000 keys.

55.   A. The certificate revocation list contains the serial numbers of digital certificates issued by a certificate authority that have later been revoked.

56.   A. The point of the digital certificate is to prove to Alison that the server belongs to the bank, so she does not need to have this trust in advance. To trust the certificate, she must verify the CA's digital signature on the certificate, trust the CA, verify that the certificate is not listed on a CRL, and verify that the certificate contains the name of the bank.

57.   C. Self-signed digital certificates should be used only for internal-facing applications, where the user base trusts the internally generated digital certificate.

58. C. Quantum may choose to use any or all of these security controls, but data encryption is, by far, the most important control. It protects the confidentiality of data stored on the tapes, which are most vulnerable to theft while in transit between two secure locations.

59. C. The formula for determining the number of encryption keys required by a symmetric algorithm is $((n*(n − 1))/2)$. With six users, you will need $((6*5)/2)$, or 15 keys.

60. C. ESP's Transport mode encrypts IP packet data but leaves the packet header unencrypted. Tunnel mode encrypts the entire packet and adds a new header to support transmission through the tunnel.

61. D. Nonrepudiation is possible only with an asymmetric encryption algorithm. RSA is an asymmetric algorithm. AES, DES, and Blowfish are all symmetric encryption algorithms that do not provide nonrepudiation.

62. C. Certificates may only be added to a Certificate Revocation List by the certificate authority that created the digital certificate.

63. C. Salting adds random text to the password before hashing in an attempt to defeat automated password cracking attacks that use precomputed values. MD5 and SHA-1 are both common hashing algorithms, so using them does not add any security. Double-hashing would only be a minor inconvenience for an attacker and would not be as effective as the use of salting.

64. D. When using symmetric cryptography, the sender encrypts a message using a shared secret key, and the recipient then decrypts the message with that same key. Only asymmetric cryptography uses the concept of public and private key pairs.

65. A. Skip should use SCP—Secure Copy is a secure file transfer method. SSH is a secure command-line and login protocol, whereas HTTP is used for unencrypted web traffic. Telnet is an unencrypted command-line and login protocol.

Chapter 6: Network and Communications Security (Domain 6)

1. C. Denial-of-service (DoS) attacks and distributed denial-of-service (DDoS) attacks try to disrupt the availability of information systems and networks by flooding a victim with traffic or otherwise disrupting service.

2. A. A repeater or concentrator will amplify the signal, ensuring that the 100-meter distance limitation of 1000BaseT is not an issue. A gateway would be useful if network protocols were changing, while Cat7 cable is appropriate for a 10Gbps network at much shorter distances. STP cable is limited to 155 Mbps and 100 meters, which would leave Chris with network problems.

3. D. Ethernet uses a bus topology. While devices may be physically connected to a switch in a physical topology that looks like a star, systems using Ethernet can all transmit on the bus simultaneously, possibly leading to collisions.

4. B. WPA2 enterprise uses RADIUS authentication for users rather than a preshared key. This means a password attack is more likely to fail as password attempts for a given user may result in account lockout. WPA2 encryption will not stop a password attack, and WPA2's preshared key mode is specifically targeted by password attacks that attempt to find the key. Not only is WEP encryption outdated, but it can also frequently be cracked quickly by tools like aircrack-ng.

5. D. Fully connected mesh networks provide each system with a direct physical link to every other system in the mesh. This is expensive but can provide performance advantages for specific types of computational work.

6. D. Network segmentation can reduce issues with performance as well as diminish the chance of broadcast storms by limiting the number of systems in a segment. This decreases broadcast traffic visible to each system and can reduce congestion. Segmentation can also help provide security by separating functional groups who don't need to be able to access each other's systems. Installing a firewall at the border would only help with inbound and outbound traffic, not cross-network traffic. Spanning tree loop prevention helps prevent loops in Ethernet networks (for example, when you plug a switch into a switch via two ports on each), but it won't solve broadcast storms that aren't caused by a loop or security issues. Encryption might help prevent some problems between functional groups, but it won't stop them from scanning other systems, and it definitely won't stop a broadcast storm!

7. A. Wardriving and warwalking are both processes used to locate wireless networks but are not typically as detailed and thorough as a site survey, and design map is a made-up term.

8. C. The Physical layer includes electrical specifications, protocols, and standards that allow control of throughput, handling line noise, and a variety of other electrical interface and signaling requirements. The OSI layer doesn't have a Device layer. The Transport layer connects the Network and Session layers, and the Data Link layer packages packets from the network layer for transmission and receipt by devices operating on the Physical layer.

9. D. The RST flag is used to reset or disconnect a session. It can be resumed by restarting the connection via a new three-way handshake.

10. The OSI layers in order from layer 1 to layer 7 are:

D. Physical

B. Data Link

C. Network

G. Transport

F. Session

E. Presentation

A. Application

11. A. A well-designed set of VLANs based on functional groupings will logically separate segments of the network, making it difficult to have data exposure issues between VLANs. Changing the subnet mask will only modify the broadcast domain and will not fix issues with packet sniffing. Gateways would be appropriate if network protocols were different on different segments. Port security is designed to limit which systems can connect to a given port.

12. D. 802.1x provides port-based authentication and can be used with technologies like EAP, the Extensible Authentication Protocol. 802.11a is a wireless standard, 802.3 is the standard for Ethernet, and 802.15.1 was the original Bluetooth IEEE standard.

13. D. WEP uses an initialization vector (IV) that is too short, making it relatively trivial to brute-force. The IV is also static, meaning that key streams will repeat after a short period of time, giving attackers who have dwell time in a network sufficient opportunity to capture traffic and then crack the key. Hashes don't work to secure traffic since they are a one-way function. WEP uses RC4, not DES, and encrypts data traffic fully to clients, but it uses weak encryption, making it unsuitable to provide secure connectivity.

14. B. The firewall in the diagram has two protected zones behind it, making it a two-tier firewall design.

15. D. Remote PCs that connect to a protected network need to comply with security settings and standards that match those required for the internal network. The VPN concentrator logically places remote users in the protected zone behind the firewall, but that means user workstations (and users) must be trusted in the same way that local workstations are.

16. C. An intrusion protection system can scan traffic and stop both known and unknown attacks. A web application firewall, or WAF, is also a suitable technology, but placing it at location C would only protect from attacks via the organization's VPN, which should only be used by trusted users. A firewall typically won't have the ability to identify and stop cross-site scripting attacks, and IDS systems only monitor and don't stop attacks.

17. C. A bus can be linear or tree-shaped and connects each system to trunk or backbone cable. Ethernet networks operate on a bus topology.

18. B. Screen scrapers copy the actual screen displayed and display it at a remote location. RDP provides terminal sessions without doing screen scraping, remote node operation is the same as dial-up access, and remote control is a means of controlling a remote system (screen scraping is a specialized subset of remote control).

19. A. WPA2, the replacement for WPA, does not suffer from the security issues that WEP, the original wireless security protocol, and WPA, its successor, both suffer from. AES is used in WPA2 but is not specifically a wireless security standard.

20. B. The Remote Authentication Dial-in User Service (RADIUS) protocol was originally designed to support dial-up modem connections but is still commonly used for VPN-based authentication. HTTPS is not an authentication protocol. ESP and AH are IPsec protocols but do not provide authentication services for other systems.

21. C. Double NATing isn't possible with the same IP range; the same IP addresses cannot appear inside and outside a NAT router. RFC 1918 addresses are reserved, but only so they are not used and routable on the Internet, and changing to PAT would not fix the issue.

22. C. Stateful packet inspection firewalls, also known as dynamic packet filtering firewalls, track the state of a conversation and can allow a response from a remote system based on an internal system being allowed to start the communication. Static packet filtering and circuit-level gateways only filter based on source, destination, and ports, whereas application-level gateway firewalls proxy traffic for specific applications.

23. C. The assignment of endpoint systems to VLANs is normally performed by a network switch.

24. C. A three-tier design separates three distinct protected zones and can be accomplished with a single firewall that has multiple interfaces. Single- and two-tier designs don't support the number of protected networks needed in this scenario, while a four-tier design would provide a tier that isn't needed.

25. B. Not only should active scanning be expected to cause wireless IPS alarms, but they may actually be desired if the test is done to test responses. Accidentally scanning guests or neighbors or misidentifying devices belonging to third parties are all potential problems with active scanning and require the security assessor to carefully verify the systems that she is scanning.

26. B. ARP and RARP operate at the Data Link layer, the second layer of the OSI model. Both protocols deal with physical (MAC) hardware addresses, which are used above the Physical layer (layer 1) and below the Network layer (layer 3), thus falling at the Data Link layer.

27. A. A smurf attack is an example of a denial-of-service attack, which jeopardizes the availability of a targeted network.

28. B. Category 3 UTP cable is primarily used for phone cables and was also used for early Ethernet networks where it provided 10 Mbps of throughput. Cat 5 cable provides 100 Mbps (and 1000 Mbps if it is Cat 5e). Cat 6 cable can also provide 1000 Mbps.

29. B. The use of TCP port 80 indicates that the messaging service is using the HTTP protocol. Slack is a messaging service that runs over HTTPS, which uses port 443. SMTP is an email protocol that uses port 25.

30. C. HTTP traffic is typically sent via TCP 80. Unencrypted HTTP traffic can be easily captured at any point between A and B, meaning that the messaging solution chosen does not provide confidentiality for the organization's corporate communications.

31. B. If a business need requires messaging, using a local messaging server is the best option. This prevents traffic from traveling to a third-party server and can offer additional benefits such as logging, archiving, and control of security options like the use of encryption.

32. A. The File Transfer Protocol (FTP) operates on TCP ports 20 and 21. UDP port 69 is used for the Trivial File Transfer Protocol, or TFTP, while UDP port 21 is not used for any common file transfer protocol.

33. D. Bluetooth active scans can determine both the strength of the PIN and what security mode the device is operating in. Unfortunately, Bluetooth scans can be challenging because of the limited range of Bluetooth and the prevalence of personally owned Bluetooth-enabled devices. Passive Bluetooth scanning only detects active connections and typically requires multiple visits to have a chance of identifying all devices.

34. B. A proxy is a form of gateway that provide clients with a filtering, caching, or other service that protects their information from remote systems. A router connects networks, while a firewall uses rules to limit traffic permitted through it. A gateway translates between protocols.

35. A. When a data stream is converted into a segment (TCP) or a datagram (UDP), it transitions from the Session layer to the Transport layer. This change from a message sent to an encoded segment allows it to then traverse the Network layer.

36. B. Media Access Control (MAC) addresses are the hardware address the machine uses for layer 2 communications. The MAC addresses include an organizationally unique identifier (OUI), which identifies the manufacturer. MAC addresses can be changed, so this is not a guarantee of accuracy, but under normal circumstances you can tell what manufacturer made the device by using the MAC address.

37. A. Passive scanning can help identify rogue devices by capturing MAC address vendor IDs that do not match deployed devices, by verifying that systems match inventories of organizationally owned hardware by hardware address, and by monitoring for rogue SSIDs or connections.

38. A. A ring connects all systems like points on a circle. A ring topology was used with Token Ring networks, and a token was passed between systems around the ring to allow each system to communicate. More modern networks may be described as a ring but are only physically a ring and not logically using a ring topology.

39. B. VLANs can be used to logically separate groups of network ports while still providing access to an uplink. Per-room VPNs would create significant overhead for support as well as create additional expenses. Port security is used to limit what systems can connect to ports, but it doesn't provide network security between systems. Finally, while firewalls might work, they would add additional expense and complexity without adding any benefits over a VLAN solution.

40. The TCP ports match with the protocols as follows:

  1. TCP port 23: D. Telnet

  2. TCP port 25: A. SMTP

3. TCP port 143: C. IMAP

4. TCP port 515: B. LPD

41. A. John's design provides multiple processing sites, distributing load to multiple regions. Not only does this provide business continuity and disaster recovery functionality, but it also means that his design will be more resilient to denial-of-service attacks.

42. C. PPTP, L2F, L2TP, and IPsec are the most common VPN protocols. TLS is also used for an increasingly large percentage of VPN connections and may appear at some point in the CISSP® exam. PPP is a dial-up protocol, LTP is not a protocol, and SPAP is the Shiva Password Authentication Protocol sometimes used with PPTP.

43. A. VLAN hopping between the voice and computer VLANs can be accomplished when devices share the same switch infrastructure. Using physically separate switches can prevent this attack. Encryption won't help with VLAN hopping because it relies on header data that the switch needs to read (and this is unencrypted), while Caller ID spoofing is an inherent problem with VoIP systems. A denial of service is always a possibility, but it isn't specifically a VoIP issue and a firewall may not stop the problem if it's on a port that must be allowed through.

44. B. While it may be tempting to tell her staff to simply not connect to any network, Susan knows that they will need connectivity to do their work. Using a VPN to connect their laptops and mobile devices to a trusted network and ensuring that all traffic is tunneled through the VPN is her best bet to secure their Internet usage. Susan may also want to ensure that they take "clean" laptops and devices that do not contain sensitive information or documents and that those systems are fully wiped and reviewed when they return.

45. B. ARP cache poisoning occurs when false ARP data is inserted into a system's ARP cache, allowing the attacker to modify its behavior. RARP flooding, denial-of-ARP attacks, and ARP buffer blasting are all made-up terms.

46. D. Egress filtering scans outbound traffic for potential security policy violations. This includes traffic with a private IP address as the destination, traffic with a broadcast address as the destination, and traffic that has a falsified source address not belonging to the organization.

47. B. A teardrop attack uses fragmented packets to target a flaw in how the TCP stack on a system handles fragment reassembly. If the attack is successful, the TCP stack fails, resulting in a denial of service. Christmas tree attacks set all of the possible TCP flags on a packet, thus "lighting it up like a Christmas tree." Stack killer and frag grenade attacks are made-up answers.

48. C. By default, RADIUS uses UDP and only encrypts passwords. RADIUS supports TCP and TLS, but this is not a default setting.

49. A. The Transport layer provides logical connections between devices, including end-to-end transport services to ensure that data is delivered. Transport layer protocols include TCP, UDP, SSL, and TLS.

50. A. In a man-in-the-middle attack, attackers manage to insert themselves into a connection between a user and a legitimate website, relaying traffic between the two parties while eavesdropping on the connection. Although similarly named, the meet-in-the-middle attack is a cryptographic attack that does not necessarily involve connection tampering. Fraggle is a network-based denial-of-service attack using UDP packets. Wardriving is a reconnaissance technique for discovering open or weakly secured wireless networks.

51. C. WEP has a weak security model that relies on a single, predefined, shared static key. This means that modern attacks can break WEP encryption in less than a minute.

52. D. Bluesnarfing targets the data or information on Bluetooth-enabled devices. Bluejacking occurs when attackers send unsolicited messages via Bluetooth.

53. B. Since Bluetooth doesn't provide strong encryption, it should only be used for activities that are not confidential. Bluetooth PINs are four-digit codes that often default to 0000. Turning it off and ensuring that your devices are not in discovery mode can help prevent Bluetooth attacks.

54. D. Ping uses ICMP, the Internet Control Message Protocol, to determine whether a system responds and how many hops there are between the originating system and the remote system. Lauren simply needs to filter out ICMP to not see her pings.

55. B. Joseph may be surprised to discover FTP (TCP port 21) and Telnet (TCP port 23) open on his network since both services are unencrypted and have been largely replaced by SSH, and SCP or SFTP. SSH uses port 22, SMTP uses port 25, and POP3 uses port 110.

56. B. While non-IP protocols like IPX/SPX, NetBEUI, and AppleTalk are rare in modern networks, they can present a challenge because many firewalls are not capable of filtering them. This can create risks when they are necessary for an application or system's function because they may have to be passed without any inspection. Christmas tree attacks set all of the possible flags on a TCP packet (and are thus related to an IP protocol), IPX is not an IP-based protocol, and while these protocols are outdated, there are ways to make even modern PCs understand them.

57. D. ARP spoofing is often done to replace a target's cache entry for a destination IP, allowing the attacker to conduct a man-in-the-middle attack. A denial-of-service attack would be aimed at disrupting services rather than spoofing an ARP response, a replay attack will involve existing sessions, and a Trojan is malware that is disguised in a way that makes it look harmless.

58. B. A denial-of-service attack is an attack that causes a service to fail or to be unavailable. Exhausting a system's resources to cause a service to fail is a common form of denial-of-service attack. A worm is a self-replicating form of malware that propagates via a network, a virus is a type of malware that can copy itself to spread, and a smurf attack is a distributed denial-of-service (DDoS) that spoofs a victim's IP address to systems using an IP broadcast, resulting in traffic from all of those systems to the target.

59. C. A full mesh topology directly connects each machine to every other machine on the network. For five systems, this means four connections per system.

60. B. LEAP, the Lightweight Extensible Authentication Protocol, is a Cisco proprietary protocol designed to handle problems with TKIP. Unfortunately, LEAP has significant security issues as well and should not be used. Any modern hardware should support WPA2 and technologies like PEAP or EAP-TLS. Using WEP, the predecessor to WPA and WPA2, would be a major step back in security for any network.

61. C. Intrusion detection systems (IDSs) provide only passive responses, such as alerting administrators to a suspected attack. Intrusion prevention systems and firewalls, on the other hand, may take action to block an attack attempt. Antivirus software also may engage in active response by quarantining suspect files.

62. B. All stateful inspection firewalls enforce an implicit deny rule as the final rule of the rulebase. It is designed to drop all inbound traffic that was not accepted by an earlier rule. Stealth rules hide the firewall from external networks, but they are not included by default. This firewall does not contain any egress filtering rules, and egress filtering is not enforced by default. Connection proxying is an optional feature of stateful inspection firewalls and would not be enforced without a rule explicitly implementing it.

63. A. SMTP uses ports 25 and 465. The presence of an inbound rule allowing SMTP traffic indicates that this is an email server.

64. C. The HTTP connection will be allowed, despite the presence of rule 2, because it matches rule 1. The HTTPS connection will be blocked because there is no rule allowing HTTPS connections to this server.

65. D. The firewall should be configured to accept inbound connections from any port selected by the source system. The vast majority of inbound firewall rules allow access from any source port.

66. A. A single-tier firewall deployment is simple and does not offer useful design options like a DMZ or separate transaction subnets.

67. B. Disabling SSID broadcast can help prevent unauthorized personnel from attempting to connect to the network. Since the SSID is still active, it can be discovered by using a wireless sniffer. Encryption keys are not related to SSID broadcast, beacon frames are used to broadcast the SSID, and it is possible to have multiple networks with the same SSID.

68. C. The DARPA TCP/IP model was used to create the OSI model, and the designers of the OSI model made sure to map the OSI model layers to it. The Application layer of the TCP model maps to the Application, Presentation, and Session layers, while the TCP and OSI models both have a distinct Transport layer.

69. B. Ethernet networks use Carrier-Sense Multiple Access/Collision Detection (CSMA/CD) technology. When a collision is detected and a jam signal is sent, hosts wait a random period of time before attempting retransmission.

70. C. Layer 6, the Presentation layer, transforms data from the Application layer into formats that other systems can understand by formatting and standardizing the data. That means that standards like JPEG, ASCII, and MIDI are used at the Presentation layer for data. TCP, UDP, and TLS are used at the Transport layer; NFS, SQL, and RPC operate at the Session layer; and HTTP, FTP, and SMTP are Application layer protocols.

71. C. WPA2's CCMP encryption scheme is based on AES. As of the writing of this book, there have not been any practical real-world attacks against WPA2. DES has been successfully broken, and neither 3DES nor TLS is used for WPA2.

72. B. A two-tier firewall uses a firewall with multiple interfaces or multiple firewalls in series. This image shows a firewall with two protected interfaces, with one used for a DMZ and one used for a protected network. This allows traffic to be filtered between each of the zones (Internet, DMZ, and private network).

73. B. DNS poisoning occurs when an attacker changes the domain name to IP address mappings of a system to redirect traffic to alternate systems. DNS spoofing occurs when an attacker sends false replies to a requesting system, beating valid replies from the actual DNS server. ARP spoofing provides a false hardware address in response to queries about an IP, and Cain & Abel is a powerful Windows hacking tool, but a Cain attack is not a specific type of attack.

74. A. The correct answer is the tape that is being shipped to a storage facility. You might think that the tape in shipment is "in motion," but the key concept is that the data is not being accessed and is instead in storage. Data in a TCP packet, in an e-commerce transaction, or in local RAM is in motion and is actively being used.

75. C. A fail open configuration may be appropriate in this case. In this configuration, the firewall would continue to pass traffic without inspection while it is restarting. This would minimize downtime, and the traffic would still be protected by the other security controls described in the scenario. Failover devices and high availability clusters would indeed increase availability, but at potentially significant expense. Redundant disks would not help in this scenario because no disk failure is described.

76. B. When a workstation or other device is connected simultaneously to both a secure and a nonsecure network like the Internet, it may act as a bridge, bypassing the security protections located at the edge of a corporate network. It is unlikely that traffic will be routed improperly leading to the exposure of sensitive data, as traffic headed to internal systems and networks is unlikely to be routed to the external network. Reflected DDoS attacks are used to hide identities rather than to connect through to an internal network, and security administrators of managed systems should be able to determine both the local and wireless IP addresses his system uses.

77. D. 1000BaseT is capable of a 100-meter run according to its specifications. For longer distances, a fiber-optic cable is typically used in modern networks.

78. The wireless attack terms match with their descriptions as follows:

1. Rogue access point: B. An access point intended to attract new connections by using an apparently legitimate SSID

2. Replay: C. An attack that retransmits captured communication to attempt to gain access to a targeted system

3. Evil twin: A. An attack that relies on an access point to spoof a legitimate access point's SSID and MAC address

4. War driving: D. The process of using detection tools to find wireless networks

79. D. This question is asking you to identify the blocking rule that should *not* be set on the firewall. Packets with public IP addresses will routinely be allowed to enter the network, so you should not create a rule to block them, making this the correct answer. Packets with internal source addresses should never originate from outside the network, so they should be blocked from entering the network. Packets with external source addresses should never be found on the internal network, so they should be blocked from leaving the network. Finally, private IP addresses should never be used on the Internet, so packets containing private IP addresses should be blocked from leaving the network.

80. C. A collision domain is the set of systems that could cause a collision if they transmitted at the same time. Systems outside a collision domain cannot cause a collision if they send at the same time. This is important, as the number of systems in a collision domain increases the likelihood of network congestion due to an increase in collisions. A broadcast domain is the set of systems that can receive a broadcast from each other. A subnet is a logical division of a network, while a supernet is made up of two or more networks.

81. A. Application firewalls add layer 7 functionality to other firewall solutions. This includes the ability to inspect Application-layer details such as analyzing HTTP, DNS, FTP, and other application protocols.

82. C. The TCP three-way handshake consists of initial contact via a SYN, or synchronize flagged packet; which receives a response with a SYN/ACK, or synchronize and acknowledge flagged packet; which is acknowledged by the original sender with an ACK, or acknowledge packet. RST is used in TCP to reset a connection, PSH is used to send data immediately, and FIN is used to end a connection.

83. D. Application-specific protocols are handled at layer 7, the Application layer of the OSI model.

84. D. MAC addresses and their organizationally unique identifiers are used at the Data Link layer to identify systems on a network. The Application and Session layers don't care about physical addresses, while the Physical layer involves electrical connectivity and handling physical interfaces rather than addressing.

85. A. A data loss prevention (DLP) system or software is designed to identify labeled data or data that fits specific patterns and descriptions to help prevent it from leaving the organization. An IDS is designed to identify intrusions. Although some IDS systems can detect specific types of sensitive data using pattern matching, they have no ability to stop traffic. A firewall uses rules to control traffic routing, while UDP is a network protocol.

86. C. EAP-TLS uses certificate-based authentication. This requires management of certificates, but is useful for security reasons due to the ease of supporting full encryption. EAP-FAST uses Protected Access Credentials rather than certificates. The Lightweight Extensible Authentication Protocol (LEAP) uses dynamically generated WEP keys for encryption. EAP-PKI does not exist.

87. A. Software-defined networking allows exactly this type of control, moving and creating security boundaries and virtual firewalls as workloads move through a network. OSI-based span control and hardware-controlled networking do not exist, and a VPN is useful for connecting to or from security zones but isn't a solution that is well suited to this scenario.

88. C. Using virtual appliances in a deployment where they can protect virtual machines in the same infrastructure allows Mikayla to easily manage the devices using the same tools she uses for the other machines. At the same time, she can take advantage of virtual network fabrics for high-speed connectivity and flexibility. Inline placement is useful for IPS and firewall systems that are protecting specific devices and is often used for physical devices, but physical devices require either physical network changes or changes done in a separate management layer, making them take extra steps when flexibility and ease of management are important. Software-based IPS might work, but placing them on each virtual machine does not allow the IPS devices to cover clusters of systems since each is running on a single host.

89. B. 4G networks encrypt traffic between the cellular device and the base station but do not provide encryption after that point. If Charles wanted to provide end-to-end encryption, he would need to use a technology such as TLS to encrypt data at the device and then decrypt it once it reaches his servers.

90. A. Virtual extensible local area networks (VXLANs) allow virtual layer 2 networks to be created overlaid on top of layer 3 networks. This can provide a powerful tool when multiple networks need to appear to be part of the same network such as between distinct physical buildings or sites. The rest of the answers for this question do not exist.

91. B. SQL injection attacks use valid SQL code added to existing queries. The DROP command can be used to drop (delete) data from a database. While the other commands could be used as part of an attack, DROP is the only command that specifically threatens to perform data deletion like Henry is concerned about.

92. A. WPA2's preshared keys (PSK) mode uses a passcode, but does not require each user to have an account or an authentication server. This provides encryption unlike an open, unencrypted network, but does not provide the same level of security that enterprise mode does since you cannot identify individual users based on their accounts.

93. A. A content delivery network (CDN) is designed to host copies of a site at strategic points around the world, allowing greater scalability and throughput while reducing latency. They can also provide a high degree of resilience against distributed denial-of-service attacks due to their scale and built-in defenses against attacks. A WAF that is designed to prevent SQL injection will not stop most distributed denial-of-service attacks since they focus on bandwidth and other resource exhaustion rather than injection attacks. Scaling machines inside a local or remote data center, even with containers or VMs, will still result in scalability issues during a large distributed denial-of-service attack.

94. C. Internet of Things (IoT) devices often have limitations on their capabilities, and it isn't uncommon to have devices on a network that cannot handle enterprise authentication modes for WPA2 or WPA3. That means segmenting those devices onto a separate VLAN to keep them away from other users and devices is a common best practice. WEP is less secure and older than WPA and should not be used. Changing the preshared key on a regular basis could create a massive amount of additional work to reconfigure devices that may not allow central or enterprise management. Forcing all traffic to use TLS may also be challenging since the devices may not support TLS for all data traffic or may not even use HTTPS as their primary communication mode.

95. D. Software-defined wide area networking (SD-WAN) solutions provide central control of wide area networks, learning what traffic needs to flow and how, often with templates guiding initial configurations. Monitoring tools then allow the network to be adjusted to handle issues such as packet loss, latency, and jitter through techniques such as traffic classification, optimization, and routing changes. They also support capabilities like micro-segmentation and quality-of-service controls.

Chapter 7: Systems and Application Security (Domain 7)

1. D. While it won't be a perfect solution, Valerie should implement an awareness campaign including simulated phishing attacks. This will decrease the chances of staff members falling for attacks like this as well as other techniques that rely on impersonation as part of phishing attempts. Requiring digital signatures for all email will not prevent phishing attacks that appear to come from personal email or external entities. While DKIM, DMARC, and SPF help to ensure that email sent via a domain is legitimate, there is nothing in this question that indicates that the email was sent from an internal email address.

2. C. The Microsoft Baseline Security Analyzer, or MBSA, is a tool provided by Microsoft that can identify installed or missing patches as well as common security misconfigurations. Since it is run with administrative rights, it will provide a better view than normal nmap and Nessus scans. MBSA provides more detailed information about specific patches that are installed. Metasploit provides some limited scanning capabilities but is not the best tool for the situation.

3.   B. Heuristic detection methods run the potential malware application and track what occurs. This can allow the anti-malware tool to determine whether the behaviors and actions of the program match those common to malware, even if the file does not match the fingerprint of known malware packages.

4.   A. The 192.168.0.0/16 address range, which includes 192.168.163.109 is one of the address ranges reserved for use as private IP addresses. These addresses should not appear on packets inbound to a network from the Internet. The other addresses mentioned here are all normal public IP addresses.

5.   D. Caitlyn is preparing a decomposition diagram that maps the high-level functions to lower-level components. This will allow her to better understand how the malware package works and may help her identify areas she should focus on.

6.   B. Lauren's team should use full disk encryption or volume encryption and should secure the encryption keys properly. This will ensure that any data that remains cannot be exposed to future users of the virtual infrastructure. While many cloud providers have implemented technology to ensure that this won't happen, Lauren can avoid any potential issues by ensuring that she has taken proactive action to prevent data exposure. Using a zero wipe is often impossible because virtual environments may move without her team's intervention, data masking will not prevent unmasked data or temporary data stored on the virtual disks from being exposed, and spanning multiple virtual disks will still leave data accessible, albeit possibly in fragmented form.

7.   C. When endpoints are connected without a network control point between them, a host-based solution is required. In this case, Lucca's specific requirement is to prevent attacks, rather than simply detect them, meaning that a HIPS is required to meet his needs. Many modern products combine HIPS capabilities with other features such as data loss prevention and system compliance profiling, so Lucca may end up with additional useful capabilities if he selects a product with those features.

8.   B. Most SaaS providers do not want their customers conducting port scans of their service, and many are glad to provide security assertions and attestations including audits, testing information, or contractual language that addresses potential security issues. Using a different scanning tool, engaging a third-party tester, and even using a VPN are not typically valid answers in a scenario like this.

9.   B. Changing the hosts file has been used by various malware packages to prevent updates by stopping DNS resolution of the antivirus update server. Lauren should check to see whether the antivirus software on the system is up-to-date, but she will probably need to recommend a rebuild or reinstallation of the system.

10.   D. Geoff's only sure bet to prevent these services from being accessed is to put a network firewall in front of them. Many appliances enable services by default, but since they are appliances, they may not have host firewalls available to enable. They also often don't have patches available, and many appliances do not allow the services they provide to be disabled or modified.

11. D. The uses described for the workstation that Tim is securing do not require inbound access to the system on any of these ports. Web browsing and Active Directory domain membership traffic can be handled by traffic initiated by the system.

12. C. Relying on hashing means that Charles will only be able to identify the specific versions of malware packages that have already been identified. This is a consistent problem with signature-based detections and malware. Packages commonly implement polymorphic capabilities, meaning that two instances of the same package will not have identical hashes because of changes meant to avoid signature-based detection systems.

13. B. Lauren can determine only that the default administrative shares are enabled. While administrative shares are useful for remote administration, they can pose a threat for systems that do not require them, and some security baselines suggest disabling them in the registry if they are not used.

14. A. Susan's best option is to submit the file to a tool like VirusTotal, which will scan it for virus-like behaviors and known malware tools. Checking the hash using either a manual check or by using the National Software Reference Library can tell her whether the file matches a known good version but won't tell her if it includes malware. Running a suspect file is the worst option on the list!

15. A. Windows 10 Pro and Enterprise support application whitelisting. Chris can whitelist his allowed programs and then set the default mode to disallowed, preventing all other applications from running and thus blacklisting the application. This can be a bit of a maintenance hassle but can be useful for high security environments or those in which limiting what programs can run is critical.

16. B. Most infrastructure as a service providers will allow their customers to perform security scans as long as they follow the rules and policies around such scans. Ian should review his vendor's security documentation and contact them for details if he has questions.

17. D. DNS blackholing uses a list of known malicious domains or IP addresses and relies on listing the domains on an internal DNS server that provides a fake reply. Route poisoning prevents networks from sending data to a destination that is invalid. Routers do not typically have an anti-malware filter feature, and subdomain whitelisting was made up for this question.

18. B. In many cases, backups are the best method to minimize the impact of a ransomware outbreak. While preventative measures can help, malware packages continue to change more quickly than detective controls like anti-malware software and NGFW device manufacturers can react. A honeypot won't help Adam prevent ransomware, so it can be easily dismissed when answering this question.

19. C. Lauren's screenshot shows behavioral analysis of the executed code. From this, we can determine that malwr is a dynamic analysis sandbox that runs the malware sample to determine what it does while also analyzing the file.

20. C. The label A designates the guest operating systems in this environment. Each virtualization platform may run multiple guest operating systems, all of which share physical resources.

21. A. The label B designates the hypervisor in this environment. In a bare-metal virtualization environment, the hypervisor sits beneath the guest operating systems and controls access to memory, disk, CPU, and other system resources.

22. D. The label C designates the physical hardware in this environment. In a bare-metal virtualization environment, the physical hardware sits beneath the hypervisor, which moderates access by guest operating systems. There is no host operating system in a bare-metal virtualization approach.

23. A. Virtualized systems run full versions of operating systems. If Frank's scan revealed a missing operating system patch when he scanned a virtualized server, the patch should be applied directly to that guest operating system.

24. A. This is an informational-level report that will be discovered on any server that supports the OPTIONS method. This is not a serious issue and is listed as an informational item, so Mike does not need to take any action to address it.

25. A. Because both of these hosts are located on the same virtualization platform, it is likely that the network traffic never leaves that environment and would not be controlled by an external network firewall or intrusion prevention system. Ed should first look at the internal configuration of the virtual network to determine whether he can apply the restriction there.

26. A. The Simple Network Management Protocol (SNMP) uses traps and polling requests to monitor and manage both physical and virtual networks. The Simple Mail Transfer Protocol (SMTP) is an email transfer protocol. The Border Gateway Protocol (BGP) and Enhanced Interior Gateway Routing Protocol (EIGRP) are used to make routing decisions.

27. A. Although the vulnerability scan report does indicate that this is a low-severity vulnerability, Don must take this information in context. The management interface of a virtualization platform should never be exposed to external hosts, and it also should not use unencrypted credentials. In that context, this is a critical vulnerability that could allow an attacker to take control of a large portion of the computing environment. Don should work with security and network engineers to block this activity at the firewall as soon as possible. Shutting down the virtualization platform is not a good alternative because it would be extremely disruptive, and the firewall adjustment is equally effective from a security point of view.

28. D. The best practice for securing virtualization platforms is to expose the management interface only to a dedicated management network, accessible only to authorized engineers. This greatly reduces the likelihood of an attack against the virtualization platform.

29. B. Angela has performed interactive behavior analysis. This process involves executing a file in a fully instrumented environment and then tracking what occurs. Angela's ability to interact with the file is part of the interactive element and allows her to simulate normal user interactions as needed or to provide the malware with an environment where it can interact like it would in the wild.

30. A. Derek has created a malware analysis sandbox and may opt to use tools like Cuckoo, Truman, Minibis, or a commercial analysis tool. If he pulls apart the files to analyze how they work, he would be engaging in reverse engineering, and doing code-level analysis of executable malware would require disassembly. Darknets are used to identify malicious traffic and aren't used in this way.

31. B. The diagram already shows a firewall in place on both sides of the network connection. Ian should place a VPN at the point marked by question marks to ensure that communications over the Internet are encrypted. IPS and DLP systems do provide added security controls, but they do not provide encrypted network connections.

32. D. Bare-metal virtualization does not impose any requirements on the diversity of guest operating systems. It is common to find Linux and Windows systems running on the same platform. Bare-metal virtualization does not use a host operating system. Instead, it runs the hypervisor directly on top of the physical hardware.

33. B. John has discovered a program that is both accepting connections and has an open connection, neither of which are typical for the Minesweeper game. Attackers often disguise trojans as innocuous applications, so John should follow his organization's incident response plan.

34. B. Improper usage, which results from violations of an organization's acceptable use policies by authorized users can be reduced by implementing a strong awareness program. This will help ensure users know what they are permitted to do and what is prohibited. Attrition attacks focus on brute-force methods of attacking services, impersonation attacks include spoofing, man-in-the-middle attacks, and similar threats. Finally, web-based attacks focus on websites or web applications. Awareness may help with some specific web-based attacks like fake login sites, but many others would not be limited by Lauren's awareness efforts.

35. C. Bring your own device (BYOD) strategies allow users to operate personally owned devices on corporate networks. These devices are more likely to contain vulnerabilities than those managed under a mobile device management (MDM) system or a corporate-owned, personally enabled (COPE) strategy. Transport Layer Security (TLS) is a network encryption protocol, not a mobile device strategy.

36. D. While application sharding and query optimization can help services respond under heavy loads, Jarett's best bet is to work with a content distribution network, or CDN, that has built-in DDoS mitigation technologies. This will allow his content to be accessible even if his primary service is taken offline and will spread the load to other servers during attacks, even if the CDN's anti-DDoS capabilities can't entirely mitigate the attack. Aggressive aging can help when implemented on a firewall and may help somewhat with survivability but is less useful for large scale DDoS attacks.

37. C. Jennifer can push an updated hosts file to her domain-connected systems that will direct traffic intended for known bad domains to the localhost or a safe system. She might want to work with a security analyst or other IT staff member to capture queries sent to that system to track any potentially infected workstations. A DNS sinkhole would work only if all the systems were using local DNS, and off-site users are likely to have DNS settings set by the local networks they connect to. Anti-malware applications may not have an update yet or may fail to detect the malware, and forcing a BGP update for third-party networks is likely a bad idea!

38. A. Full disk encryption prevents anyone who gains possession of a device from accessing the data it contains, making it an ideal control to meet Martin's goal. Strong passwords may be bypassed by directly accessing the disk. Cable locks are not effective for devices used by travelers. Intrusion prevention systems are technical controls that would not affect someone who gained physical access to a device.

39. C. One of the visibility risks of virtualization is that communication between servers and systems using virtual interfaces can occur "inside" the virtual environment. This means that visibility into traffic in the virtualization environment has to be purpose-built as part of its design. Option D is correct but incomplete because inter-hypervisor traffic isn't the only traffic the IDS will see.

40. B. Cut and paste between virtual machines can bypass normal network-based data loss prevention tools and monitoring tools like an IDS or IPS. Thus, it can act as a covert channel, allowing the transport of data between security zones. So far, cut and paste has not been used as a method for malware spread in virtual environments and has not been associated with denial-of-service attacks. Cut and paste requires users to be logged in and does not bypass authentication requirements.

41. A. While virtual machine escape has been demonstrated only in laboratory environments, the threat is best dealt with by limiting what access to the underlying hypervisor can prove to a successful tracker. Segmenting by data types or access levels can limit the potential impact of a hypervisor compromise. If attackers can access the underlying system, restricting the breach to only similar data types or systems will limit the impact. Escape detection tools are not available on the market, restoring machines to their original snapshots will not prevent the exploit from occurring again, and Tripwire detects file changes and is unlikely to catch exploits that escape the virtual machines themselves.

42. C. Michael should conduct his investigation, but there is a pressing business need to bring the website back online. The most reasonable course of action would be to take a snapshot of the compromised system and use the snapshot for the investigation, restoring the website to operation as quickly as possible while using the results of the investigation to improve the security of the site.

43. B. The Trusted Platform Module (TPM) is a hardware security technique that stores an encryption key on a chip on the motherboard and prevents someone from accessing an encrypted drive by installing it in another computer.

44. D. In an infrastructure as a service environment, security duties follow a shared responsibility model. Since the vendor is responsible for managing the storage hardware, the vendor would retain responsibility for destroying or wiping drives as they are taken out of service. However, it is still the customer's responsibility to validate that the vendor's sanitization procedures meet their requirements prior to utilizing the vendor's storage services.

45. A. Mobile device management (MDM) products provide a consistent, centralized interface for applying security configuration settings to mobile devices.

46. B. In a software as a service environment, the customer has no access to any underlying infrastructure, so firewall management is a vendor responsibility under the cloud computing shared responsibility model.

47. A. The blacklisting approach to application control allows users to install any software they want except for packages specifically identified by the administrator as prohibited. This would be an appropriate approach in a scenario where users should be able to install any nonmalicious software they want to use.

48. B. The hypervisor is responsible for coordinating access to physical hardware and enforcing isolation between different virtual machines running on the same physical platform.

49. C. The most reasonable choice presented is to move the devices to a secure and isolated network segment. This will allow the devices to continue to serve their intended function while preventing them from being compromised. All of the other scenarios either create major new costs or deprive her organization of the functionality that the devices were purchased to provide.

50. A. Resilience on a transactional level is best accomplished at the application level. Load balancers and clusters can ensure that a single failed container or system does not interrupt processing, but first the application or service must know to try again if it does not get a proper or timely response. A content delivery network (CDN) is useful for ensuring that failures of web servers or denial-of-service conditions do not prevent a site or service from responding.

51. B. Since physical access to the workstations is part of the problem, setting application timeouts and password-protected screensavers with relatively short inactivity timeouts can help prevent unauthorized access. Using session IDs for all applications and verifying system IP addresses would be helpful for online attacks against applications.

52. C. Cross-site scripting (XSS) attacks seek to inject script code into a web application through unvalidated input. By removing the <SCRIPT> tag from that input, Harold is seeking to prevent this type of attack from succeeding.

53. D. Software-defined networking separates the control plane from the data plane. Network devices then do not contain complex logic themselves but receive instructions from the SDN.

54. D. Hotfixes, updates, and security fixes are all synonyms for single patches designed to correct a single problem. Service packs are collections of many different updates that serve as a major update to an operating system or application.

55. D. The scenario describes a mix of public cloud and private cloud services. This is an example of a hybrid cloud environment.

56. D. In a software as a service solution, the vendor manages both the physical infrastructure and the complete application stack, providing the customer with access to a fully managed application.

57. C. Zero-day attacks are those that are previously unknown to the security community and, therefore, have no available patch. These are especially dangerous attacks because they may be highly effective until a solution becomes available.

58. C. A host-based intrusion detection system (HIDS) may be able to detect unauthorized processes running on a system. The other controls mentioned, network intrusion detection systems (NIDSs), firewalls, and DLP systems, are network-based and may not notice rogue processes.

59. B. The scenario describes a privilege escalation attack where a malicious insider with authorized access to a system misused that access to gain privileged credentials.

60. C. In an infrastructure as a service environment, the vendor is responsible for hardware- and network-related responsibilities. These include configuring network firewalls, maintaining the hypervisor, and managing physical equipment. The customer retains responsibility for patching operating systems on its virtual machine instances.

61. C. In a platform as a service solution, the customer supplies application code that the vendor then executes on its own infrastructure.

62. C. A whitelist of allowed applications will ensure that Lauren's users can run only the applications that she preapproves. Blacklists would require her to maintain a list of every application that she doesn't want to allow, which is an almost impossible task. Graylisting is not a technology option, and configuration management can be useful for making sure the right applications are on a PC but typically can't directly prevent users from running undesired applications or programs.

63. A. Macro viruses are most commonly found in office productivity documents, such as Microsoft Word documents that end in the .doc or .docx extension. They are not commonly found in executable files with the .com or .exe extensions.

64. D. Worms have built-in propagation mechanisms that do not require user interaction, such as scanning for systems containing known vulnerabilities and then exploiting those vulnerabilities to gain access. Viruses and Trojan horses typically require user interaction to spread. Logic bombs do not spread from system to system but lie in wait until certain conditions are met, triggering the delivery of their payload.

65. D. One possibility for the clean scan results is that the virus is using stealth techniques, such as intercepting read requests from the antivirus software and returning a correct-looking version of the infected file. The system may also be the victim of a zero-day attack, using a virus that is not yet included in the signature definition files provided by the antivirus vendor.

66. D. Messages similar to the one shown in the figure are indicative of a ransomware attack. The attacker encrypts files on a user's hard drive and then demands a ransom, normally paid in Bitcoin, for the decryption key required to restore access to the original content. Encrypted viruses, on the other hand, use encryption to hide themselves from antivirus mechanisms and do not alter other contents on the system.

67. C. PowerShell is frequently used by fileless viruses to perform actions on compromised systems. Ghita may want to recommend additional monitoring tools and capabilities for systems as well as utilities that can track the state of a system to monitor for unexpected changes. Remote Desktop is sometimes used for remote control, but is not commonly exploited by fileless malware; Defender might be part of the solution to stop the malware; and Windows Hello is used for local login.

68. A. Liu should validate the digital signature of the container to ensure that the container matches the original. Scanning the container for malicious software can be helpful, but scripts and other malicious tools might still be resident, or malware might not be detected. One of the advantages of containers is frequent easy updates, and waiting a week for each update might leave Liu's infrastructure vulnerable. Finally, preventing updates to avoid malware is also likely to leave the containers vulnerable.

69. C. While advanced persistent threats (APTs) take advantage of a wide range of techniques and capabilities, unexpected data flows, use of remote access Trojans, and abuse of elevated privileges from unauthorized accounts are all common artifacts of an APT. Increases in spam email are not a direct indicator of an APT, but an increase in targeted phishing email might be.

70. D. Endpoint detection and response (EDR) tools do not collect data like network traffic or cloud infrastructure. They do collect data from endpoints and centralize it for analysis and response, including forensic and threat detection capabilities.

71. C. This is an example of a directory traversal attack. In this case, it is aimed at accessing the /etc/passwd file on a Linux server. There is no indication of a denial-of-service attack that would attempt to crash a service or consume resources, and SQL injection will have escape characters and SQL code. Brute-force attacks simply try to gain access through minor variations until they succeed, and this doesn't have any indications of that type of attack.

72. B. Whole-disk (often also called full-disk) encryption protects data at rest. When a user logs in, data from the drive can be accessed in unencrypted form.

73. D. By default, modern versions of iOS encrypt data when the device is locked using a passcode, TouchID, or FaceID. Locked devices that do not have a code set up will not be encrypted, and data can be accessed in unencrypted form on unlocked devices.

74. C. Olivia should look for systems that provide behavior-based analytics that rely on AI, machine learning, or other data analytics capabilities to detect common indicators of compromise and malicious behavior. Signature-based detection often misses modern malware due to design features that change signatures to avoid detection. Trend-based analytics may be helpful to determine patterns, but behavior-based analytics will allow Olivia to detect issues rather than just trends. Finally, regression analysis techniques look at the relationship between multiple variables and are used for statistical modeling rather as a specific APT detection technique.

75. B. Containers can allow controls to be applied at the container level, and using a mobile device management system can help keep data from being shared between personal applications and corporate applications. Similarly, controls on screenshots and other security concerns can also be controlled while keeping containerized apps secure. While a remote desktop environment would work, it can be a challenge if bandwidth is restricted or if reception is poor. SIM swaps wouldn't change the applications or controls, just which cellular provider or account is in use. Finally, SIEMs are used to centralize security information and events, not to manage mobile devices.

76. C. Data loss prevention (DLP) tools rely on tagging, pattern recognition, and other techniques to identify data that should be protected and to detect if it is being sent or used in ways that do not fit organizational policy. DLP can be a useful control against both inadvertent exposures and intentional data exfiltration attempts. COPE is a mobile device deployment scheme for company owned, personally enabled devices; APTs are advanced persistent threats; and SLAs are service level agreements.

77. C. A mobile application management (MAM) tool, or an MDM tool that has MAM capabilities built in, will allow Keisha to control what applications are installed, what version they are, and other important settings. TPM is a trusted platform module, used for security and encryption on devices. SCCM was Microsoft's System Center Configuration Manager, which has now become the Microsoft Endpoint Configuration Manager, and MTM isn't a security-related term or acronym.

Chapter 8: Practice Test 1

1. C. Dictionary, brute-force, and man-in-the-middle attacks are all types of attacks that are frequently aimed at access controls. Teardrop attacks are a type of denial-of-service attack.

2. D. The hearsay rule says that a witness cannot testify about what someone else told them, except under specific exceptions. The courts have applied the hearsay rule to include the concept that attorneys may not introduce logs into evidence unless they are authenticated by the system administrator. The best evidence rule states that copies of documents may not be submitted into evidence if the originals are available. The parol evidence rule states that if two parties enter into a written agreement, that written document is assumed to contain all the terms of the agreement. Testimonial evidence is a type of evidence, not a rule of evidence.

3. D. Device fingerprinting via a web portal can require user authentication and can gather data like operating systems, versions, software information, and many other factors that can uniquely identify systems. Using an automated fingerprinting system is preferable to handling manual registration, and pairing user authentication with data gathering provides more detail than a port scan. MAC addresses can be spoofed, and systems may have more than one depending on how many network interfaces they have, which can make unique identification challenging.

4. C. The whitelisting approach to application control allows users to install only those software packages specifically approved by administrators. This would be an appropriate approach in a scenario where application installation needs to be tightly controlled.

5. B. Biometric systems can face major usability challenges if the time to enroll is long (more than a couple of minutes) and if the speed at which the biometric system is able to scan and accept or reject the user is too slow. FAR and FRR may be important in the design decisions made by administrators or designers, but they aren't typically visible to users. CER and ERR are the same and are the point where FAR and FRR meet. Reference profile requirements are a system requirement, not a user requirement.

6. B. Category 5e and Category 6 UTP cable are both rated to 1000 Mbps. Cat 5 (not Cat 5e) is rated only to 100 Mbps, whereas Cat 7 is rated to 10 Gbps. There is no Cat 4e.

7. B. Provisioning that occurs through an established workflow, such as through an HR process, is workflow-based account provisioning. If Alex had set up accounts for his new hire on the systems he manages, he would have been using discretionary account provisioning. If the provisioning system allowed the new hire to sign up for an account on their own, they would have used self-service account provisioning, and if there was a central, software-driven process, rather than HR forms, it would have been automated account provisioning.

8. C. As Alex has changed roles, he retained access to systems that he no longer administers. The provisioning system has provided rights to workstations and the application servers he manages, but he should not have access to the databases he no longer administers. Privilege levels are not specified, so we can't determine whether he has excessive rights. Logging may or may not be enabled, but it isn't possible to tell from the diagram or problem.

9. C. When a user's role changes, they should be provisioned based on their role and other access entitlements. Deprovisioning and reprovisioning is time-consuming and can lead to problems with changed IDs and how existing credentials work. Simply adding new rights leads to privilege creep, and matching another user's rights can lead to excessive privileges because of privilege creep for that other user.

10. C. The blacklist approach to application control blocks certain prohibited packages but allows the installation of other software on systems. The whitelist approach uses the reverse philosophy and allows only approved software. Antivirus software would only detect the installation of malicious software after the fact. Heuristic detection is a variant of antivirus software.

11. C. Capacitance motion detectors monitor the electromagnetic field in a monitored area, sensing disturbances that correspond to motion.

12. A. In this scenario, the vendor is providing object-based storage, a core infrastructure service. Therefore, this is an example of infrastructure as a service (IaaS).

13. D. Individuals with specific business continuity roles should receive training on at least an annual basis.

14. D. The log entries contained in this example show the allow/deny status for inbound and outbound TCP and UDP sessions. This is, therefore, an example of a firewall log.

15. B. MDM products do not have the capability of assuming control of a device not currently managed by the organization. This would be equivalent to hacking into a device owned by someone else and might constitute a crime.

16. B. White-box penetration testing provides the tester with information about networks, systems, and configurations, allowing highly effective testing. It doesn't simulate an actual attack like black- and gray-box testing can and thus does not have the same realism, and it can lead to attacks succeeding that would fail in a zero- or limited-knowledge attack.

17. B. TACACS+ is the most modern version of TACACS, the Terminal Access Controller Access-Control System. It is a Cisco proprietary protocol with added features beyond what RADIUS provides, meaning it is commonly used on Cisco networks. XTACACS is an earlier version, Kerberos is a network authentication protocol rather than a remote user authentication protocol, and RADIUS+ is a made-up term.

18. B. Class B fire extinguishers use carbon dioxide, halon, or soda acid as their suppression material and are useful against liquid-based fires. Water may not be used against liquid-based fires because it may cause the burning liquid to splash, and many burning liquids, such as oil, will float on water.

19. A. The emergency response guidelines should include the immediate steps an organization should follow in response to an emergency situation. These include immediate response procedures, a list of individuals who should be notified of the emergency, and secondary response procedures for first responders. They do not include long-term actions such as activating business continuity protocols, ordering equipment, or activating DR sites.

20. C. During a parallel test, the team activates the disaster recovery site for testing, but the primary site remains operational. A simulation test involves a roleplay of a prepared scenario overseen by a moderator. Responses are assessed to help improve the organization's response process. The checklist review is the least disruptive type of disaster recovery test. During a checklist review, team members each review the contents of their disaster recovery checklists on their own and suggest any necessary changes. During a tabletop exercise, team members come together and walk through a scenario without making any changes to information systems.

21. D. Implementations of syslog vary, but most provide a setting for severity level, allowing configuration of a value that determines what messages are sent. Typical severity levels include debug, informational, notice, warning, error, critical, alert, and emergency. The facility code is also supported by syslog but is associated with which services are being logged. Security level and log priority are not typical syslog settings.

22. A. Network address translation (NAT) translates an internal address to an external address. VLANs are used to logically divide networks, BGP is a routing protocol, and S/NAT is a made-up term.

23. B. While full device encryption doesn't guarantee that data cannot be accessed, it provides Michelle's best option for preventing data from being lost with a stolen device when paired with a passcode. Mandatory passcodes and application management can help prevent application-based attacks and unwanted access to devices but won't keep the data secure if the device is lost. Remote wipe and GPS location is useful if the thief allows the device to connect to a cellular or Wi-Fi network. Unfortunately, many modern thieves immediately take steps to ensure that the device will not be trackable or allowed to connect to a network before they capture data or wipe the device for resale.

24. D. Dogs, guards, and fences are all examples of physical controls. While dogs and guards might detect a problem, fences cannot, so they are not all examples of detective controls. None of these controls would help repair or restore functionality after an issue, and thus they are not recovery controls, nor are they administrative controls that involve policy or procedures, although the guards might refer to them when performing their duties.

25. A. System A should send an ACK to end the three-way handshake. The TCP three-way handshake is SYN, SYN/ACK, ACK.

26. A. In the public cloud computing model, the vendor builds a single platform that is shared among many different customers. This is also known as the shared tenancy model.

27. D. Sending logs to a secure log server, sometimes called a bastion host, is the most effective way to ensure that logs survive a breach. Encrypting local logs won't stop an attacker from deleting them, and requiring administrative access won't stop attackers who have breached a machine and acquired escalated privileges. Log rotation archives logs based on time or file size and can also purge logs after a threshold is hit. Rotation won't prevent an attacker from purging logs.

28. C. A security information and event management (SIEM) tool is designed to provide automated analysis and monitoring of logs and security events. A SIEM tool that receives access to logs can help detect and alert on events like logs being purged or other breach indicators. An IDS can help detect intrusions, but IDSs are not typically designed to handle central logs. A central logging server can receive and store logs but won't help with analysis without taking additional actions. Syslog is simply a log format.

29. B. Requiring authentication can help provide accountability by ensuring that any action taken can be tracked back to a specific user. Storing logs centrally ensures that users can't erase the evidence of actions that they have taken. Log review can be useful when identifying issues, but digital signatures are not a typical part of a logging environment.

Logging the use of administrative credentials helps for those users but won't cover all users, and encrypting the logs doesn't help with accountability. Authorization helps, but being able to specifically identify users through authentication is more important.

30. B. An application-level gateway firewall uses proxies for each service it filters. Each proxy is designed to analyze traffic for its specific traffic type, allowing it to better understand valid traffic and to prevent attacks. Static packet filters and circuit-level gateways simply look at the source, destination, and ports in use, whereas a stateful packet inspection firewall can track the status of communication and allow or deny traffic based on that understanding.

31. D. The recovery point objective (RPO) identifies the maximum amount of data, measured in time, that may be lost during a recovery effort. The recovery time objective (RTO) is the amount of time expected to return an IT service or component to operation after a failure. The maximum tolerable downtime (MTD) is the longest amount of time that an IT service or component may be unavailable without causing serious damage to the organization. Service-level agreements (SLAs) are written contracts that document service expectations.

32. D. The four canons of the (ISC)² code of ethics are to protect society, the common good, necessary public trust and confidence, and the infrastructure; act honorably, honestly, justly, responsibly, and legally; provide diligent and competent service to principals; and advance and protect the profession.

33. B. Rainbow tables use precomputed password hashes to conduct cracking attacks against password files. They may be frustrated by the use of salting, which adds a specified value to the password prior to hashing, making it much more difficult to perform precomputation. Password expiration policies, password complexity policies, and user education may all contribute to password security, but they are not direct defenses against the use of rainbow tables.

34. C. The process of removing a header (and possibly a footer) from the data received from a previous layer in the OSI model is known as de-encapsulation. Encapsulation occurs when the header and/or footer are added. Payloads are part of a virus or malware package that are delivered to a target, and packet unwrapping is a made-up term.

35. C. Static packet filtering firewalls are known as first-generation firewalls and do not track connection state. Stateful inspection, application proxying, and next-generation firewalls all add connection state tracking capability.

36. D. Integrity ensures that unauthorized changes are not made to data while stored or in transit.

37. D. The Network Time Protocol (NTP) allows the synchronization of system clocks with a standardized time source. The Secure Shell (SSH) protocol provides encrypted administrative connections to servers. The File Transfer Protocol (FTP) is used for data exchange. Transport Layer Security (TLS) is an encryption process used to protect information in transit over a network.

38. D. Fire suppression systems do not stop a fire from occurring but do reduce the damage that fires cause. This is an example of reducing risk by lowering the impact of an event.

39. A. Load balancing helps to ensure that a failed server will not take a website or service offline. Dual power supplies only work to prevent failure of a power supply or power source. IPS can help to prevent attacks, and RAID can help prevent a disk failure from taking a system offline.

40. B. The use of an electromagnetic coil inside the card indicates that this is a proximity card.

41. D. Authorization provides a user with capabilities or rights. Roles and group management are both methods that could be used to match users with rights. Logins are used to validate a user.

42. B. Triple DES functions by using either two or three encryption keys. When used with only one key, 3DES produces weakly encrypted ciphertext that is the insecure equivalent of DES.

43. A. Gina's actions harm the SSCP certification and information security community by undermining the integrity of the examination process. While Gina also is acting dishonestly, the harm to the profession is more of a direct violation of the code of ethics.

44. D. When the owner of a file makes the decisions about who has rights or access privileges to it, they are using discretionary access control. Role-based access controls would grant access based on a subject's role, while rule-based controls would base the decision on a set of rules or requirements. Nondiscretionary access controls apply a fixed set of rules to an environment to manage access. Nondiscretionary access controls include rule-, role-, and lattice-based access controls.

45. A. Administrators and processes may attach security labels to objects that provide information on an object's attributes. Labels are commonly used to apply classifications in a mandatory access control system.

46. C. The user has successfully explained a valid need to know the data—completing the report requested by the CFO requires this access. However, the user has not yet demonstrated that he or she has appropriate clearance to access the information. A note from the CFO would meet this requirement.

47. D. The DES modes of operation are Electronic Codebook (ECB), Cipher Block Chaining (CBC), Cipher Feedback (CFB), Output Feedback (OFB), and Counter (CTR). The Advanced Encryption Standard (AES) is a separate encryption algorithm.

48. C. Voice pattern recognition is "something you are," a biometric authentication factor, because it measures a physical characteristic of the individual authenticating.

49. D. Kerberos, Active Directory Federation Services (ADFS), and Central Authentication Services (CAS) are all SSO implementations. RADIUS is not a single sign-on implementation, although some vendors use it behind the scenes to provide authentication for proprietary SSO.

50. B. The single loss expectancy (SLE) is the amount of damage that a risk is expected to cause each time that it occurs.

51. A. Tara first must achieve a system baseline. She does this by applying the most recent full backup to the new system. This is Sunday's full backup. Once Tara establishes this baseline, she may then proceed to apply differential backups to bring the system back to a more recent state.

52. B. To restore the system to as current a state as possible, Tara must first apply Sunday's full backup. She may then apply the most recent differential backup, from Wednesday at noon. Differential backups include all files that have changed since the most recent full backup, so the contents of Wednesday's backup contain all of the data that would be contained in Monday and Tuesday's backups, making the Monday and Tuesday backups irrelevant for this scenario.

53. A. In this scenario, the differential backup was made at noon, and the server failed at 3 p.m. Therefore, any data modified or created between noon and 3 p.m. will not be contained on any backup and will be irretrievably lost.

54. D. By switching from differential to incremental backups, Tara's weekday backups will contain only the information changed since the previous day. Therefore, she must apply all the available incremental backups. She would begin by restoring the Sunday full backup and then apply the Monday, Tuesday, and Wednesday incremental backups.

55. D. Each incremental backup contains only the information changed since the most recent full or incremental backup. If we assume that the same amount of information changes every day, each of the incremental backups would be roughly the same size.

56. C. She has placed compensation controls in place. Compensation controls are used when controls like the locks in this example are not sufficient. While the alarm is a physical control, the signs she posted are not. Similarly, the alarms are not administrative controls. These controls do not help to recover from an issue and are thus not recovery controls.

57. B. During the preservation phase, the organization ensures that information related to the matter at hand is protected against intentional or unintentional alteration or deletion. The identification phase locates relevant information but does not preserve it. The collection phase occurs after preservation and gathers responsive information. The processing phase performs a rough cut of the collected information for relevance.

58. D. This broad access may indirectly violate all of the listed security principles, but it is most directly a violation of least privilege because it grants users privileges that they do not need for their job functions.

59. C. Metasploit is a tool used to exploit known vulnerabilities. Nikto is a web application and server vulnerability scanning tool, Ettercap is a man-in-the-middle attack tool, and THC Hydra is a password brute-force tool.

60. C. The parol evidence rule states that when an agreement between two parties is put into written form, it is assumed to be the entire agreement unless amended in writing. The best evidence rule says that a copy of a document is not admissible if the original document is available. Real evidence and testimonial evidence are evidence types, not rules of evidence.

61. D. During the Reporting phase, incident responders assess their obligations under laws and regulations to report the incident to government agencies and other regulators.

62. A. The annualized loss expectancy is the amount of damage that the organization expects to occur each year as the result of a given risk.

63. D. The Physical layer deals with the electrical impulses or optical pulses that are sent as bits to convey data.

64. A. All packets leaving Angie's network should have a source address from her public IP address block. Packets with a destination address from Angie's network should not be leaving the network. Packets with source addresses from other networks are likely spoofed and should be blocked by egress filters. Packets with private IP addresses as sources or destinations should never be routed onto the Internet.

65. D. In the subject/object model, the object is the resource being requested by a subject. In this example, Harry would like access to the document, making the document the object of the request.

66. C. Personally identifiable information (PII) includes data that can be used to distinguish or trace that person's identity and also includes information such as their medical, educational, financial, and employment information. PHI is personal health information, EDI is Electronic Data Interchange, and proprietary data is used to maintain an organization's competitive advantage.

67. B. The recovery time objective (RTO) is the amount of time expected to return an IT service or component to operation after a failure. The maximum tolerable downtime (MTD) is the longest amount of time that an IT service or component may be unavailable without causing serious damage to the organization. The recovery point objective (RPO) identifies the maximum amount of data, measured in time, that may be lost during a recovery effort. Service-level agreements (SLAs) are written contracts that document service expectations.

68. C. Detective access controls operate after the fact and are intended to detect or discover unwanted access or activity. Preventive access controls are designed to prevent the activity from occurring, whereas corrective controls return an environment to its original status after an issue occurs. Directive access controls limit or direct the actions of subjects to ensure compliance with policies.

69. C. Change management typically requires sign-off from a manager or supervisor before changes are made. This helps to ensure proper awareness and communication. SDN stands for software-defined networking, release management is the process that new software releases go through to be accepted, and versioning is used to differentiate versions of software, code, or other objects.

70. C. In a risk acceptance strategy, the organization chooses to take no action other than documenting the risk. Purchasing insurance would be an example of risk transference. Relocating the data center would be risk avoidance. Reengineering the facility is an example of a risk mitigation strategy.

71. C. The sender of a message encrypts the message using the public key of the message recipient.

72. D. The recipient of a message uses his or her own private key to decrypt messages that were encrypted with the recipient's public key. This ensures that nobody other than the intended recipient can decrypt the message.

73. D. Digital signatures enforce nonrepudiation. They prevent an individual from denying that he or she was the actual originator of the message.

74. B. An individual creates a digital signature by encrypting the message digest with his or her own private key.

75. C. Wave pattern motion detectors transmit ultrasonic or microwave signals into the monitor area, watching for changes in the returned signals bouncing off objects.

76. A. In an IaaS server environment, the customer retains responsibility for most server security operations under the shared responsibility model. This includes managing OS security settings, maintaining host firewalls, and configuring server access control. The vendor would be responsible for all security mechanisms at the hypervisor layer and below.

77. B. A callback to a landline phone number is an example of a "somewhere you are" factor because of the fixed physical location of a wired phone. A callback to a mobile phone would be a "something you have" factor.

78. A. Using encryption reduces risk by lowering the likelihood that an eavesdropper will be able to gain access to sensitive information.

79. B. Worms have built-in propagation mechanisms that do not require user interaction, such as scanning for systems containing known vulnerabilities and then exploiting those vulnerabilities to gain access. Viruses and Trojan horses typically require user interaction to spread. Logic bombs do not spread from system to system but lie in wait until certain conditions are met, triggering the delivery of their payload.

80. C. Both a logical bus and a logical ring can be implemented as a physical star. Ethernet is commonly deployed as a physical star by placing a switch as the center of a star, but Ethernet still operates as a bus. Similarly, Token Ring deployments using a multistation access unit (MAU) were deployed as physical stars but operated as rings.

81. B. As an employee's role changes, they often experience privilege creep, which is the accumulation of old rights and roles. Account review is the process of reviewing accounts and ensuring that their rights match their owners' role and job requirements. Account revocation removes accounts, while reprovisioning might occur if an employee was terminated and returned or took a leave of absence and returned.

82. A. The ping flood attack sends echo requests at a targeted system. These pings use inbound ICMP echo request packets, causing the system to respond with an outbound ICMP echo reply.

83. C. Social engineering is the best answer, as it can be useful to penetration testers who are asked to assess whether staff members are applying security training and have absorbed the awareness messages the organization uses. Port scanning and vulnerability scanning find technical issues that may be related to awareness or training issues but that are less likely to be directly related. Discovery can involve port scanning or other data-gathering efforts but is also less likely to be directly related to training and awareness.

84. A. Encrypting the files reduces the probability that the data will be successfully stolen, so it is an example of risk mitigation. Deleting the files would be risk avoidance. Purchasing insurance would be risk transference. Taking no action would be risk acceptance.

85. C. Sally needs to provide nonrepudiation, the ability to provably associate a given email with a sender. Digital signatures can provide nonrepudiation and are her best option. IMAP is a mail protocol, encryption can provide confidentiality, and DKIM is a tool for identifying domains that send email.

86. C. Multipartite viruses use multiple propagation mechanisms to spread between systems. This improves their likelihood of successfully infecting a system because it provides alternative infection mechanisms that may be successful against systems that are not vulnerable to the primary infection mechanism.

87. D. A fingerprint scan is an example of a "something you are" factor, which would be appropriate for pairing with a "something you know" password to achieve multifactor authentication. A username is not an authentication factor. PINs and security questions are both "something you know," which would not achieve multifactor authentication when paired with a password because both methods would come from the same category, failing the requirement for multifactor authentication.

88. A. The maximum tolerable downtime (MTD) is the amount of time that a business may be without a service before irreparable harm occurs. This measure is sometimes also called maximum tolerable outage (MTO).

89. C. Software-defined networking (SDN) is a converged protocol that allows virtualization concepts and practices to be applied to networks. MPLS handles a wide range of protocols like ATM, DSL, and others, but isn't intended to provide the centralization capabilities that SDN does. Content distribution network (CDN) is not a converged protocol, and FCoE is Fibre Channel over Ethernet, a converged protocol for storage.

90. A. RSA is an asymmetric encryption algorithm that requires only two keys for each user. IDEA, 3DES, and Skipjack are all symmetric encryption algorithms and would require a key for every unique pair of users in the system.

91. A. TKIP is used only as a means to encrypt transmissions and is not used for data at rest. RSA, AES, and 3DES are all used on data at rest as well as data in transit.

92. A. Applying a digital signature to a message allows the sender to achieve the goal of nonrepudiation. This allows the recipient of a message to prove to a third party that the message came from the purported sender. Symmetric encryption does not support nonrepudiation. Firewalls and IDS are network security tools that are not used to provide nonrepudiation.

93. D. Privileged access reviews are one of the most critical components of an organization's security program because they ensure that only authorized users have access to perform the most sensitive operations. They should take place whenever a user with privileged access leaves the organization or changes roles as well as on a regular, recurring basis.

94. D. Nessus, OpenVAS, and SAINT are all vulnerability scanning tools. All provide port scanning capabilities as well but are more than simple port scanning tools.

95. B. Network access control (NAC) systems can be used to authenticate users and then validate their system's compliance with a security standard before they are allowed to connect to the network. Enforcing security profiles can help reduce zero-day attacks, making NAC a useful solution. A firewall can't enforce system security policies, whereas an IDS can only monitor for attacks and alarm when they happen. Thus, neither a firewall nor an IDS meets Kolin's needs. Finally, port security is a MAC address-based security feature that can restrict only which systems or devices can connect to a given port.

96. C. Binary keyspaces contain a number of keys equal to 2 raised to the power of the number of bits. Two to the eighth power is 256, so an 8-bit keyspace contains 256 possible keys.

97. B. In the private cloud computing model, the cloud computing environment is dedicated to a single organization and does not follow the shared tenancy model. The environment may be built by the company in its own data center or built by a vendor at a co-location site.

98. B. Decentralized access control can result in less consistency because the individuals tasked with control may interpret policies and requirements differently and may perform their roles in different ways. Access outages, overly granular control, and training costs may occur, depending on specific implementations, but they are not commonly identified issues with decentralized access control.

99. C. In the community cloud computing model, two or more organizations pool their resources to create a cloud environment that they then share.

100. B. Password complexity is driven by length, and a longer password will be more effective against brute-force attacks than a shorter password. Each character of additional length increases the difficulty by the size of the potential character set (for example, a single lowercase character makes the passwords 26 times more difficult to crack). While each of the other settings is useful for a strong password policy, they won't have the same impact on brute-force attacks.

101. C. Heuristic-based antimalware software has a higher likelihood of detecting a zero-day exploit than signature-based methods. Heuristic-based software does not require frequent signature updates because it does not rely upon monitoring systems for the presence of known malware. The trade-off with this approach is that it has a higher false positive rate than signature detection methods.

102. B. Worms have built-in propagation mechanisms that do not require user interaction, such as scanning for systems containing known vulnerabilities and then exploiting those vulnerabilities.

103. B. Registration is the process of adding a user to an identity management system. This includes creating their unique identifier and adding any attribute information that is associated with their identity. Proofing occurs when the user provides information to prove who they are. Directories are managed to maintain lists of users, services, and other items. Session management tracks application and user sessions.

104. D. Fred should choose a router. Routers are designed to control traffic on a network while connecting to other similar networks. If the networks are very different, a bridge can help connect them. Gateways are used to connect to networks that use other protocols by transforming traffic to the appropriate protocol or format as it passes through them. Switches are often used to create broadcast domains and to connect endpoint systems or other devices.

105. The testing methodologies match with the level of knowledge as follows:

1. Black box: C. No prior knowledge of the system

2. White box: A. Full knowledge of the system

3. Gray box: B. Partial or incomplete knowledge

106. The cloud service offerings in order from the case where the customer bears the least responsibility to where the customer bears the most responsibility are:

B. SaaS

C. PaaS

A. IaaS

In an infrastructure as a service (IaaS) cloud computing model, the customer retains responsibility for managing operating system and application security while the vendor manages security at the hypervisor level and below. In a platform as a service (PaaS) environment, the vendor takes on responsibility for the operating system, but the customer writes and configures any applications. In a software as a service (SaaS) environment, the vendor takes on responsibility for the development and implementation of the application while the customer merely configures security settings within the application. TaaS is not a cloud service model.

107. B. RAID level 5 is also known as disk striping with parity. It uses three or more disks, with one disk containing parity information used to restore data to another disk in the event of failure. When used with three disks, RAID 5 is able to withstand the loss of a single disk.

108. C. A star topology uses a central connection device. Ethernet networks may look like a star, but they are actually a logical bus topology that is sometimes deployed in a physical star.

109. A. Access control lists (ACLs) are used for determining a user's authorization level. Usernames are identification tools. Passwords and tokens are authentication tools.

110. A. Rainbow tables rely on being able to use databases of precomputed hashes to quickly search for matches to known hashes acquired by an attacker. Making passwords longer can greatly increase the size of the rainbow table required to find the matching hash, and adding a salt to the password will make it nearly impossible for the attacker to generate a table that will match unless they can acquire the salt value. MD5 and SHA1 are both poor choices for password hashing compared to modern password hashes, which are designed to make hashing easy and recovery difficult. Rainbow tables are often used against lists of hashes acquired by attacks rather than over-the-wire attacks, so over-the-wire encryption is not particularly useful here. Shadow passwords simply make the traditionally world-readable list of password hashes on Unix and Linux systems available in a location readable only by root. This doesn't prevent a rainbow table attack once the hashes are obtained.

111. C. During a parallel test, the team actually activates the disaster recovery site for testing, but the primary site remains operational. During a full interruption test, the team takes down the primary site and confirms that the disaster recovery site is capable of handling regular operations. The full interruption test is the most thorough test but also the most disruptive. The checklist review is the least disruptive type of disaster recovery test. During a checklist review, team members each review the contents of their disaster recovery checklists on their own and suggest any necessary changes. During a tabletop exercise, team members come together and walk through a scenario without making any changes to information systems.

112. A. Confidentiality ensures that data cannot be read by unauthorized individuals while stored or in transit.

113. D. Notifications and procedures like the signs posted at the company Chris works for are examples of directive access controls. Detective controls are designed to operate after the fact. The doors and the locks on them are examples of physical controls. Preventive controls are designed to stop an event and could also include the locks that are present on the doors.

114. A. Identity as a service (IDaaS) provides an identity platform as a third-party service. This can provide benefits, including integration with cloud services and removing overhead for maintenance of traditional on-premise identity systems but can also create risk because of third-party control of identity services and reliance on an offsite identity infrastructure.

115. D. Binary keyspaces contain a number of keys equal to 2 raised to the power of the number of bits. Two to the sixth power is 64, so a 6-bit keyspace contains 64 possible keys. The number of viable keys is usually smaller in most algorithms because of the presence of parity bits and other algorithmic overhead or security issues that restrict the use of some key values.

116. B. Social engineering exploits humans to allow attacks to succeed. Since help desk employees are specifically tasked with being helpful, they may be targeted by attackers posing as legitimate employees. Trojans are a type of malware, whereas phishing is a targeted attack via electronic communication methods intended to capture passwords or other sensitive data. Whaling is a type of phishing aimed at high-profile or important targets.

117. A. Developing a business impact assessment is an integral part of the business continuity planning effort. The selection of alternate facilities, activation of those facilities, and restoration of data from backup are all disaster recovery tasks.

118. C. The file clearly shows HTTP requests, as evidenced by the many GET commands. Therefore, this is an example of an application log from an HTTP server.

119. D. Kerberos uses realms, and the proper type of trust to set up for an Active Directory environment that needs to connect to a K5 domain is a realm trust. A shortcut trust is a transitive trust between parts of a domain tree or forest that shortens the trust path, a forest trust is a transitive trust between two forest root domains, and an external trust is a nontransitive trust between AD domains in separate forests.

120. B. A captive portal can require those who want to connect to and use Wi-Fi to provide an email address to connect. This allows Ben to provide easy-to-use wireless while meeting his business purposes. WPA3 PSK is the preshared key mode of WPA and won't provide information about users who are given a key. Sharing a password doesn't allow for data gathering either. Port security is designed to protect wired network ports based on MAC addresses.

121. B. Many modern wireless routers can provide multiple SSIDs. Ben can create a private, secure network for his business operations, but he will need to make sure that the customer and business networks are firewalled or otherwise logically separated from each other. Running WPA3 on the same SSID isn't possible without creating another wireless network and would cause confusion for customers (SSIDs aren't required to be unique). Running a network in Enterprise mode isn't used for open networks, and WEP is outdated and incredibly vulnerable.

122. D. Unencrypted open networks broadcast traffic in the clear. This means that unencrypted sessions to websites can be easily captured with a packet sniffer. Some tools like FireSheep have been specifically designed to capture sessions from popular websites. Fortunately, many now use TLS by default, but other sites still send user session information in the clear. Shared passwords are not the cause of the vulnerability, ARP spoofing isn't an issue with wireless networks, and a Trojan is designed to look like safe software, not to compromise a router.

123. A. This is a clear example of a denial-of-service attack—denying legitimate users authorized access to the system through the use of overwhelming traffic. It goes beyond a reconnaissance attack because the attacker is affecting the system, but it is not a compromise because the attacker did not attempt to gain access to the system. There is no reason to believe that a malicious insider was involved.

124. C. SYN floods rely on the TCP implementation on machines and network devices to cause denial-of-service conditions.

125. A. The Advanced Encryption Standard (AES) supports the use of encryption keys that are 128 bits, 192 bits, or 256 bits in length.

Chapter 9: Practice Test 2

1. C. The first thing Casey should do is notify her management, but after that, replacing the certificate and using proper key management practices with the new certificate's key should be at the top of her list.

2. B. Phishing is not an attack against an access control mechanism. While phishing can result in stolen credentials, the attack itself is not against the control system and is instead against the person being phished. Dictionary attacks and man-in-the-middle attacks both target access control systems.

3. C. One of the core capabilities of infrastructure as a service is providing servers on a vendor-managed virtualization platform. Web-based payroll and email systems are examples of software as a service. An application platform managed by a vendor that runs customer code is an example of platform as a service.

4. B. Soda acid and other dry powder extinguishers work to remove the fuel supply. Water suppresses temperature, while halon and carbon dioxide remove the oxygen supply from a fire.

5. B. Warm sites contain the hardware necessary to restore operations but do not have a current copy of data.

6. A. 201.19.7.45 is a public IP address. RFC 1918 addresses are in the ranges 10.0.0.0 to 0.255.255.255, 172.16.0.0 to 172.31.255.255, and 192.168.0.0 to 192.168.255.255. APIPA addresses are assigned between 169.254.0.0 to 169.254.255.254, and 127.0.0.1 is a loopback address (although technically the entire 127.x.x.x network is reserved for loopback).

7. B. A post-admission philosophy allows or denies access based on user activity after connection. Since this doesn't check the status of a machine before it connects, it can't prevent the exploit of the system immediately after connection. This doesn't preclude out-of-band or in-band monitoring, but it does mean that a strictly post-admission policy won't handle system checks before the systems are admitted to the network.

8. B. Encapsulation is a process that adds a header and possibly a footer to data received at each layer before handoff to the next layer. TCP wrappers are a host-based network access control system, attribution is determining who or what performed an action or sent data, and data hiding is a term from object-oriented programming that is not relevant here.

9. A. The four canons of the (ISC)² code of ethics are to protect society, the common good, necessary public trust and confidence, and the infrastructure; act honorably, honestly, justly, responsibly, and legally; provide diligent and competent service to principals; and advance and protect the profession.

10. A. The purpose of a digital certificate is to provide the general public with an authenticated copy of the certificate subject's public key.

11. D. The last step of the certificate creation process is the digital signature. During this step, the certificate authority signs the certificate using its own private key.

12. C. When an individual receives a copy of a digital certificate, he or she verifies the authenticity of that certificate by using the CA's public key to validate the digital signature contained on the certificate.

13. A. Mike uses the public key that he extracted from Renee's digital certificate to encrypt the message that he would like to send to Renee.

14. A. Guidelines provide advice based on best practices developed throughout industry and organizations, but they are not compulsory. Compliance with guidelines is optional.

15. C. Privilege creep occurs when users retain from roles they held previously rights they do not need to accomplish their current job. Unauthorized access occurs when an unauthorized user accesses files. Excessive provisioning is not a term used to describe permissions issues, and account review would help find issues like this.

16. C. Routing Information Protocol (RIP), Open Shortest Path First (OSPF), and Border Gateway Protocol (BGP) are all routing protocols and are associated with routers.

17. B. Susan has used two distinct types of factors: the PIN and password are both Type 1 factors, and the retina scan is a Type 3 factor. Her username is not a factor.

18. B. TCP's use of a handshake process to establish communications makes it a connection-oriented protocol. TCP does not monitor for dropped connections, nor does the fact that it works via network connections make it connection-oriented.

19. A. The goal of the business continuity planning process is to ensure that your recovery time objectives are all less than your maximum tolerable downtimes.

20. B. Awareness training is an example of an administrative control. Firewalls and intrusion detection systems are technical controls. Security guards are physical controls.

21. B. RAID level 1 is also known as disk mirroring. RAID 0 is called disk striping. RAID 5 is called disk striping with parity. RAID 10 is known as a stripe of mirrors.

22. C. Service Provisioning Markup Language, or SPML, is an XML-based language designed to allow platforms to generate and respond to provisioning requests. SAML is used to make authorization and authentication data, while XACML is used to describe access controls. SOAP, or Simple Object Access Protocol, is a messaging protocol and could be used for any XML messaging but is not a markup language itself.

23. C. TCP, UDP, and other transport layer protocols like SSL and TLS operate at the Transport layer.

24. B. Linda should choose a warm site. This approach balances cost and recovery time. Cold sites take a long time to activate, measured in weeks or months. Hot sites activate immediately but are quite expensive. Mutual assistance agreements depend on the support of another organization.

25. D. Differential backups do not alter the archive bit on a file, whereas incremental and full backups reset the archive bit to 0 after the backup completes. Partial backups are not a backup type.

26. C. The Remediation phase of incident handling focuses on conducting a root-cause analysis to identify the factors contributing to an incident and implementing new security controls, as needed.

27. The services match with the network ports as follows:

1. DNS: D. UDP port 53

2. HTTPS: A. TCP port 443

3. SSH: E. TCP port 22

4. RDP: B. TCP port 3389

5. MSSQL: C. TCP port 1433

28. C. Windows system logs include reboots, shutdowns, and service state changes. Application logs record events generated by programs, security logs track events like logins and uses of rights, and setup logs track application setup.

29. D. The system is set to overwrite the logs and will replace the oldest log entries with new log entries when the file reaches 20 MB. The system is not purging archived logs because it is not archiving logs. Since there can only be 20 MB of logs, this system will not have stored too much log data, and the question does not provide enough information to know whether there will be an issue with not having the information needed.

30. D. Modification of audit logs will prevent repudiation because the data cannot be trusted, and thus actions cannot be provably denied. The modification of the logs is also a direct example of tampering. It might initially be tempting to answer elevation of privileges and tampering, as the attacker made changes to files that should be protected, but this is an unknown without more information. Similarly, the attacker may have accessed the files, resulting in information disclosure in addition to tampering, but again, this is not specified in the question. Finally, this did not cause a denial of service, and thus that answer can be ignored.

31. The disaster recovery test types, listed in order of their potential impact on the business from the least impactful to the most impactful, are as follows:

A. Checklist review

B. Parallel test

C. Tabletop exercise

D. Full interruption test

Checklist reviews are the least impactful type of exercise because they do not even require a meeting. Each team member reviews the checklist on his or her own. Table-top exercises are slightly more impactful because they require bringing together the DR team in the same room. Parallel tests require the activation of alternate processing sites and require significant resources. Full interruption tests are the most impactful type of exercise because they involve shifting operations to the alternate site and could disrupt production activity.

32. A. Resource-based access controls match permissions to resources like a storage volume. Resource-based access controls are becoming increasingly common in cloud-based infrastructure as a service environments. The lack of roles, rules, or a classification system indicate that role-based, rule-based, and mandatory access controls are not in use here.

33. B. Fred's company needs to protect integrity, which can be accomplished by digitally signing messages. Any change will cause the signature to be invalid. Encrypting isn't necessary because the company does not want to protect confidentiality. TLS can provide in-transit protection but won't protect integrity of the messages, and of course a hash used without a way to verify that the hash wasn't changed won't ensure integrity either.

34. C. Deterrence is the first functional goal of physical security mechanisms. If a physical security control presents a formidable challenge to a potential attacker, they may not attempt the attack in the first place.

35. B. In this scenario, all the files on the server will be backed up on Monday evening during the full backup. Tuesday's incremental backup will include all files changed since Monday's full backup: files 1, 2, and 5. Wednesday's incremental backup will then include all files modified since Tuesday's incremental backup: files 3 and 6.

File Modifications
Monday 8AM - File 1 created
Monday 10AM - File 2 created
Monday 11AM - File 3 created
Monday 4PM - File 1 modified
Monday 5PM - File 4 created
Tuesday 8AM - File 1 modified
Tuesday 9AM - File 2 modified
Tuesday 10AM - File 5 created
Wednesday 8AM - File 3 modified
Wednesday 9AM - File 6 created

36. C. Identity proofing can be done by comparing user information that the organization already has, such as account numbers or personal information. Requiring users to create unique questions can help with future support by providing a way for them to do password resets. Using a phone call only verifies that the individual who created the account has the phone that they registered and won't prove their identity. In-person verification would not fit the business needs of most websites.

37. C. Interviews, surveys, and audits are all useful for assessing awareness. Code quality is best judged by code review, service vulnerabilities are tested using vulnerability scanners and related tools, and the attack surface of an organization requires both technical and administrative review.

38. D. The three-way handshake is SYN, SYN/ACK, ACK. System B should respond with "Synchronize and Acknowledge" to System A after it receives a SYN.

39. D. The Advanced Encryption Standard supports encryption with 128-bit keys, 192-bit keys, and 256-bit keys.

40. B. Multipartite viruses use multiple propagation mechanisms to defeat system security controls but do not necessarily include techniques designed to hide the malware from antivirus software. Stealth viruses tamper with the operating system to hide their existence. Polymorphic viruses alter their code on each system they infect to defeat signature detection. Encrypted viruses use a similar technique, employing encryption to alter their appearance and avoid signature detection mechanisms.

41. A. Cellular networks have the same issues that any public network does. Encryption requirements should match those that the organization selects for other public networks such as hotels, conference Wi-Fi, and similar scenarios. Encrypting all data is difficult and adds overhead, so it should not be the default answer unless the company specifically requires it. WAP is a dated wireless application protocol and is not in broad use; requiring it would be difficult. WAP does provide TLS, which would help when in use.

42. D. Fred's best option is to use an encrypted, trusted VPN service to tunnel all of his data usage. Trusted Wi-Fi networks are unlikely to exist at a hacker conference, normal usage is dangerous due to the proliferation of technology that allows fake towers to be set up, and discontinuing all usage won't support Fred's business needs.

43. B. Remote wipe tools are a useful solution, but they work only if the phone can access either a cellular or Wi-Fi network. Remote wipe solutions are designed to wipe data from the phone regardless of whether it is in use or has a passcode. Providers unlock phones for use on other cellular networks rather than for wiping or other feature support.

44. B. Risk transference involves actions that shift risk from one party to another. Purchasing insurance is an example of risk transference because it moves risk from the insured to the insurance company.

45. C. For systems running in System High mode, the user must have a valid security clearance for all information processed by the system, access approval for all information processed by the system, and a valid need to know for some, but not necessarily all, information processed by the system.

46. D. Risk acceptance occurs when an organization determines that the costs involved in pursuing other risk management strategies are not justified and they choose not to pursue any action.

47. B. Carla's account has experienced aggregation, where privileges accumulated over time. This condition is also known as privilege creep and likely constitutes a violation of the least privilege principle.

48. A. The service-level agreement (SLA) is between a service provider and a customer and documents in a formal manner expectations around availability, performance, and other parameters. An MOU may cover the same items but is not as formal a document. An OLA is between internal service organizations and does not involve customers. An SOW is an addendum to a contract describing work to be performed.

49. C. Both TCP and UDP port numbers are a 16-digit binary number, which means there can be 216 ports, or 65,536 ports, numbered from 0 to 65,535.

50. D. When users have more rights than they need to accomplish their job, they have excessive privileges. This is a violation of the concept of least privilege. Unlike creeping privileges, this is a provisioning or rights management issue rather than a problem of retention of rights the user needed but no longer requires. Rights collision is a made-up term and thus is not an issue here.

51. C. Jim has agreed to a black-box penetration test, which provides no information about the organization, its systems, or its defenses. A crystal- or white-box penetration test provides all of the information an attacker needs, whereas a gray-box penetration test provides some, but not all, information.

52. C. An access control matrix is a table that lists objects, subjects, and their privileges. Access control lists focus on objects and which subjects can access them. Capability tables list subjects and what objects they can access. Subject/object rights management systems are not based on an access control model.

53. B. Identity as a service (IDaaS) provides capabilities such as account provisioning, management, authentication, authorization, reporting, and monitoring. Platform as a service (PaaS), infrastructure as a service (IaaS), and software as a service (SaaS) are other types of cloud computing capabilities that are not specialized identity management services.

54. A. If the (ISC)² peer review board finds that a certified individual has violated the (ISC)² code of ethics, the board may revoke their certification. The board is not able to terminate an individual's employment or assess financial penalties.

55. C. They need a key for every possible pair of users in the cryptosystem. The first key would allow communication between Matthew and Richard. The second key would allow communication between Richard and Christopher. The third key would allow communication between Christopher and Matthew.

56. B. Syslog uses UDP port 514. TCP-based implementations of syslog typically use port 6514. The other ports may look familiar because they are commonly used TCP ports: 443 is HTTPS, 515 is the LPD print service, and 445 is used for Windows SMB.

57. D. During a tabletop exercise, team members come together and walk through a scenario without making any changes to information systems. The checklist review is the least disruptive type of disaster recovery test. During a checklist review, team members each review the contents of their disaster recovery checklists on their own and suggest any necessary changes. During a parallel test, the team actually activates the disaster recovery site for testing, but the primary site remains operational. During a full interruption test, the team takes down the primary site and confirms that the disaster recovery site is capable of handling regular operations. The full interruption test is the most thorough test but also the most disruptive.

58.   D. Procedures are formal, mandatory documents that provide detailed, step-by-step actions required from individuals performing a task.

59.   B. Tammy should choose a warm site. This type of facility meets her requirements for a good balance between cost and recovery time. It is less expensive than a hot site but facilitates faster recovery than a cold site. A red site is not a type of disaster recovery facility.

60.   C. Signature detection is extremely effective against known strains of malware because it uses a reliable pattern matching technique to identify known malware. Signature detection is, therefore, the most reliable way to detect known malware. This technique is not, however, effective against the zero-day malware typically used by advanced persistent threats (APTs) that does not exploit vulnerabilities identified in security bulletins. While malware authors once almost exclusively targeted Windows systems, malware now exists for all major platforms.

61.   C. Regression testing ensures proper functionality of an application or system after it has been changed. Unit testing focuses on testing each module of a program instead of against its previous functional state. White- and black-box testing both describe the amount of knowledge about a system or application, rather than a specific type or intent for testing.

62.   A. Heartbeat sensors send periodic status messages from the alarm system to the monitoring center. The monitoring center triggers an alarm if it does not receive a status message for a prolonged period of time, indicating that communications were disrupted.

63.   B. Polymorphic viruses mutate each time they infect a system by making adjustments to their code that assists them in evading signature detection mechanisms. Encrypted viruses also mutate from infection to infection but do so by encrypting themselves with different keys on each device.

64.   C. External auditors can provide an unbiased and impartial view of an organization's controls to third parties. Internal auditors are useful when reporting to senior management of the organization but are typically not asked to report to third parties. Penetration tests test technical controls but are not as well suited to testing many administrative controls. The employees who build and maintain controls are more likely to bring a bias to the testing of those controls and should not be asked to report on them to third parties.

65.   D. The hypervisor runs within the virtualization platform and serves as the moderator between virtual resources and physical resources.

66.   B. Google's federation with other applications and organizations allows single sign-on as well as management of their electronic identity and its related attributes. While this is an example of SSO, it goes beyond simple single sign-on. Provisioning provides accounts and rights, and a public key infrastructure is used for certificate management.

67. B. Running the program in a sandbox provides secure isolation that can prevent the malware from impacting other applications or systems. If Joe uses appropriate instrumentation, he can observe what the program does, what changes it makes, and any communications it may attempt. ASLR is a memory location randomization technology, process isolation keeps processes from impacting each other, but a sandbox typically provides greater utility in a scenario like this since it can be instrumented and managed in a way that better supports investigations, and clipping is a term often used in signal processing.

68. C. Each of the precautions listed helps to prevent social engineering by helping prevent exploitation of trust. Avoiding voice-only communications is particularly important since establishing identity over the phone is difficult. The other listed attacks would not be prevented by these techniques.

69. D. Mirai targeted Internet of Things devices, including routers, cameras, and DVRs. As organizations bring an increasing number of devices like these into their corporate networks, protecting both internal and external targets from insecure, infrequently updated, and often vulnerable IoT devices is increasingly important.

70. D. The use of a probability/impact matrix is the hallmark of a qualitative risk assessment. It uses subjective measures of probability and impact, such as "high" and "low," in place of quantitative measures.

71. B. Ben is reusing his salt. When the same salt is used for each hash, all users with the same password will have the same hash, and the attack can either attempt to steal the salt or may attempt to guess the salt by targeting the most frequent hash occurrences based on commonly used passwords. Short salts are an issue, but the salts used here are 32 bytes (256 bits) long. There is no salting algorithm used or mentioned here; salt is an added value for a hash, and plaintext salting is a made-up term.

72. C. Usernames are an identification tool. They are not secret, so they are not suitable for use as a password.

73. A. While developers may feel like they have a business need to be able to move code into production, the principle of separation of duties dictates that they should not have the ability to both write code and place it on a production server. The deployment of code is often performed by change management staff.

74. B. A security information and event management (SIEM) tool is designed to centralize logs from many locations in many formats and to ensure that logs are read and analyzed despite differences between different systems and devices. The Simple Network Management Protocol (SNMP) is used for some log messaging but is not a solution that solves all of these problems. Most non-Windows devices, including network devices among others, are not designed to use the Windows event log format, although using NTP for time synchronization is a good idea. Finally, local logging is useful, but setting clocks individually will result in drift over time and won't solve the issue with many log sources.

75. A. The emergency response guidelines should include the immediate steps an organization should follow in response to an emergency situation. These include immediate response procedures, a list of individuals who should be notified of the emergency, and secondary response procedures for first responders. They do not include long-term actions such as activating business continuity protocols, ordering equipment, or activating disaster recovery sites.

76. D. The image clearly shows a black magnetic stripe running across the card, making this an example of a magnetic stripe card.

77. A. Repudiation threats allow an attacker to deny having performed an action or activity without the other party being able to prove differently.

78. A. When operating system patches are no longer available for mobile devices, the best option is typically to retire or replace the device. Building isolated networks will not stop the device from being used for browsing or other purposes, which means it is likely to continue to be exposed to threats. Installing a firewall will not remediate the security flaws in the OS, although it may help somewhat. Finally, reinstalling the OS will not allow new updates or fix the root issue.

79. C. Mandatory access controls use a lattice to describe how classification labels relate to each other. In this image, classification levels are set for each of the labels shown. A discretionary access control (DAC) system would show how the owner of the objects allows access. RBAC could be either rule- or role-based access control and would use either system-wide rules or roles. Task-based access control (TBAC) would list tasks for users.

80. B. Cloud computing systems where the customer only provides application code for execution on a vendor-supplied computing platform are examples of platform as a service (PaaS) computing.

81. C. Rainbow tables are databases of prehashed passwords paired with high-speed lookup functions. Since they can quickly compare known hashes against those in a file, using rainbow tables is the fastest way to quickly determine passwords from hashes. A brute-force attack may eventually succeed but will be very slow against most hashes. Pass-the-hash attacks rely on sniffed or otherwise acquired NTLM or LanMan hashes being sent to a system to avoid the need to know a user's password. Salts are data added to a hash to avoid the use of tools like rainbow tables. A salt added to a password means the hash won't match a rainbow table generated without the same salt.

82. C. The blacklist approach to application control blocks certain prohibited packages but allows the installation of other software on systems. The whitelist approach uses the reverse philosophy and allows only approved software. Antivirus software would detect the installation of malicious software only after the fact. Heuristic detection is a variant of antivirus software.

83. C. This scenario describes separation of duties—not allowing the same person to hold two roles that, when combined, are sensitive. While two-person control is a similar concept, it does not apply in this case because the scenario does not say that either action requires the concurrence of two users.

84. C. These are examples of private IP addresses. RFC1918 defines a set of private IP addresses for use in internal networks. These private addresses including 10.0.0.0 to 10.255.255.255, 172.16.0.0 to 172.31.255.255, and 192.168.0.0 to 196.168.255.255 should never be routable on the public Internet.

85. A. This is an example of a vendor offering a fully functional application as a web-based service. Therefore, it fits under the definition of software as a service (SaaS). In infrastructure as a service (IaaS), compute as a service (CaaS), and platform as a service (PaaS) approaches, the customer provides their own software. In this example, the vendor is providing the email software, so none of those choices is appropriate.

86. The cable types match with the maximum lengths as follows:

1. Category 5e: B. 300 feet

2. Coaxial (RG-58): A. 500 feet

3. Fiber optic: C. 1+ kilometers

87. D. The Authentication Header provides authentication, integrity, and nonrepudiation for IPsec connections. The Encapsulating Security Payload provides encryption and thus provides confidentiality. It can also provide limited authentication. L2TP is an independent VPN protocol, and Encryption Security Header is a made-up term.

88. D. Need to know is applied when subjects like Alex have access to only the data they need to accomplish their job. Separation of duties is used to limit fraud and abuse by having multiple employees perform parts of a task. Constrained interfaces restrict what a user can see or do and would be a reasonable answer if need to know did not describe his access more completely in this scenario. Context-dependent control relies on the activity being performed to apply controls, and this question does not specify a workflow or process.

89. B. Operational investigations are performed by internal teams to troubleshoot performance or other technical issues. They are not intended to produce evidence for use in court and, therefore, do not have the rigid collection standards of criminal, civil, or regulatory investigations.

90. B. The best change that Susan can make is to allow the use of symbols in passwords. This extends the character set significantly, allowing many new characters in passwords and freeing users to make more complex passwords. Changing to a nine-character minimum would also improve the strength of passwords, but this would be a less significant change than allowing symbols in any character position. Password expiration policies are no longer considered best practices, and Susan would be better off requiring multifactor authentication and allowing users to retain the same passwords until they want to change them or the passwords are suspected to be compromised.

91. A. Purchasing insurance is a way to transfer risk to another entity.

92. B. The recovery time objective (RTO) is the amount of time that it may take to restore a service after a disaster without unacceptable impact on the business. The RTO for each service is identified during a business impact assessment.

93. A. Retina scans can reveal additional information, including high blood pressure and pregnancy, causing privacy concerns. Newer retina scans don't require a puff of air, and retina scanners are not the most expensive biometric factor. Their false positive rate can typically be adjusted in software, allowing administrators to adjust their acceptance rate as needed to balance usability and security.

94. C. The SMTP protocol does not guarantee confidentiality between servers, making TLS or SSL between the client and server only a partial measure. Encrypting the email content can provide confidentiality; digital signatures can provide nonrepudiation.

95. B. When data reaches the Transport layer, it is sent as segments (TCP) or datagrams (UDP). Above the Transport layer, data becomes a data stream, while below the Transport layer they are converted to packets at the Network layer, frames at the Data Link layer, and bits at the Physical layer.

96. A. Authenticated scans use a read-only account to access configuration files, allowing more accurate testing of vulnerabilities. Web application, unauthenticated scans, and port scans don't have access to configuration files unless they are inadvertently exposed.

97. B. A baseline is used to ensure a minimum security standard. A policy is the foundation that a standard may point to for authority, and a configuration guide may be built from a baseline to help staff who need to implement it to accomplish their task. An outline is helpful, but outline isn't the term you're looking for here.

98. B. Full disk encryption only protects data at rest. Since it encrypts the full disk, it does not distinguish between labeled and unlabeled data.

99. C. This scenario violates the least privilege principle because an application should never require full administrative rights to run. Gwen should update the service account to have only the privileges necessary to support the application.

100. B. When a message reaches the Data Link layer, it is called a frame. Data streams exist at the Application, Presentation, and Session layers, whereas segments and datagrams exist at the Transport layer (for TCP and UDP, respectively).

101. B. Criminal forensic investigations typically have the highest standards for evidence, as they must be able to help prove the case beyond a reasonable doubt. Administrative investigations merely need to meet the standards of the organization and to be able to be defended in court, while civil investigations operate on a preponderance of evidence. There is not a category of forensic investigation referred to as "industry" in the CISSP® exam's breakdown of forensic types.

102. A. Protected health information (PHI) is defined by HIPAA to include health information used by healthcare providers, such as medical treatment, history, and billing. Personally identifiable information is information that can be used to identify an individual, which may be included in the PHI but isn't specifically this type of data. Protected health insurance and individual protected data are both made-up terms.

103. D. Fiber-optic cable is more expensive and can be much harder to install than stranded copper cable or coaxial cable, but it isn't susceptible to electromagnetic interference (EMI). That makes it a great solution for Jen's problem, especially if she is deploying EMI-hardened systems to go with her EMI-resistant network cables.

104. D. Gray-box testing is a blend of crystal-box (or white-box) testing, which provides full information about a target, and black-box testing, which provides little or no knowledge about the target.

105. D. The Service Organizations Control audit program includes business continuity controls in a SOC 2, but not SOC 1, audit. Although FISMA and PCI DSS may audit business continuity, they would not apply to an email service used by a hospital.

106. C. A mantrap, which is composed of a pair of doors with an access mechanism that allows only one door to open at a time, is an example of a preventive access control because it can stop unwanted access by keeping intruders from accessing a facility because of an opened door or following legitimate staff in. It can serve as a deterrent by discouraging intruders who would be trapped in it without proper access, and of course, doors with locks are an example of a physical control. A compensating control attempts to make up for problems with an existing control or to add additional controls to improve a primary control.

107. The protocols match with the descriptions as follows:

1. TCP: C. Transports data over a network in a connection-oriented fashion

2. UDP: D. Transports data over a network in a connectionless fashion

3. DNS: B. Performs translations between FQDNs and IP addresses

4. ARP: A. Performs translations between MAC addresses and IP addresses

The Domain Name System (DNS) translates human-friendly fully qualified domain names (FQDNs) into IP addresses, making it possible to easily remember websites and hostnames. ARP is used to resolve IP addresses into MAC addresses. TCP and UDP are used to control the network traffic that travels between systems. TCP does so in a connection-oriented fashion using the three-way handshake, while UDP uses connectionless "best-effort" delivery.

108. C. A unique salt should be created for each user using a secure generation method and stored in that user's record. Since attacks against hashes rely on building tables to compare the hashes against, unique salts for each user make building tables for an entire database essentially impossible—the work to recover a single user account may be feasible, but large-scale recovery requires complete regeneration of the table each time. A single salt allows rainbow tables to be generated if the salt is stolen or can be guessed based on frequently used passwords. Creating a unique salt each time a user logs in does not allow a match against a known salted hashed password.

109. C. An important part of application threat modeling is threat categorization. It helps to assess attacker goals that influence the controls that should be put in place. The other answers all involve topics that are not directly part of application threat modeling.

110. D. There is no need to conduct forensic imaging as a preventative measure. Rather, forensic imaging should be used during the incident response process. Maintaining patch levels, implementing intrusion detection/prevention, and removing unnecessary services and accounts are all basic preventative measures.

111. C. The two most important elements of a qualitative risk assessment are determining the probability and impact of each risk upon the organization. Likelihood is another word for probability. Cost should be taken into account but is only one element of impact, which also includes reputational damage, operational disruption, and other ill effects.

112. C. The Secure File Transfer Protocol (SFTP) is specifically designed for encrypted file transfer. SSH is used for secure command-line access, whereas TCP is one of the bundles of Internet protocols commonly used to transmit data across a network. IPsec could be used to create a tunnel to transfer the data but is not specifically designed for file transfer.

113. B. Criminal investigations have high stakes with severe punishment for the offender that may include incarceration. Therefore, they use the strictest standard of evidence of all investigations: beyond a reasonable doubt. Civil investigations use a preponderance-of-the-evidence standard. Regulatory investigations may use whatever standard is appropriate for the venue where the evidence will be heard. This may include the beyond-a-reasonable-doubt standard, but it is not always used in regulatory investigations. Operational investigations do not use a standard of evidence.

114. A. During a full interruption test, the team takes down the primary site and confirms that the disaster recovery site is capable of handling regular operations. The full interruption test is the most thorough test but also the most disruptive. During a parallel test, the team actually activates the disaster recovery site for testing but the primary site remains operational. The checklist review is the least disruptive type of disaster recovery test. During a checklist review, team members each review the contents of their disaster recovery checklists on their own and suggest any necessary changes. During a tabletop exercise, team members come together and walk through a scenario without making any changes to information systems.

115. B. Personally identifiable information (PII) can be used to distinguish a person's identity. Protected health information (PHI) includes data such as medical history, lab results, insurance information, and other details about a patient. Personal protected data is a made-up term, and PID is an acronym for process ID, the number associated with a running program or process.

116. A. Information that is modifiable between a client and a server also means that it is accessible, pointing to both tampering and information disclosure. Spoofing in STRIDE is aimed at credentials and authentication, and there is no mention of this in the question. Repudiation would require that proving who performed an action was important, and elevation of privilege would come into play if privilege levels were involved.

117. C. Risk transference involves shifting the impact of a potential risk from the organization incurring the risk to another organization. Insurance is a common example of risk transference.

118. C. Turnstiles are unidirectional gates that prevent more than a single person from entering a facility at a time.

119. C. The goal of business continuity planning exercises is to reduce the amount of time required to restore operations. This is done by minimizing the recovery time objective (RTO).

120. B. The maximum allowed length of a Cat 6 cable is 100 meters, or 328 feet. Long distances are typically handled by a fiber run or by using network devices like switches or repeaters.

121.   A. Hot sites contain all of the hardware and data necessary to restore operations and may be activated very quickly.

122.   C. A hybrid authentication service can provide authentication services in both the cloud and on-premise, ensuring that service outages due to interrupted links are minimized. An on-site service would continue to work during an Internet outage, but would not allow the e-commerce website to authenticate, while a cloud service would leave the corporate location offline. Outsourcing authentication does not indicate whether the solution is on or off premise, and thus isn't a useful answer.

123.   C. Federation links identity information between multiple organizations. Federating with a business partner can allow identification and authorization to occur between them, making integration much easier. Single sign-on would reduce the number of times a user has to log in, but will not facilitate the sharing of identity information. Multifactor can help secure authentication, but again, doesn't help integrate with a third party. Finally an Identity as a Service provider might provider federation, but doesn't guarantee it.

124.   B. SAML, the Security Assertion Markup Language is frequently used to integrate cloud services, and provides the ability to make authentication and authorization assertions. Active Directory integrations are possible, but are less common for cloud service providers, and RADIUS is not typically used for integrations like this. SPML, the Service Provisioning Markup Language is used to provision users, resources, and services.

125.   A. The RSA algorithm supports key lengths between 1,024 and 4,096 bits. All of these key lengths are currently considered secure. Some cryptographers believe that attacks will surface that render 1,024 bit keys insecure in the future, but no such attacks are yet public. RSA does not support 512 bit keys.

Index

captive portal, 166, 268
Category 3 UTP cable, 103, 238
Category 6 cable, 194, 281
CCTV, 13, 201
cellular hot spot, 114
Central Authentication Services
   (CAS), 152, 260
centralized authentication records, 74, 227
CER, 24, 205
certificate authority (CA), 172, 270
certificate management, 81
Certificate Revocation List, 92, 93, 235
chain of custody, 64, 70, 222, 225
change control board (CCB), 7, 199
change log, 39, 165, 212
change management
   about, 18, 156, 262
   goals of, 8, 200
   process of, 7, 199
change manager, 8, 200
change request, 8, 200
checklist review, 71, 74, 146, 164, 176, 182,
   193, 225, 227–228, 257, 267, 271–272,
   274, 281
chief information officer, 7
Christmas tree attack, 108, 240
ciphers, 90
ciphertext, 90
circuit-level gateway firewall, 102,
   148, 238, 259
civil tort, 66
civilian data classifications, 82, 230
clearance, 152
clearing, 10, 200
clipping, 56, 184, 219, 276
cloud computing model, 147, 161,
   187, 265, 277
cloud-based authentication services, 195
cluster, 133
code auditing, 51, 216
code quality, 177
cold site, 71, 73, 107, 171, 174, 182,
   195, 225, 226
collision domain, 115, 244
command injection, 56
command.com, 135

command.exe, 135
Common Vulnerability Scoring System
   (CVSS), 56, 219
community cloud, 147, 161, 265
compartmentalized environment, 24
compensating access control, 15,
   192, 202, 280
composition, 121
compromise, 166
compute as a service (CaaS), 134, 135, 144,
   187, 188, 277
computer security incident, 72
computer security incident response team
   (CSIRT), 65, 223, 224
confidentiality breach, 17, 203
confidentiality principle, 5, 6, 7, 9, 89, 90, 97,
   103, 149, 164, 199, 233, 267
configuration management, 18, 135, 204
conflict of interest, 3
connection proxy, 111
constrained interfaces, 188
containment phase, of incident response
   process, 62, 75, 221, 228
content delivery network (CDN), 76, 133,
   160, 228, 252, 264
content filter, 22
context-dependent control, 188
contractual risk, 58, 221
corporate-owned, personally enabled (COPE)
   strategy, 130, 138, 250, 255
corrective access control, 15, 16, 156, 202
cost metric, 192, 280
Counter Mode Cipher Block Chaining
   Message Authentication Mode Protocol
   (CCMP), 113
credential management system, 27, 207
credit card security requirements, 9
criminal forensics, 66
crisis management process, 77–78, 229
crossover error rate, 24, 205
cross-site request forgery (CSRF), 134
cross-site scripting (XSS), 100, 134, 252
cryptographic algorithm, 93, 165
cryptographic erase, 63, 222
cryptographic hashing, 81, 89, 230
cryptographic keys, 151

crystal-box penetration test, 181, 191, 274
cubicle work areas, 15
customer relationship management
    (CRM), 134
cyber production, 66

D

darknet analysis, 129
DARPA, 112, 242
data at rest, 81, 83, 84, 87, 190,
    230, 231, 232
data breach, 81
data center, 15
data center firewall, 127
data classification, 7, 199
data corruption, 50, 216
Data Encryption Standard (DES), 83, 85, 87,
    91, 93, 152, 230, 231, 232, 235, 260
data gathering, 51
data hiding, 171
data in motion, 81, 114, 230
data in transit, 160, 190, 264
Data Link layer (OSI model), 98, 99, 105,
    116, 155, 190, 236, 279
Data Loss Prevention (DLP), 81, 116, 129,
    135, 138, 245, 250, 253, 255
data minimization, 15, 81, 202
data modeling, 50
data storage, 12, 201
data storage policy, 12, 201
data stream, 190, 279
database logs, 57
datagram, 190
decentralized access control, 25, 34,
    161, 206, 265
decompiler sandbox, 126
decomposition, 121, 247
dedicated cloud, 134
de-encapsulation, 149
defense in depth, 5, 6, 8, 16, 18, 90, 199,
    200, 203, 204
deluge, 13
Demilitarized Zone (DMZ), 102
denial principle, 5, 6, 7, 9, 103

denial-of-ARP attack, 108
denial-of-service (DoS), 49, 50, 52, 97, 108,
    110, 135, 137, 166, 184, 216, 217,
    235, 241, 268
design map, 98
detection phase, of incident response process,
    74, 75, 155, 228
detection technology, 12, 62, 201
detective access control, 156, 164, 262, 267
deterrent access control, 16, 192
device authentication, 22, 204
dictionary attack, 48, 52, 142, 170, 215,
    217, 255, 269
differential backup, 153, 154, 174, 261
Diffie-Hellman, 86, 89, 232, 233
digital certificate, 22, 86, 91, 92, 156–157,
    172, 205, 234, 270
digital content management, 5, 199
digital signatures, 5, 48, 49, 86, 89, 159, 160,
    189, 199, 216, 232, 264, 265
direct evidence, 76, 228
directive access control, 156, 164, 262
directory management, 162
directory traversal attack, 56, 137, 219, 254
disaster recovery plan, 72, 73, 146, 148,
    156, 164, 174, 176, 182, 193, 227,
    267, 271, 281
disaster recovery test, 71
discovery of assets, 58, 158, 220, 264
discretionary access control (DAC), 22, 25,
    28, 30, 32, 33, 34–35, 143, 151, 187,
    204, 206, 208, 209, 210–211, 260, 277
discretionary model, 30
disk mirroring, 174, 270
distributed denial-of-service (DDoS),
    97, 118, 235
documentary evidence, 76, 228
documentation
    for forensic investigation process, 70
    types of, 6
Domain Name System (DNS)
    about, 192, 280
    blackholing, 125, 248
    poisoning, 114, 243
    port for, 175, 271
    spoofing, 114, 243

X

Z

Comprehensive Online Learning Environment

Register to gain one year of *free* access to the Sybex online interactive learning environment and test bank to help you study for your Systems Security Certified Practitioner (SSCP) certification exam—included with your purchase of this book! The test bank includes all of the questions from the book itself in online format.

Register and Access the Online Test Bank

To register your book and get access to the online test bank, follow these steps:

1. Go to www.wiley.com/go/sybextestprep.
2. Select your book from the list.
3. Complete the required registration information, including answering the security verification to prove book ownership. You will be emailed a PIN code.
4. Follow the directions in the email or go to www.wiley.com/go/sybextestprep. Find your book in the list there and click Register Or Login.
5. Enter the PIN code you received and click the Activate button.
6. On the Create an Account or Login page, enter your username and password, and click Login or create a new account. A success message will appear.
7. Once you are logged in, you will see the online test bank you have registered for and should click the Go To Test Bank button to begin.

Do you need more practice? If you have not already read Sybex's *(ISC)² SSCP Systems Security Certified Practitioner Official Study Guide, Third Edition* by Mike Wills (ISBN: 978-1-119-85498-2) and are not seeing passing grades on these practice tests, that book is an excellent resource to master any SSCP topics causing problems. The Study Guide series maps every official exam objective to the corresponding chapter in the book to help track exam prep objective by objective, includes challenging review questions in each chapter to prepare for exam day, and offers online test prep materials with flashcards and additional practice tests.